Praise for *One of Them*

'Poignant reading' *Observer*

'Michael Cashman describes his journey from a cruel Dickensian childhood to the dignity of the House of Lords with brutal honesty. I was shocked, amused, and deeply moved by this life of a brave, good, man' Sheila Hancock

'There is brilliance in his memoir, *One of Them*, and darkness, too, enough to raise it far above the normal standard of celebrity biography ... Stunning ... The lucidity of the writing is breathtaking ... He could never be accused ... in life or literature, of not doing enough' *Herald*

'Michael Cashman's beautifully crafted memoir left me in tears and grateful that he had the courage to lay out his almost unimaginable life with such impressive honesty ... Above all, however, this is the tenderest of love stories, a proud testament to a decades-long queer romance. There are so many reasons to love this book' Armistead Maupin

'A roller coaster memoir ... Peppered with delicious anecdotes of his encounters with celebrities' *Scotsman*

'An extraordinary account of improbable leaps of faith and changes of direction ... An amazing, complicated love story' *Radio Times*

77000007412 1

MICHAEL CASHMAN CBE is a British politician and life peer. Born and raised in the East End of London, he acted throughout his childhood and into adulthood and is best known for his role as Colin Russell in BBC TV's *EastEnders*. He is the co-founder of the Stonewall Group UK and was the UK's first-ever special envoy on LGBT+ issues. He was elected as an MEP in 1999, a position he held for fifteen years. He has been awarded the Stonewall Politician of the Year, a *Pink News* Lifetime Achievement Award, and a Lifetime Achievement Award from the European Diversity Awards. He was made a CBE in 2013 and was raised to the peerage the following year. He lives in the East End of London.

lordmichaelcashman.com / @mcashmanCBE

Michael Cashman

One of Them

BLOOMSBURY PUBLISHING

LONDON · OXFORD · NEW YORK · NEW DELHI · SYDNEY

BLOOMSBURY PUBLISHING
Bloomsbury Publishing Plc
50 Bedford Square, London, WC1B 3DP, UK
29 Earlsfort Terrace, Dublin 2, Ireland

BLOOMSBURY, BLOOMSBURY PUBLISHING and the Diana
logo are trademarks of Bloomsbury Publishing Plc

First published in Great Britain 2020
This edition published 2021

Copyright © Michael Cashman, 2020

Michael Cashman has asserted his right under the Copyright,
Designs and Patents Act, 1988, to be identified as Author of this work

All rights reserved. No part of this publication may be reproduced or
transmitted in any form or by any means, electronic or mechanical,
including photocopying, recording, or any information storage or retrieval
system, without prior permission in writing from the publishers

Plate sections: *The Sun* article printed with permission of News Corp;
Sir Ian McKellen and Michael Cashman at 'Never Going Underground,'
Shirlaine Forest/Getty Images; Paul Cottingham and Michael Cashman
wedding photos, Les Wilson; Michael Cashman at Labour Conference, Gus Campbell

A catalogue record for this book is available from the British Library

ISBN: PB: 978-1-5266-1236-6; EBOOK: 978-1-5266-1235-9

2 4 6 8 10 9 7 5 3 1

Typeset by Newgen KnowledgeWorks Pvt. Ltd., Chennai, India
Printed and bound in Great Britain by CPI Group (UK) Ltd, Croydon CR0 4YY

To find out more about our authors and books visit
www.bloomsbury.com and sign up for our newsletters

For Paul,
the man who put the F in fun

PROLOGUE

The winter sun is dropping quickly. The room is already dark – even in summer it is dark. It's north-facing. Easier to sleep in.

He opens the torn, dusty grey folder and is surprised. After a few seconds he picks up an envelope. He recognises who it's addressed to, but he doesn't know what's written inside. It doesn't occur to him to turn on a light or to get closer to the window. He's been searching, looking, but never been able to find what he has been looking for. Until today. The letter, freed from years of confinement, rests in his open hands. He takes a deep breath, holds himself upright and begins to read:

It was smashing talking to you over the weekend, and I was so pleased about the honest chat we had late on Friday.

It does worry me that you are having some difficulties. I want to help you all I can, and so the best I can do is to love you. I will love you, give you the knowledge that whatever happens to you, whatever you do I will love you and give you the security of a relationship as long as you (and I) need it. I hope that it is forever, but only time will tell, and we must not live for tomorrow, but for now, for today.

All I am trying to say in my confusing style is that whatever anyone thinks, feels, or says about you, remember that you love someone, they love you. That is enviable. Not everyone experiences that. End of lecture.

He folds the letter back along its original lines and places it inside the envelope.

PART ONE

I

We are getting married, even though they call it a civil partnership. We will have the same rights, the same responsibilities and I never thought it would happen in my lifetime.

Three months after the civil partnership legislation came into effect, which we had helped to become a reality, Paul and I arrived at our venue on 11 March 2006, nervous, awkward and excited. Paul had found a brilliant location, Vinopolis, a huge Victorian wine warehouse nestled beside the infamous Clink prison at London Bridge. Paul quietened my nerves, thrust a cup of coffee at me and then ran through the programme with the staff: after the ceremony everyone would go upstairs for the drinks reception while the room was rearranged for the buffet dinner for the 300 guests. When that was over, the free bar would continue and we would dance away to an Abba tribute band until midnight and beyond. Ever the organiser, Paul wanted to be there from the beginning to make certain it went okay. Hidden away from our guests we perched upstairs and waited as the staff gave us a running commentary.

Outside, the media spilled over into the street – and so did the security, as half the Cabinet was in attendance: Gordon and Sarah Brown, the first female foreign secretary, Margaret Beckett, her husband Leo, Cherie Blair, as well as casts of soaps, dramas and the crème de la crème of British theatre. Oh, and Lily Savage, aka Paul O'Grady.

All the guests had assembled; it was going like clockwork. But by 3.45 there was still no sign of the registrar. By quarter past four I had started to panic. When it approached 4.30 I saw that Paul was worried too. So was the manager of the venue.

Repeated calls made to the registrar's number were met by an answerphone. Sweat broke out across my top lip. The blood had drained from my cheeks, and from Paul's. The manager asked us what we wanted to do.

Paul and I now had to face the reality that the ceremony was not going to happen. We discussed options: I would go downstairs and announce that we had been let down by a Lib Dem council, that it was sabotage, but we would celebrate our union anyway, which would be legally undertaken another day. Paul begged for a bit more time.

I screamed out: 'I can see it now, I can see it now—'

'What?'

'The headlines: "Labour can't organise a piss-up in Vinopolis".'

Downstairs there was a sudden flurry of activity. Two Amazonian women crashed through the doors, brushing security guards aside and pleading: 'Is this Vinopolis?'

'Are you the registrars?' I begged.

They nodded, one nearly breaking down in tears. They'd been driving around in circles for nearly an hour but the police and security services wouldn't let them stop, let alone park. After a pause so they could get their breath, Paul issued instructions to the manager and we made our way round to the back of the hall. Through the crack in the door we watched as our witnesses, Michelle Collins and Ian McKellen, took their places and an expectant buzz started to fill the room.

Paul looked at me. 'Ready?' he whispered.

I nodded and beamed.

'I love you,' I mouthed.

'I love you too,' he mouthed back.

He raised his thumb to the man on the sound deck, and we took a deep breath, placing our hands on the doors. My eyes were fixed firmly on his, awaiting the signal.

We hadn't rehearsed this but I knew instinctively that I had to follow his lead.

The music began gently with the tender swirls of 'L'Amore Sei Tu' ('I Will Always Love You'), sung in Italian. After about

4

thirty seconds romance gave way to the dramatic sax and piano opening of Abba's 'I Do, I Do, I Do, I Do, I Do'. We pushed our weight against the back doors and stepped into the hall. As one, the congregation turned and cheered. Cottingham had quietly, and painstakingly, done it again.

We were on our way, like never before.

2

It was a cold December. But it wasn't the cold that brought me into the world, it was a street fight outside Stepney East station. A group of men jumped my dad, fists and boots flying in all directions. My mum did the thing any decent wife would do, she waded in.

It was a vicious fight, she threw a few punches, extracted my dad and then they escaped home on a passing bus.

Inside their threadbare council flat my dad inspected his cuts and bruises and my mum let out a cry, clutched her stomach and, three weeks earlier than planned, went into labour with me. The following morning, I was born at Bancroft Road Hospital, Mile End. My dad turned up to look over his second son. He hadn't been around for the first. After a quick glance he told my mum to take care of herself and went to put my name down at the Port Labour Board, so that when I left school I would follow in his footsteps as a docker. Then he embarked on a pub crawl with Grandad Cashman to 'wet the baby's head' and to settle scores from the day before.

The post-war East End was both mesmerising and bloody awful, but there wasn't a better place to be alive and poor. The docks were thriving. Ships and boats were double-berthed along the Thames, and cargo arrived from across the world to be bundled into lorries and carts or on to the backs of strong men. For us kids the war was far enough behind that it felt like a fascinating game, as we rushed between bombsites playing Germans and English, Cowboys and Indians, and sex versions of 'Doctors and Nurses'.

And we, the Cashmans, lived right in the middle of it all – on a council estate on the edge of the River Thames.

St Vincent's in Limehouse was a newly built estate of flats – with blocks with names such as Bahama, Cayman, Garford, Grenada, Jamaica, Nevis, Trinidad and Windward. It accommodated around 2,000 of us, all shapes, all sizes, and Josie the prostitute. In our block lived the Kamaras, the only black family on the estate, and there was someone we called the 'Chinaman'. Another of our neighbours, Mrs Cootes, had lost the use of her legs and travelled around on what looked like a lay-on-your-back bicycle that she pedalled with her hands.

And everywhere there was noise.

The sounds pulled and pushed at you – men shouting, lorries revving up and snarling through streets, cranes and chains descending, ropes and barges pulling against the Thames tides. Then the ships and tugs blasting one another in the queue to be unloaded or pass downriver. Us crying for mums and dads and ice cream from the Wall's ice cream man. Knife grinders on their bikes, wheels forever spinning, the baker's van, the coal lorry, the money lender hammering at a door and always some poor woman inside screaming that nobody's in. Little Mr Pittaway banging away on his rented piano; Jacko the tramp quietly drinking a bottle of tea outside the cafe; a row going on with the caretaker over whose turn it was to wash the stairs. Then there was the rag-and-bone man in search of any old iron, older boys incessantly pretending to be Stanley Matthews and banging a football against the air-raid shelter, cargo crashing to the ground, an ambulance or police bell. And always the women chatting beneath their makeshift turbans – headscarves scooped up from the back of the neck and wrapped around encased hair, invariably teased into plastic curlers or pipe cleaners. Women were rarely seen without this badge of work.

Everywhere the sound of work. As it got dark that noise quietly drifted off along the Thames, following the carts and cargoes, and a hum began that told you night was on its way. Other men and women commenced their labours: nightwatchmen, gate keepers, office cleaners and Josie the prostitute. Other sounds came into play: the pubs, the pianos, radios and televisions – for those of us lucky enough to have one. The evenings spent playing in the playground and stairwells when the noise could be our own, women huddled now in their doorways quietly swapping stories, and laughter and puffs of a shared cigarette.

And then that unspoken moment when everyone had to be indoors, at home. It was the silence watching the little black and white TV in the dark – so we appreciated the picture – that I remember most clearly. And some nights we lay in bed, the lamplight from outside shedding a yellow glow into our bed-room, and waited for noise. It made life interesting, like the films they showed at the Troxy Picture House down the Commercial Road.

Autumn was approaching. You could smell it. A warm, sweet smell riding on the backs of strong winds. You could see it in the trees on our estate. Leaves turning red, then brown. And we knew that through the foot tunnel, under the river, in Greenwich, the conkers would be growing and, any week soon, would be ready to be plucked.

Then, as it got colder, the smells got stronger. From the coal fires, the air thick with soot, and spices, wood drying in the kilns, hops and yeast coming from Taylor Walker's brewery, bananas ripening in Narrow Street warehouses, and horse shit. Horse shit from the carthorses carrying all sorts from West India Docks to Wapping or Buchanan's Wharf, the tea warehouse opposite where we lived. The horses would stand for hours on the cobblestones, as the canvas-backed trailers were loaded with wooden tea chests. Often we waited in the hope that a chest would fall from the grip of the cast-iron cranes and in the shouts and the free-for-all we'd get some tea to take home. If that failed we scavenged the barges tied up on the river, or got into the warehouses themselves.

It was a place where everything was possible, where you could run riot, and, so long as you didn't get caught, nobody cared. It seemed like paradise, even when we were hungry.

I was running home one evening. From where I can't remember, but I was ahead of my two brothers as I sprinted along Narrow Street, and then ran into Three Colt Street. I looked back to see if they were catching me up but there was no sign of them and I was thrilled. I would be the first home.

Suddenly in the deserted street a young man appeared. He was on the corner of the alley that went down to the river, and he was dressed like my dad, like a docker. He was looking straight at me like I had done something and he put his cigarette out as he crossed the road towards me.

I stopped running but kept on walking. I was nearly home, just passing the Enterprise, where my mum and dad went drinking.

The man stood in front of me, smiled and asked me what I was up to, like we were sharing a secret.

I told him I was going home, that I'd done nothing wrong, and pointed to our flats. He laughed and told me that boys were always up to something wrong.

Then he asked if I wanted to earn a shilling. A shilling! I couldn't believe it; you could drown in Tizer and ice cream with a shilling, it was a fortune. So I quickly said yes in case he changed his mind.

He nodded and told me to follow him, and we walked down the alley to the river where he lifted me up onto the wall. On the other side of the alley was Dundee Wharf. It was then I thought I knew what he wanted: 'You want me to break in for yer?' I asked.

He put his finger to his lips, got up onto the wall with me, and then pulled us both down onto the other side, keeping hold of my arm. He pressed himself back against the wall and I mimicked him.

The light from the nightwatchman's office suddenly made me aware how dark it was. It was that silence, too, that always meant you had to be at home, or be careful. I was going to tell him that I didn't want the shilling after all and that I should go. My heart was racing, beating, jumping in my chest. I'd broken in before, usually going in through a fanlight window then opening the door, but it had always been for my dad, and normally when he'd had too much to drink on a Sunday or Saturday afternoon.

This was different. This was real.

He looked in the direction of the nightwatchman, then smiled at me. His hand tightened around my arm and he started to walk me up the ramp where the trailers were backed up ready to be loaded. It was then that I noticed his smell. It was really strong; you could almost taste it, like salt and sweet.

Away from the street lights it got darker. I could hardly see where we were going. Then he suddenly stopped. I tried to make sense of what was happening and looked up at him. His hand came over my mouth and he pushed me into a trailer. I struggled but he was forcing me down. His other hand was tugging at his belt.

I tried to push back, but I couldn't breathe. I thought my head was going to explode.

He then went very still and looked at me. He raised his fist and snarled like a dog. I didn't know why he was doing this to me. I'd done nothing wrong. All I'd wanted was a shilling.

My heart was banging in my chest but everything else was quiet. Except his breathing. Then he started to pull my shorts down.

I didn't want him to. I wanted to scream, I wanted my brothers, I wanted to be home and I wanted my mum. But he kept pulling and then they were down. I was ashamed because I had nothing on underneath and I started to cry.

He pushed me down onto the floor, and his hand pressed harder against my mouth. I still couldn't breathe.

Outside everything was silence. I wanted to hear something. Anything. Then he put his hand between my legs, grabbed my cock and pushed himself harder onto me. I thought I was going to be crushed. My head was swimming and I was hitting him because I couldn't breathe, but he didn't care.

He stood up and pulled me with him and I tried to get my shorts up but I couldn't. Then he made me play with his cock.

I didn't want to but he made me touch it.

And I didn't know why he was doing this to me. He had been nice. He had talked to me like I was important and smiled at me. I thought he liked me. But now he was touching me, and I sobbed because it was wrong and if anyone found out I knew I would get into trouble. But it wasn't my fault. I'd just wanted the shilling.

He was quietly laughing, but it wasn't a nice laugh, he was telling me my prick was like a little sparrow. Saying it again and again, and then he threw me back onto the floor and shoved his cock between my legs. His grip on my mouth tightened and I felt my face starting to explode like a balloon. Then something happened.

I was wet. Wet between my legs and I didn't know why. He started making sounds like he was hurt, then it went quiet and he stood up, quickly did his trousers up and looked down at me.

I waited for a noise outside to tell me I was safe, but still there was only silence. He told me to stay where I was, that I was to be good, then pointed his finger at me and said he knew where I lived. I nodded and just kept nodding and trying not to cry. And I wished I had never wanted that fucking shilling.

Then he ran into the silence outside. I heard him running and although I wanted to run too I wasn't sure if he would get me, so I sat in the trailer until the sound of his boots went away.

Eventually I wiped my face on my T-shirt and pulled up my shorts. That was when I knew I would really be in trouble because he had broken the snake buckle on my elastic belt.

I tried to climb back over the wall, but I couldn't. So I just walked past the nightwatchman's office and he didn't even see me.

My dad gave me a clip behind the ear when he opened our front door and told me off for being out late. I made my way along our unlit hallway towards the light coming from the black and white television in the living room. Everyone there ignored me and carried on watching telly. I sat down on the hard chair by the door, pleased that no one was looking at me. That they couldn't see I had been crying, or that my belt buckle was broken. Then I suddenly got really angry because I realised that the bastard hadn't given me the shilling either.

Weeks later I remembered how he had smiled at me. I would remember that often.

The secret of that night I kept to myself. I knew I couldn't tell anyone because of what they would think of me. They would say that I had 'asked' for it, and that I was really a 'bummer'.

Then one day, when we were all playing on the river, I saw him. We were larking around on the long iron barges at high tide, jumping as the waves crashed against the sides and the barges boomed and collided. We were laughing and shouting but when he appeared I went quiet and watched him.

He came over and chatted to us and, because he was so ordinary and so nice, I thought I must have imagined it was him.

Then I smelt him.

My heart jumped, but I knew I mustn't do or say anything. The smell filled my head. I knew for sure it was him. And he knew I knew. I got up and told my mates to come with me. But they wouldn't.

I stood there watching him with them; he wasn't even looking at me; it was as if I didn't exist. He just kept smiling that smile that made everything seem all right. He took off his coat and lay on the canvas top of the barge as my mates sat around him.

I walked away. But a part of me really wanted to shout out that they should watch their cocks, and that he owed me a fucking shilling.

3

After that night I started wetting the bed.

My mum and dad couldn't understand it and my brothers screamed blue murder as I drenched them in our shared bed every night. They tried wrapping me in towels and blankets but nothing worked; I could piss for Britain. It was terrible for everyone, as they dragged me out of bed and the shouting started. My brothers always joined in because they didn't know any different.

Mum washed me in the scullery every morning and dried me out in front of the gas oven. It was awful being stood up in the sink naked, my mum holding me like a plucked turkey and then scraping the skin off my bones with an old cloth and a bar of Lifebuoy, all the time muttering under her breath.

I didn't like upsetting them. I told my mum that I was sorry. But I don't think she heard me. As my brothers ate their cornflakes they shouted that I stank, and that the fumes would kill the budgies our dad was breeding on the top of the scullery cupboard. But I ignored them, and the budgies had chicks anyway so the smell couldn't have been that bad. And once we were out of our flat and off to school the night-time waterworks were forgotten. The Cashman boys stuck up for one another.

We went to St Mary's and St Joseph's Catholic Primary School on Poplar High Street. Every morning we walked up Garford Street, past West India Docks and the sailors coming out and the crowds of men waiting for work, or for Charlie Brown's pub to open, and lorry after lorry coming out or going in. And there was always the noise of people shouting, bells on bikes, hooters and horses.

We crossed over the busy road and walked up to China Town, Pennyfields, and we'd stare at what we called the 'Chinamen' with their hats and pigtails, or cover our faces against the smells billowing out from the Chinese restaurants. On past the White Horse pub with its horse standing on a big pole and then into school, that great big building spread over two floors, with a rarely used playground on the roof.

It was a walk where you kept your wits about you, and it was exciting, except when it was raining or wet and the water came through the holes in our shoes and into our socks. On those days it was no use telling the nuns at school because you knew everyone else was soaking from the feet up. There were times when I was soaking from the crotch down too, when the teachers wouldn't let me go to the toilet. 'You've been already,' they'd snort, and that would start me off like a tap. And I would have to try and wrap my shorts over themselves so no one could see the spreading wet patch.

But I felt different at school. Like I belonged. We had school dinners, when our mum could afford it, and a bottle of milk to drink, and cod liver oil tablets, and a nurse and a doctor who were always looking for fleas, or nits, or checking your balls. I hated those medicals after what that man did to me. It felt like the worst kind of torture that anyone could think up. So I avoided them and went missing whenever I had an appointment. But the school soon caught on and they gave me notes to take home for my mum, never my dad. Knowing what the letters were about I tore them up and buried them on a bomb site. Finally a letter in a brown envelope would be held up to my face by my dad, posted by the school, and I got a wallop from him, and a doctor feeling my balls into the bargain. It just seemed sometimes with adults that you couldn't win, they always got their way.

Apart from the 'bastard nuns' as my dad called them, most of the teachers were interested in me, and I could make them smile, sometimes even laugh.

Sister Mary Ann wasn't like the other nuns. She laughed – a lot – and she liked me because I was good at country dancing and could 'fly around the room like a whippet'. She would wind up the gramophone in the corner of junior assembly, place the needle on the record and, after a few seconds of cracks and spits, an accordion would be heard and we'd be off! Highland Fling, Eightsome Reel, Scottish country dancing! I was in another world.

And oh the joy, the utter Wall's ice-cream-eating sensation, of being asked to read aloud to the class by Miss O'Sullivan. With a book in my hand everything went quiet as the whole class looked at me expectantly, even Miss O'Sullivan. I'd play with the words, making them sound big or small, I'd use different voices like in the cartoons, and I read it to them like they wanted to hear it. It made me feel special. Afterwards no one ever punched me, hit me or called me names like 'teacher's pet'. They were just quiet. And that was really, really good.

I wanted to be liked and I wanted the teacher's praise, but most of all, I wanted to belong with the 'Holy Joes'.

So it was the same old routine every Monday morning. In the ground-floor assembly hall we'd stand in our classes with the teachers in front of us, Sister Mary Ann poised at the piano, then as the headmistress Sister Mary Ita's wimple appeared through the doorway we were off! Singing our hearts out – 'All Things Bright and Beautiful' usually – then praying for the lost souls in Africa, saying a few words about the Catechism and wrapping it all up with a Hail Mary and the Sign of the Cross: 'In the Name of the Father, and of the Son, and of the Holy Ghost. Amen.'

That's when Sister Mary Ita would walk forward and stare out of her starched white wimple. I'd tell myself not to say a word, but my imagination always got hold of my tongue. 'Put your hands up who went to Mass of a Sunday,' she'd say, and my arm, having a mind of its own, would shoot up like a rocket. Each 'Holy Joe' tried to outreach the other with squeaks of 'Miss. Miss. Me, Miss,' but I would go one better: 'Sister! Sister!'

Eventually she always chose me.

She'd ask me, for instance, whether as I went to Mass I'd like to tell them all what colour the priest's vestments were. The trouble was I didn't know the answer; I hadn't been to Mass, so I'd pluck a colour from thin air.

'Pink!' I'd say confidently, almost like I was bragging.

'Is that right?' she'd reply with a sharp intake of breath. That's when I knew I was in for it.

I honestly thought she would take me at my word, but no, every week began with the same old caning. So I finally decided it would be easier to go to Mass on a Sunday. The shock on her hard, scrubbed face when I not only gave her the right colour but described the trimmings and announced that I was going to serve as an altar boy, and that it 'wasn't a lie neither', was a joy to behold. With a satisfied glow I knew she couldn't cane me, even though I could see her eager hand twitching (and Sister Mary Ann suppressing a smile). Sister Mary Ita was never a woman to be silenced and responded that she had great sympathy for the priest, and that God worked in mysterious ways that even she sometimes found hard to understand.

When I turned eight and had to leave junior school I was really upset and wouldn't let go of Miss O'Sullivan. I didn't want to cry, it just happened. I stood at the top of the iron staircase that led to the playground and the big building just on the other side. I had felt safe at school until now, and I was terrified that it wouldn't be the same again.

Miss O'Sullivan stood in her green brogues, her grey hair tucked up into a kind of crown shape, dressed in a long, green, woollen tweed dress, and watched me as I descended the staircase, her arms crossed. I looked up at her. She waved me on. I walked out of the school gate, back along Poplar High Street, past the 'Chinamen' and the Chinese restaurants and home to Garford House. And although the six weeks of summer holidays were now beginning, and I could run riot with my mates, all I felt was sad.

When I went back to school, after our hop-picking holiday and the summer, it was to the big building and to different teachers.

I'd look out for Miss O'Sullivan across the way but she seemed never to notice me. Eventually Miss Donkin became my class teacher, and though I did see her smile a couple of times, she was very strict and made me feel stupid. Then one day we were told that we had to prepare for the 'eleven-plus', whatever that was. And school didn't feel the same again.

4

What I lost from Miss O'Sullivan I got from Lou Clench.

Lou Clench ran the tiny, overstuffed shop on the corner of Emmett Street and West Ferry Road with her husband Ned Murray and her dad Tom.

Tom was old and round and always wore a brown full-length porter's coat with a shirt and tie underneath; one of the coat sleeves was tucked neatly into the pocket as he had lost an arm. Various explanations for the loss were often discussed: some said he lost it in the Great War, others claimed that a woman had asked for credit while Tom had the till open and he slammed it shut with such force that he ripped his arm off.

Whatever the truth, it was my way of coming to the attention of Lou. Tall, thin and stooped, she too had a long brown porter's coat. In the shop she never wore any make-up and her silver-white hair just hung limp and lifeless, held back from her glasses by a single metal hairclip. Perpetually in her right hand was a white hanky which she'd dab her face with or rub agitatedly under her nose when working out someone's bill.

Lou had decided that she needed someone to help her father with his evening and morning paper rounds. My brother Johnny had done it but was now interested in other things. Like always being round our Uncle Charlie's where no one knew the mischief he got up to, except Uncle Charlie, who encouraged him. Anyway, I spotted an opportunity and went for it.

It was simple enough. I would hold her dog, Jip, on his lead, and simultaneously open the letter box so that old man Clench could shove the paper through. After that I would go with him to the Enterprise, get a bottle of MacKintosh Cream label for Lou and a bottle of stout for Ned and then head back to the shop.

Not that Ned was often there. He would go missing for days on end and was a man of very few words, even to Lou. According to the women, he was 'always up Aldgate' where the prostitutes could be found; and I heard the men say that, looking at Lou, they'd go up Aldgate too.

With Ned so often on the missing list I was promoted to helping out in the shop after school, in school holidays and at weekends. I was given a wooden box to stand on in order to see the customers, young and old. Perched on my crate I could look out across the sweet counter at my empire.

The shop was tiny, even to someone as small as me, but there was nothing that Lou didn't have. In the shop a bench and narrow table were squeezed up against the front window and in the summer the bench was placed outside. From the overhead lights hung brown flypapers stuck with unlucky flies, on the counter in enamel bins and glass display cabinets were fresh bread and rolls, home-cooked hams, corned beef, rolls of Spam, cheeses, and cigarettes in packets of twos, fives and tens. The overstocked shelves rose from floor to ceiling, and an L-shaped counter separated us from the public. In the mornings it was also a snack bar. The dock workers would take their mugs of tea and massive crusty white-bread sandwiches of ham cut from the bone, or Cheddar cheese and pickle.

Upstairs one of the two bedrooms had been turned into the store room, and it was packed to the rafters with boxes. Boxes were placed upon other boxes: Izal toilet tissue (which ripped your arse off), Harpic, Omo and Daz washing powders, bleach, carbolic soaps, Vosene shampoo. Separated away were cases of sugar, tins and tins of fruit, beans, peas, Carnation milk, fly paper, flour, and sweets by the jar load. Under the window were the mysterious Dr White's 'STs' which the women never actually asked for, they wordlessly mouthed, after which Lou would nod and quietly wrap them in newspaper.

On the same floor was the Clenches' living room, with a radio, but no telly, and a tiny kitchen. The downstairs toilet, which had a tin bath hanging on the door, was the most forbidding place imaginable: freezing in the winter and fly-ridden in the summer. I once mentioned to Lou that it was dark in there too, to which she replied: 'It's for shitting in Nobby, not loafing in.' And the subject was closed.

Why she named me Nobby I never knew, but I was never called anything else, even if she came to our flat looking for me. 'Is Nobby in?' she'd ask. And my dad would shake his head like she'd escaped from the 'local loony bin' and just to piss her off would ask her how Ned was. This was another question she was fond of ignoring. She rarely talked about Ned. In fact, apart from Jip and the stray cats, which she loved, she rarely talked about anything.

In the morning the shop smelt of fresh bread and rolls from the bakers, and home-cooked hams cooling in the back. I loved to be at 'Clenchie's'. I'd run from school to get there, and at the weekend would jump out of bed before my mum could drag me to the sink. If I was early I would bang on the door and upon opening it Lou would say: 'Have you shit the bed'? But, as with most of Lou's questions, it was just better to ignore them and pretend she hadn't said anything. She never expected an answer anyway, that was what was lovely about her; she was different from other adults.

Once I was in the shop my day would start. 'Nobby, get me some STs. Blues and Pinks. And tea. And sugar. And some condensed milk...' Lou would mutter orders until the list was done. I'd be off up the stairs, scampering across a room that housed everything that everyone downstairs wanted but could only get from Lou. Or me. In the evenings, after Lou had taken a mop and brush to the place, the shop would smell of bleach and pine. And in that lovely evening silence, as the traffic lumbered past, Lou would give me the delicate job of knowing exactly when to lay cardboard on the drying lino floors. 'If it's worth doing Nobby, it's worth doing well,' she would say.

At the end of the week, on Saturday, I was paid two shillings and sixpence – half a crown – given a large brown egg ('that's for yer tea, Nobby') and half a pound of the most expensive sweets in the shop: sugared almonds. The longer I worked in the shop the more I began to realise why Lou was so fond of dishing out the sugared almonds. They were shop-soiled, literally: Jip loved cocking his leg over the boxes of them stashed behind the counter.

One day I witnessed the pissing offence and called Lou over, but she dismissed it. 'You gotta eat a bit of dirt before you die, Nobby,' she said, and the subject was never spoken of again.

After that I enjoyed watching my mum and dad and brothers tucking into the sugared almonds on Saturday nights, while I sucked on a bag of aniseed twists, or a couple of gobstoppers.

The best part of the shop job was asking adults, and especially kids, if I could help them and adding up what they had spent as I went along. In the early days Lou would watch me out of the corner of her National Health glasses, and I could see her counting along with me, just to check. I then passed her the money and she counted the change out for the customer or counted it out to me and watched me repeat it.

If it was a kid being served she wrote the calculations on the shopping list and screwed the paper into a twist to hold the change. I must have been doing the sums right because she gave up watching and counting alongside me and even let me serve my own brothers. But she never let me serve my mum.

The worst part of the job was taking Jip for his walk. He hated other dogs and they hated him. It would be a nightly struggle as he heaved one way towards the barking warriors and I pulled the other, dragging him towards the Enterprise off-licence at the other end of the street. There I'd get Lou's bottle of Cream Label, stuff it into the shopping bag and then try to make my way back without smashing it in the canine battles ahead.

Sometimes I'd take a rest at our flat on the first floor of Garford House. Because we lived at the corner flat, I could chain Jip up to the pipes on the landing balcony and go inside and have my tea before heading back to Lou's. Once I took Jip inside our scullery, where he lay out on the floor like he was bored. I must have given my mum some lip, because she swept out her hand to cuff me and Jip jumped to his hind legs and snarled at her. Seeing Jip do that for me made me love him. I didn't know that he even liked me, let alone that he would fight for me. And it felt really good, especially when I smiled at my mum and whistled as I left the flat.

Ned disappeared more and more frequently, especially after Lou's dad died. For a while she'd ask him where he was going, but he said nothing, put on his brown trilby hat and went. When he came back she'd just ignore him: the bell would ring as the shop door opened, she'd turn to see him, and then go back to whatever she'd been doing. She never said anything; it was like he wasn't there. But sometimes when they were together they were really nice to me.

Once they told me I was going to spend Christmas Day with them. Lou said it was going to be red ribbons, the Queen's Speech and a goose. I went round there in my Christmas suit that mum had bought with a provident cheque on the never-never from Harry Neeve's. Ned got drunk, and me and Lou pulled a cracker between us, sitting at the table wearing paper hats as Ned sat there smiling and nodding all afternoon.

At other times Lou would take me out for a treat to the Troxy. She'd always put on her smart topcoat with a fur collar for these occasions and we'd set off from the shop. Approached from the Commercial Road at night, ablaze with lights, the Troxy looked amazing. Inside, the manager – black suit, white shirt, black bow tie – would approach us and say: 'Evening, Miss Clench', and stand there holding out his hand. But Lou never shook it; she'd just hand him her complimentary tickets (she had a cinema advertisement board outside the shop). Once he escorted us up a long staircase to the posh bit of the cinema where I had never been before, and into our seats.

We didn't go to the pictures very often but when we did it was always to see a film that made Lou cry, and she'd get full use out of the hanky that always hung from her right hand. I regularly went to the Troxy though with my brothers and mates for the kids' Saturday matinee, when we would shout through the films, boo the Indians, cheer Roy Rogers, laugh at Spanky and his Gang, throw things at the organist as he descended into the ground, and search for the two seats that 'Old Fat Minnie', the barber, sat in. But when I went there with Lou, into the posh seats, I was quiet and well behaved. It felt like the films came out and captured me. It was magical.

Other times we ventured further afield. Occasionally on a Sunday afternoon Lou would take me to her sister's in Catford, on the 'other side of the water'. At five o'clock, after we finished our tea, which consisted of tinned pilchards in tomato sauce, lettuce, tomatoes and spring onions, washed down with a cup of tea, we'd all stand around the piano on which Lou would bash out song after song as we sang along. She'd make me stand on a footstool and I'd sing 'Slow Boat to China' or one of her other favourites. And we clapped and cheered and it felt really warm and lovely to be with them, and to see a Lou that nobody else could see, except in Catford – a smiling, happy Lou. I noticed how different she was as her face came to life. Then, without any notice, she'd stand up, close the piano and say it was time for hats and coats, and off we'd go, on the bus back to West Ferry Road. She'd watch as I walked onto our estate: 'Straight home, Nobby', she'd say. Then she'd turn and walk up the street to the darkened rooms above the corner shop, and me to Garford House, the place I called home.

Then one day it all came to an end. I wanted to be out playing with my mates, but I still really enjoyed my time with Lou. My mates kept saying that if I really liked them then I would be with them. I should have acted like a grown-up and talked to Lou about it. I loved being there; I loved that there was never any fuss, and that she liked me being there too. But with all the confusion in my head, of wanting to please my mates, and then of that man interfering with me, one day, I played up and refused to go to the store room, so that she would sack me.

Which she did. 'Collect yer cards, Nobby,' she said. Except I was too young to have a national insurance card. So I just left.

Whenever I went back, on an errand for my mum or a neighbour, it was as if she didn't know me. Nobby didn't exist any more and deep down I knew I had upset her, that I had let her down. But I always smiled and thanked her, and called her Lou. And she always looked straight back into my eyes without smiling.

5

At Garford House we originally lived on the top floor, at number 55. From there you could see all of the St Vincent's estate and sometimes the tops of the ships in West India Docks. It was a U-shaped block with mates on nearly every floor, and a great big air-raid shelter in the middle of the playground that had been bricked up after the war. Other smaller blocks of flats – Cayman House, Windward House and Jamaica House – ran alongside the road that bordered the estate and this was our manor. Here you were safe. If you ventured across the road into Providence House or the other blocks you were in hostile territory and the boys would either beat you up or try to 'bum' you.

It was later that we moved down to the first floor. Mum and Dad had their own bedroom there and I was in the other one with Johnny and Stevie, sharing the same bed, until I got into the pissing for Britain mode. Then it all changed. Our fourth brother, Danny, had come along by then.

Along the same landing as us were my mum's best friends, Betty Wood and Eva Marston, who she went office cleaning with. Eva was slim and thin and dark, and her sons were our best friends. Betty was the 'size of a house' and her legs were etched with vari-cose veins from always standing in front of the coal fire. One day when my mum and Betty were leaning over the balcony, chewing the fat, my younger brother Stevie rushed in and shouted: 'Dad, Dad! Betty Woods's got no drawers on!'

'That's why she's got seven kids,' my dad responded.

Her husband, who we only knew as Mr Wood, was a long-distance lorry driver and polisher of his car, which he only used on Sundays. On those rare occasions when he was home he had an uncanny knack of knowing when someone was around his precious vehicle and he'd rush out onto the communal balcony, shouting: 'You go near that car again and I will stick my big toe right up your arse.'

And we knew he would, so we'd scarper.

We careered around the estate on go-karts – which consisted of a plank and four pram wheels. If you were really lucky and had a dad or brother who was handy with a hammer and nails then the kart would have front steering wheels that meant you and the kart could always go in the same direction round the corner.

As soon as one game was over another was invented. Nothing could interrupt us, not even the Sisters of Holy Charity, or Josie with another drunken punter in tow. Happy as we were, we knew money was short, but what someone else had you could have too – a few coppers for the gas or electric meter, or even the odd shilling. So people would lend one another money if they could. Betty Wood was always good for a loan because Mr Wood worked regular. Others, like Flo Thompson, were not so lucky. She had a son and a mother and 'no man in the house'. Sometimes my mum would try to borrow from her mum and dad, but Grandad Clayton didn't approve. He was a quiet man who wore a collar and tie to work and lived in a place called Ratcliffe Orchard. But it wasn't really an orchard, it was a row of houses in an alley just off Stepney Highway. My mum would sit in the corner of their front room, biting her nails, as she waited for the same response that always came: 'You have to manage, Mary. You have to manage.' Then, when Grandad wasn't looking, Nan Clayton would slip her a few shillings. If it was really bad my mum would load us all onto the pram and we'd go and visit Nan Cashman. When all else failed it was the pawn shop or the loan man.

All that mattered was that you had the money you needed to get the gas on and the food on the table. How you paid it back was for another day.

Life was never dull at Garford House. If there was no enter-tainment then you made your own. I loved doing shows for the mums, and dancing, not just Scottish country dancing like at school, but jiving, and wiggling my hips and kicking my legs up like the dancers from *Sunday Night at the London Palladium*, which was on telly.

One day when my favourite aunt, Eileen, was in our flat my mum put on a record and asked me to dance for them. I obliged, and jigged and jumped, and they laughed and whooped and clapped and then I heard my mum say: 'I think he's one of *them*.' I panicked. In my heart I stopped dancing because I knew that what she had said meant I was different. And I knew I was different from the other boys. I just knew. I wanted to shout at her and Eileen and tell them to stop laughing at me. Instead I carried on dancing and I hoped they would forget what Mum had said.

When I finished they hugged me and Eileen kissed me, but I knew they knew I was different. It made me feel a little bit scared, and a little bit nice too.

Besides, I was only seven or eight and soon was distracted by other things. As long as I had my special mate Micky our secret games would be all right. Micky lived on the same estate, we were the same age and we got into the same trouble, which was good. One day, long before that man came along, he showed me how to play Doctors and Nurses without the nurse, just the two of us, and I preferred that, but I had to promise never to tell anyone. That was why he was special.

My dad worked near the Tower of London in the London Docks, loading and unloading the cargo, frequently into his own pockets. This meant that we had things that other kids never had, like oranges, tangerines and Brazil nuts.

But there were months when he couldn't get any work and he had to wait in line with the other men, hoping to be taken on, even for a day. Sometimes he did other work, like at Christmas when he sorted letters throughout the night, or went cleaning with my mum. At other times he borrowed money and went drinking with Grandad Cashman, who had one leg. We knew where Grandad had lost his leg, unlike Tom Clench and his arm. It was in the war, the first one, in which he had also been gassed. In his pub people would send Grandad over a beer; they knew he went looking for work but rarely got it. Sometimes we saw him in agony as he lay on my nan's floor trying to strap the leg onto his ulcerated stump. On those days he needed the booze more than on any other.

Maybe that was why he was always clever at being able to get a few pounds together, like when our families went hop-picking in Kent. The Cashmans and our relatives the Claytons, the Treumanns, the Ealeses, the Marshes and various neighbours would join thousands of other families at the end of summer to pick the hops from the vines that grew across the Kent fields. People came from all parts of London and the farmers knew which Londoners to keep apart; there were enough fights and rivalries over the docks and jobs to start them again over a bale of hops. Harmony only presided when they kept those of us from north of the river away from those from the south side.

We'd arrive on lorries and vans with everything but the kitchen sink, then we'd spend weeks living in wooden huts with everyone crammed into the same straw bed and cooking on a makeshift fire outside. There was no electricity, just paraffin oil lamps, bonfires, cold water and toilets dug over holes. And it was heaven. We kids chased anything that moved and, although we didn't know the difference between a cow and a bull, we did know how to pinch apples and pears and anything else that wasn't nailed down.

The men who stayed all week with their families were often the grandparents or the men who'd been shell-shocked or injured in the wars. They never picked the hops, that was 'women's work', they just lurked. Grandad Cashman was one such lurker. Down hopping it was always harder for him to get some drink money. That was until he saw me singing outside the village pub. The next night he produced a couple of beer crates for me to stand on and announced that I was going to give a few songs. Affecting a good limp with his wooden leg and his crutch, he toured the onlookers with his cap held out to them as I sang.

We developed a good relationship. He'd collect the money, go in the pub and consume more drink, which ultimately meant there were more empty crates for me to stand on. When my dad arrived on Friday nights with money, the two of them disappeared for a booze-up and my speciality act was quickly deemed unnecessary and forgotten. But I'd tasted my first audience, and I liked it.

Some evenings in London we were taken to Grandad's canvas hut where he was a nightwatchman overlooking the road works, and he and my dad would huddle together silently, drinking bottles of beer, staring at the coke fire. The days when Dad went drinking with Grandad in the pub were not good ones. They always ended in a row. Either with my nan, or at home in Garford House.

They would roll back to Grandad's drunk and Dad would sit in Nan's scullery giving her backchat. Because she was deaf she often couldn't hear him; then, all of a sudden, she would make a grab for him and scream: 'Come 'ere you hook-nosed bastard', but she never caught him.

At our home it was worse. The rows were followed by days of silence. Then, one day, my mum decided that if he was going drinking in the evenings, then she was going with him.

Fridays and Saturdays were always the worst. Sometimes my brothers and I accompanied them to the pub and sat on the bench outside with the other kids, listening to the piano and the singing. At times like that it was perfect: everyone together, laughing, making nice noises as they got drunk and silly. Then, when our lemonade or crisps or arrowroot biscuits ran out, we'd pop our heads inside and get fresh supplies. Some nights we were even given a bottle of Mann's sweet Brown Ale, which we had to keep hidden under the bench. Other nights we waited at home, listening for the sound of the key turning in the lock, at which point we would all go quiet. Poised to listen for the silence.

If Mum and Dad were talking and chatting we knew it would be lovely; but silence meant trouble. My brothers always said that I made it worse, but I couldn't help myself. I wished I could. As soon as I heard my dad bolt the front door from the inside I'd jump up. Dressed only in my vest I'd listen by our half-open bedroom door, the light from the living room streaming into the hallway. Johnny and Stevie told me to mind my own business, to get back into bed. Danny, the youngest, knew it was best to say nothing. Then suddenly out of the silence my dad would say something about the money it cost him because my mum had accepted a drink from someone and he had to buy them all a drink back, or accuse her of being 'after' someone. Though I never really understood what the arguments were about, from their voices I knew it was bad. I could feel him hitting her with his words, and she said nothing in reply. If she did say any-thing he would shout over her that she was a 'fucking whore', or a bastard this and another fucking that. And those words churned inside my stomach and my head felt like it was going to explode, like when that man put his hand over my mouth and held me down. From the living room the words came in all different directions and my fingers would find the door handle even though Johnny and Stevie pleaded with me not to. I knew it was terrible and bad because his voice cut like a knife.

'Cunt. You fucking cunt.'

I'd rush in and tell him to leave her alone, but at that moment I knew my brothers were right.

It always made it worse. Especially when I stood between them and tried to hit him. He'd push me away or hold my head like he was dangling me off a ledge. All the time I was hitting out and never managing to touch him. My brothers were so lucky because they stayed where they were. They could help to make the peace and pretend that they hadn't heard the fight, and that everything was all right.

If the row was serious Mum would run out onto the common balcony. He'd slam the door behind her and bolt it, with her out-side in the dark, and go to bed. I'd wait until Dad was asleep and whisper to my mum through the letter box. And she'd tell me to be a good boy and go to bed. But I couldn't. So I'd sit on one side of the front door knowing she was on the other. If we thought the coast was clear I'd get a chair from the scullery, unbolt the door and let her in. Other nights she'd stay there, and ask me to push her cleaning things through the fanlight so that she could go to work the next morning, and then she'd fall asleep on the step.

On these nights I could never go to bed. And I really wanted to hurt him for what he had done to her.

Despite this he could be really nice, like when she was ill.

We all watched in our scullery in the early hours of the morning as he strapped a scalding hot kaolin and morphine poultice onto her back so she wouldn't get pleurisy and she could go office cleaning, and he would tell her that it was going to be 'all right', soothing her by repeating: 'It'll be all right. It'll be all right.' Johnny, Stevie, Danny and I sat there wanting and hoping for it to be okay.

At other times when he was 'in the drink' he could be funny. Especially at weddings, when he had a habit of disappearing and then returning dressed up like an old lady, or a little boy in shorts. Or when he came down to the hop fields in Kent – Yording – everyone said he was the 'life and soul of the party'. And he was. On those occasions it was perfect. It was the other times that I remembered more though.

It must have been difficult to put up with me. I had an 'over-active imagination'; I was always singing and dressing up, inventing stories and games. I craved attention, and I never knew when to keep my mouth shut – especially when the neighbours chastised me.

Now I was at the bigger side of the school I wasn't really happy there either. It seemed I could never do the right thing. Not even when I went through the 'Holy Joe' phase and became an altar boy. During Bible class the young priest, tired of my persistent questions, bounced the Good Book off my head and told me to 'get the fuck out'.

6

Most of my friends were going to the grammar schools, while I would join my eldest brother Johnny at the secondary modern school in Poplar. I had failed my eleven-plus, but as I didn't even know what it was it didn't matter, and Mum and Dad seemed relieved that they wouldn't have to get a provident cheque to pay for grammar school clothes. My special mate Micky was going to the same school also, but he no longer seemed interested in me, or our games. He had other friends now, and, like him, they played sports.

Cardinal Griffin School was next door to the Catholic Church where we would be taken for Mass, Communion, Benediction and – especially – Confession. The school was bigger than any-where I had ever been: rows and rows of two-storey buildings looking out onto tarmac that passed as a space for recreation. There were science labs, metal workshops, woodwork shops, a fearsome gym with 'horses', and ropes that went to an unreach-ably high ceiling; then room after room for French, history, algebra and any other torture that they could dream up. At the other school they knew who we were, but here they didn't care, and called you by your surname like it was a piece of shit. The teachers seemed permanently at war and always on the lookout for enemy spies. The school stank of piss and bleach and despair. It dared you to get it wrong, and possessed a ready arsenal for when you did. I had walked into a battlefield and I was com-pletely unprepared. The war was fought in the classrooms and corridors, and often spread with you and the other kids onto the streets.

I lusted after the PE teacher as soon as I saw him, and the fact that he looked right through me made him even more attractive. The other exotic person was a real Frenchwoman, Miss René, who taught French. She looked like a film star, and I adored going off at lunchtime to buy her an 'apple and fromage'. The eccentrics were the two Miss Youleses. They were known as Big Miss Youles, who was thinner, taller and the deputy head, and Little Miss Youles, who also taught French. Except, she didn't. She taught cockney French, along the lines of 'Parlez Français, son. Parlez Français!' Accompanied by a screwing-up of her face and blinking her eyes as if Jesus had just taken off his loincloth.

Then there was our poor form teacher, Miss Davicci. I was in 1X1, the top stream, and we were considered to be the cleverest. We showed how good we were over the space of a couple of months by destroying her so thoroughly that she never returned.

As for the other teachers, they were either nondescript, professional misfits or thugs. The thugs were there to administer discipline. Usually six strokes of the cane either across your arse or your hand, and always witnessed by a class, or assembly. We were told that we were there to learn a trade, to get a job; they made us feel that we would count for nothing and that our lives were going to be tough so we had better get used to it. I rose to the challenge and became rebellious (I could indulge my overactive imagination), as I thought that way the other boys would want to be with me. I knew I didn't fit in with them, that I was different, but I wanted to hide it, and I wanted to be with them. Especially the sporty ones, and the prefects, but it was as if I didn't exist. I waited for them, was nice to them, smiled and laughed. I wanted more than anything in the world for them to ask me to do something for them. But they told me I was stupid, and crap at football, which I was.

So I gave up and told them to go fuck themselves, but I never meant it because I sat in the changing room after PE just to look at them. I pretended that I couldn't find my socks, or my vest, as I waited for the ones who would take their time getting dressed.

Standing naked or in their underpants I snatched glances that would be hidden away until later. My heart pounded so much I was convinced they could hear it.

One boy was friendly, even though he was from the Isle of Dogs, and he would smile. He was good at sports and let me watch him get dressed. When I realised he was happy for me to observe him I breathed out like I had never breathed before. Without having to hide my eyes or look away I sat the other side of the changing room and ran my eyes over every bit of his body. I wanted to touch him. I looked forward to those afternoons like nothing else on earth.

On the football pitch I lived up to being 'useless' and when they forced me to play I kicked the ball into my own goal so that they'd send me off. But not before I had had a good beating from the teachers and the boys. Sports terrified me, I felt inadequate. Particularly on the days we went to Goresbrook. Every Monday we'd board coaches to take us to playing fields in Essex. After running round pitches, chasing balls and boys, it was then the cruelty of the cold showers. We were packed into a long communal shower, followed by cock waving and comparing as they looked, not for the biggest, but for the smallest. No matter how much I tried to hide myself they always picked on me. I knew I wasn't small, I was just petrified.

And there, doing the laughing and the pointing, was my special friend Micky, who now loved humiliating me, while forgetting that he had played with my dick and I had played with his.

If the boys wouldn't have me I decided to hang around with the girls, so that we could pretend to hate the boys together. I'd been at school for nearly three months and I was often in serious trouble, regularly being caned for insolence or creating anarchy in the classroom. Then out of the blue one of the girls took me to Mr Everett's drama class in the lunch break. I had to volunteer to go because I couldn't take drama for another year. Some of the lads told me to watch myself there, unless I was a bummer as well, but that only made me more curious. They even said I had to watch Mr Everett, but it was rumoured that he had eyes for the headmaster's wife, and besides, he was posh and had been in the army so I reckoned he couldn't possibly be a bummer.

His lunchtime class was like a different world! The elegant and interesting teachers were there, all three of them: the two who we thought were having an affair with one another, and the PE teacher! I thought I might get a chance to finally touch him, but he avoided me like the clap and looked right through me to the older Maltese and Cypriot boys, who had his undivided attention. Yet even he was confusing because one of the women teachers was in love with him, and he used to hold her hand and kiss her.

Despite the confusion I sensed I would be okay here. People ignored you and let you get on with whatever you wanted to do. Finally I could be me. I could be different. Drama became my haven; I put up with the pain of the other classes because I knew at lunchtime I could escape to that kaleidoscope on the other side of the red curtain! No longer was I among the first out of the school gates to get home to fantasise over my mates or the gym teacher; now I fantasised on the school stage.

I will never forget being in the assembly hall behind the curtain and someone putting the song 'I Want to Be in America' on the Dansette gramophone and being transported into space, even though I had never heard of or seen *West Side Story*. The words, the music, the energy, the sheer unknown magic of it all wrapped me around its fingers and I was hooked. The sounds and the silences were like nothing I had ever experienced. Not even a pilchard tea and Lou Clench on the piano could match this.

'Play it again,' I'd beg. 'Play it again.'

But no matter how often they did, it was never enough. I had found something that lifted me high into the air where no one could touch me. I was out of reach of everyone.

Behind that tired old red curtain I sang songs from other shows too, like *My Fair Lady*; did impersonations of Eartha Kitt and Louis Armstrong. I became them. The loathing of the other boys made it even more special because I knew that no matter how hard they tried or bullied me or beat me, I was in a world that they could never be a part of. And what made it really brilliant was that I knew they knew it too.

With this in my life I no longer got into trouble; the canings and the notes home from the headmaster ceased. He even gave me back my application form to be a trainee monk. This was a relief because I only wanted to be taught by the monks because it meant being in an all-boys school.

When it came to performing in front of the school and the parents, I didn't flinch. I'd done it for Betty Wood and the other mums at Garford House, so I could do it again.

The Christmas show approached and Mr Everett got me time off from the other classes to practise. Mr Kerrigan the headmaster popped in to see that everything was above board and the chaos reassured him. Not much from that Christmas show sticks in my memory except that I sang two songs: Bud Flanagan's 'Strollin," and then I did Eartha Kitt. When Mr Everett announced that they had a star all the way from America, a silence descended. He continued: 'Here she is. The fabulous, the wonderful, Miss Eartha Kitt,' and two boys brought me in reclining on the back of a chair, wearing one of my mum's best dresses.

There was a commotion as she stood up and shouted "'Ere, 'ere, he's got my bleeding cocktail dress on!' and they all started laughing. But I ignored them, singing and acting my way like Eartha through 'Old-Fashioned Millionaire'. The audience clapped and cheered as I complained that the boys had carried me off too soon.

After the show I felt special. My mum did too and seemed to have forgiven me for taking her dress without asking. Betty Wood said I should go into show business, like Helen Shapiro, and some of the boys I fancied started telling me I made a good tart.

Then as quickly as it had all begun it finished. No more rehearsals at lunchtime, nothing to get me through the pain and the boredom of normal lessons. The only theatrics I had to fall back on was choking on the incense at high Mass on Sunday and trying to shock the priest in the confessional. Even that lost its excitement when the priest greeted me with 'And what scandal is it this time?' That's when I knew religion wasn't for me, though. The costumes were bold, the hymns uplifting and the Latin incomprehensibly fascinating, but it didn't have the magic of real theatre.

Then one night there was a knock at the door of our flat. Hard and heavy, like a policeman's knock. 'Don't answer it,' said my dad, who sent Mum to peer through the bathroom window.

We knew it wasn't one of my mum's tally men who she had loans and bought stuff from, and who she tried to pay back weekly. They always came on a Thursday or Friday, and the 'bastard priest' always came in search of money on a Sunday. No, this was a much-feared unexpected caller, and it always spelt trouble. My brothers and I all looked at each other wondering who had been caught getting up to mischief, as we tried to sink lower into our seats.

My mum came back and shook her head, but the knocking continued, only louder. Then a voice called through the letter box, 'It's about your son, Michael', and my dad shook his fist at me and mouthed he was going to kill me. The man wasn't going away easily. If the neighbours hadn't pleaded with my dad to 'open the bleedin' door' I don't think he would ever have got inside our flat and the direction of my life would have been irrevocably changed.

7

We emerged from the darkness of the underground station. I was dressed in new Clarks red leather sandals, grey socks, khaki shorts and a white shirt, all bought from the tally man, and an overcoat. My mum had 'dolled herself up' with lipstick, like when she went off to weddings and parties, and a few men had given her the 'whistle' along the streets.

'St John's Wood' the sign said, but there wasn't a leaf to be seen, let alone a wood, and that's when I spotted them: palm trees either side of the station entrance, like you only ever saw in the films. My mum saw them too and we smiled at one another, then she looked again at the address that was written on the piece of paper and asked the newspaper seller for directions. I loved my mum on days like these. All dressed up with somewhere to go, she was in her element, and she took me by the hand as we crossed the road and made our way to the agent's office.

The unexpected guest at our front door had persevered and conducted a conversation through the letter box. He'd explained that he wasn't after money, I wasn't in trouble; in fact, on the contrary, he was the bearer of 'good tidings'. Like one of those Christmas carols. Eventually my dad gave the signal for him to be let in, the neighbours muttered their approval, the ceiling light was turned on and my parents listened. My brothers and I listened too, on the other side of the living-room door.

He was a talent scout and said he'd seen me performing at school; he thought I had real talent. My dad interrupted him and asked how much it was all going to cost. The man didn't answer him, he just kept going and said that they were on the lookout for boys like me and that he wanted me to go and sing for one of his partners. If all went well they wanted me to 'audition' for *Oliver*. For America. Then there was a lovely silence, like you get in the pictures before the ice cream. The man next said that there was a shortage of natural East End talent, and what with all these Lionel Bart musicals in the West End, someone like me could pocket a 'good few bob'.

That was it. That was how we made it to St John's Wood, though my mum had to borrow money for the fare.

'What's he gonna sing?' asked the blind agent. Except he wasn't asking us, he was asking his partner, who then asked us.

'Slow Boat to China?' I asked.

No one objected and so, unaccompanied, off I went.

When I finished there was silence. Everyone was looking at the blind man, who seemed to be looking at something on the ceiling. So we all looked there.

Finally he said: 'Good. Very good.'

After a series of questions about my behaviour at school, school reports and how tall I was, we gave the phone number of the neighbour who lived along the landing from us, and they showed us the door.

I don't remember the journey back but I do recall the palm trees and my mum's words as we left the agent's: 'Don't get yer hopes up,' she said. I just smiled and nodded because we were happy. Then she took my hand and we went home. And the men whistled at her again.

'It's full of queers yer know.'

My ears pricked up but I pretended I wasn't listening and continued watching the telly.

'Queers,' repeated my dad.

Queers.

It seemed a funny word. But it wasn't so much the word, it was the way everyone reacted to it. Like they had just eaten a turd or watched Roy Rogers have pins stuck up his fingernails by the 'Red Indians'.

To me it didn't seem a bad word. But when my dad and the other men said it, it was hard and nasty. Like when they used the cunt word. That's why I knew I had to be careful when I asked about being queer. So, a place that was full of queers seemed to me an interesting place to be.

It was a few days since we'd visited the agent's and we had given up waiting. Then, out of the blue, our letter box flipped open.

'Mary! Phone call.'

We rushed along the landing to our neighbour who was waiting at her door and nodded my mum towards the telephone table. She picked up the receiver, put on her phone voice and said yes, she was Mrs Cashman, then asked for a pen.

A small collection of neighbours had gathered in the doorway. My dad in his vest, still wearing his belt and braces, was out on the landing too.

After what felt like a lifetime to me my mum put the receiver back on its hook and announced in the same phone voice that I had an audition for *Oliver*.

Oliver! There had been a school outing to see it and I had begged my mum for the five shillings for the coach and a seat in the gallery. I'd sat peering down at the stage that seemed a million miles away. As the show went on I was there with Nancy, Bill and the Artful Dodger. And as Fagin sang that he was 'Reviewing the Situation', I thought I never wanted this to end. Never.

My mum and I put on the same clothes we'd worn for the agent, got the bus and off we went to the West End of London. Even though it was barely an hour away from where we lived, it was like a different world. Black taxi cabs, people in suits wearing bowler hats and carrying rolled-up black umbrellas. Newspaper sellers wailed out the headlines of the '*News* and *Standard*' and the air was thick with noise and petrol fumes, not horse shit. In fact, there wasn't a carthorse to be seen.

We went into the theatre through the back door and were told to take a seat and that I should wait to be called. A man led me down a long winding staircase to the side of a stage. I stood in the dark, gazing out into the brightly lit space ahead of me. The smells and the sounds were like nothing I had ever known. From the darkness someone called my name and a hand pushed me out onto the stage.

As I walked slowly into the light, my knees started to shake beneath me. I heard a woman's voice say hello, and I turned towards it, but I could see nothing except a spotlight on my face and the greatest pool of darkness beyond. My breath caught in my chest. The voice asked me to sing a song, any song. I didn't say a word. I just smiled and smiled, then launched into Lou Clench's favourite, 'Slow Boat to China'.

In the silence I heard men's voices mumbling and I was asked if I knew any hymns. 'Only Catholic ones,' I answered. Unaccompanied, as before, I sang 'Kyrie eleison'. Then I was told that I could go.

Outside, my mum asked what had happened, and I told her that I just had to sing. 'Were you nervous?' she asked. But I didn't know what she meant; I wanted to tell her that I had nearly shat myself but I shook my head instead.

Then I had to go through it all again on another day. Only this time they made me sing with the piano, then sing a song sadly, before my mum and I were sent home, as before.

The next day my mum replaced the neighbour's phone and declared that I had a nine-month contract to play one of Fagin's gang and to understudy Oliver. I found it hard to believe the words she was saying. I was going into 'show business', I was going into a show that I had seen and never wanted to end. Now I was really different and I knew they couldn't hurt me for it. I felt special and everyone was so happy for me. Lionel Bart and Peter Coe, the director, had auditioned me, I had come very close to going to Broadway as Oliver, but I was too young. You had to be fourteen for the US visa. So I was put in the West End production.

My dad was more than happy, even if the theatre was full of queers. He was over the moon. I would be earning more money each week than him. But before that could happen I had to get my 'licence'.

At school other pupils started to notice that I was taking time off, and that there were notes for the headmaster. Even the boys

I fancied started taking an interest in me, asking me if I was going into show business and whether there were any 'fit birds'. Mr Everett, the drama master, was pleased as punch. He started this all off, had given me confidence and had believed in me, so when he said that I should keep my head about me and not to get above myself, I took his words seriously.

The agent called again and explained everything. The glamour of the show-business phone calls had passed and our neighbour now resented them, even suggesting that she might have to charge for the use. Once the contract was signed my school would be contacted by the licensing authorities and I would have to attend London County Hall at Waterloo for an interview and a medical. That hated fucking word struck me with fear. After being poked and prodded by the doctor, and the obligatory squeeze of my balls – they were obsessed with boys' balls – I was then sent off with my mum to see Mr Langley, the licensing officer.

We traipsed down long dark corridors until we eventually found his office and were told to wait. No one would describe Mr Langley as a friendly man, in fact my mum said he looked like a man who had 'lost a pound and found a shilling'. And he had that habit of talking about me as if I wasn't there, constantly referring to me as 'the boy'. I would have to attend an interview after every three months of the contract, undergo the same medical: I would have to present school reports, and 'the boy's bank book—'

'Bank book?' asked my mum.

He nodded solemnly and replied that she would have to save at least a third of the money I earned each week, which was to be deposited in a post office savings account. This bank book would be inspected at the interviews.

He then asked her if she understood and looked at me as if I had the answer.

'Don't think about letting this go to your head, my boy. One false move, one bad school report and you don't get your licence. Simple as that. Understood?'

I nodded.

Now we all understood.

On 3 January 1963, two weeks after my twelfth birthday – then the earliest age at which you could be licensed to perform in the West End – I appeared on the stage of the New Theatre in St Martin's Lane.

Before the licence period I had attended a few rehearsals and instead mainly watched *Oliver!* from a box at the back of the royal circle. On my first night I was herded with the other boys backstage. In the darkness I stood with them behind the grille of the workhouse and listened as an orchestra started to play. I suddenly felt anxious, a bit frightened, and I wanted to piss. The other boys said it was 'nerves', then they started to push towards the front of the grille. As the music played I became calmer, I knew we were all in it together and that if anything went wrong they would help me.

The curtain rose and the silence from the audience was wonderful. My heart rose simultaneously; I felt so happy and as the lights started to come up we walked onto a stage I knew I never ever wanted to leave.

'Like a duck to water' they said to my mum when she collected me that first night. The other boys congratulated me and the stage manager told me I had to start learning Oliver's part. That night, going home on the number 15 bus, I saw the lights of the West End pass behind us and I couldn't wait to get back the next night. But I still hadn't met my first real queer.

Over the first couple of weeks, as I started to make new mates, I was warned by one or two of the boys to beware of certain actors who asked you to hold their hand backstage, and sometimes much more. And there was the company manager who walked along the corridor like a woman. I knew he wasn't a queer. He was what was known as a 'nancy boy', a man who lived with his mother and could only lift a bag of dolly mixtures.

Me and the other boys played around sexually, especially in the darkness backstage, but I wanted to find a real 'friend'.

Someone who I could sit with and hold his hand and cuddle and cry together watching Ingrid Bergman dying of consumption in *The Bells of St Mary's*. But there were women designed to stop any of that from happening on theatre premises: chaperones who spent their entire time trying, but often failing, to control us. They also tried to control the men who loitered with intent outside the stage door.

8

At school the novelty of my new life in the West End ended as quickly as it had begun. Teachers seemed to think that I was a challenge that needed to be beaten and overcome. In the school playground and on the playing fields at Goresbrook I was seen as something of an oddity. The glamour of showbiz had limited magic in the East End, in fact it could single you out for a good beating. And having a different routine from everyone else didn't help either. Apart from one friend, Richard, I was pretty much alone. Not even the drama teacher Mr Everett was interested any more. I felt isolated and lost.

Every day I would have to leave school ten minutes early and rush home to get my duffel bag with a flask of tea, a sandwich and a packet of crisps, and then catch the number 15 bus. I always sat on the top deck, where the air was heavy with tobacco smoke. From there I could look out at the world as it stretched ahead of me. Aldgate, where I looked for Lou Clench's husband, the Bank of England, St Paul's Cathedral, and always men in suits with their bowlers and their brollies, marching along the streets and disappearing into the underground. We passed along Fleet Street, where the newspapers and *The Beano* comic were printed, the law courts, and finally the lights of the West End appeared at the east end of the Strand.

I jumped off the bus at Charing Cross, ran all the way up St Martin's Lane, then stood outside the New Theatre, looking up at the billboards and neon lights –'*Oliver!* now in its fourth year'! In less than an hour from the East End I had left one world behind and come to another. And it was mine. I loved the warm darkness of the theatre, the unspoken rules and rituals that accompanied it, like not being allowed to whistle in dressing rooms, or, if you did, having to go outside, turn round three times, spit and then knock on the door and ask to come in. Everything was new and different, down to the nancy boys who walked arm-in-arm backstage and wore too much eye make-up.

The thrill of the orchestra starting as you lurked backstage waiting to enter the workhouse, and the light shining brightly on you, was like nothing else on earth. Sweet smells of perfume, stage make-up, and 'size', which was used to keep everything fireproof, hung in the air like a mist, and the roar of the audience when the show was over was an incredible high.

On stage I was enraptured by the performances, of Fagin, Nancy, Bill Sykes and his bulldog, and the Artful Dodger. I would repeat in my head over and over again that I had found my home. Here it didn't matter that I was different, or didn't fit in. No one did, which was why we all fitted in. Here the other boys were not the enemy, they were my friends – we were split into two dressing rooms – and our common enemy was our chaperone, the fearsome Mrs Dudley.

Outside in the West End the other boys quickly showed me the ropes, took me to the coffee shops when we had a matinee performance – like Le Macabre where you had your frothy coffee or Coca Cola on a coffin as a table, or the 2i's coffee bar in Old Compton Street where Tommy Steele had been discovered. They warned you about the men you had to be careful of, or ones who would give you a shilling just to talk to them. 'A shilling,' I thought. I'd heard that one before. But here the boys were smart, and insisted you had to get the money 'up front'.

When the shows finished there were fewer old men in raincoats waiting about because you had to be collected by a parent; it was before the show that they would try to strike up a conversation with you. Even though it was exciting to get the attention and be chased I soon finessed the art of telling them to 'fuck off'. They didn't give up that easily, their retort would be 'there's money in it for you' to which some of the older boys would respond 'suck my cock'. The men never argued with that. Some were even known to faint.

The first three months were quickly coming to an end and I knew that I would have to take the statutory three weeks off, be touched up by the doctor and then re-licensed like a performing dog. As well as doing eight shows a week I had learnt the lines for the part of Oliver and all his songs, and attended understudy rehearsals, just in case Oliver was sick, or got hit by a bus.

But our Oliver was as fit as a fiddle and could dodge a bus at any speed. That was until his balls dropped and he couldn't hit the notes. I arrived at the theatre and the stage-door keeper told me to go down into the orchestra pit where Jack, the Glaswegian pianist that nobody could understand, was waiting for me. 'Reet,' he said, and without any explanation off we went through Oliver's songs one after the other at breakneck speed. I wanted to ask him why we were doing all this now, just before a show, but I knew better than to ask. When we finished he stood up, took the fag out of his mouth and said 'Reet, noo get yersel up tee the dressin' room and get changed.'

I looked at him blankly.

'You're on toneet lad. As Oleever,' and popped his fag back in his mouth.

Backstage I put my four pennies into the phone, dialled and pressed Button A when it was answered. I told the neighbour and then my mum the news, but Mum didn't understand, so I shouted down the phone 'I'm bleedin' Oliver tonight!' Then she screamed and said they were all coming.

The stage manager took me to Oliver's dressing room, below ours, and that was it. When it was time to start, we all walked down the stairs, onto the stage and into a world that felt the most natural and supportive I could have hoped to find.

After the first song, 'Food, Glorious Food', I took the nod from the conductor in the orchestra pit, stood up from the workhouse table and, with a bowl in my outstretched hand, approached the Beadle, a spotlight tightening around my face.

'Please sir. I want some more.'

And so the journey began.

A little later, sitting on the coffin in Mr Sowerberry's funeral parlour, the lights dimmed and the spotlight narrowed its beam again. Standing in the wings of the stage were the leading actors, all dressed and made up, waiting for Oliver's solo, 'Where is Love'.

It was a night never to be forgotten. Not even when Nan Cashman stood up at the back of the theatre and shouted at Noah Claypole as he beat me. But I couldn't hear her. I was in a place far, far away, and it was mine.

I played the part of Oliver for weeks, even one night performing for a man that my dad said was famous, Senator Richard Nixon, with whom I swapped autographs. It was on one of the rare nights when my dad collected me from the stage door. Mostly my mum came. She enjoyed it. It gave her a chance to dress up and put on some make-up. Unlike with my dad, we wouldn't rush for the bus; Mum and I would stroll about near the theatres trying to see if we could spot some stars before heading home to our new council maisonette to which we had recently moved.

One night she turned up with a man. His name was Alec and we didn't go star-spotting that night, we just went to get the bus. 'There's nothing in it,' she told me. I wasn't to tell my father though, she said, because 'he would get hold of the wrong end of the stick'.

Alec said nothing. He never did. He sat beside my mum while I had to sit in the seat in front of them. He turned up with her often after that and it was like I didn't exist as they chatted away walking along the streets. When it came to our stop Alec would stay on the bus and continue his journey to wherever Mrs Alec lived. I knew there was a Mrs Alec because my mum had said that his wife didn't understand him. I soon worked out that my mum understood him perfectly, and he hovered around for many years. Their secret was safe with me – even when Mum died and I realised, forty-odd years later, that she had been paying for catalogue goods to be sent to him at an address in Plaistow.

At other times my mum's secrets exploded in front of us. She had made a new friend, Rosie, who lived next door in our new block. Rosie didn't work, she said it made her ill, and as a result she had all her debts and rent paid for by National Assistance. She didn't have a husband either; it was rumoured that he had run off with another woman, or been knocked over by a bus. Rosie introduced my mother to the delights of bingo, and my mum couldn't get enough after that. Unfortunately, one day my dad found out that she wasn't playing bingo with Rosie as she claimed, she was off 'gallivanting' somewhere. When she came home she found that he had taken every single dress and blouse from the wardrobe and slashed them to pieces with a knife. She slept downstairs on the sofa for weeks, and it was never mentioned again. It was then that I knew that I could never reveal our secret.

9

He knew I fancied him. I always did fancy the older boys. Chris was only four years my senior but at sixteen he seemed like a man. And unlike most men he had time for me.

Nothing happened between us, even though I wanted him to kiss and cuddle me. No, he would just put his arm around me and include me in everything, and we worked together well when he was playing Artful Dodger and I was playing Oliver. Then one day he told me he wanted me to meet someone, a friend of his who did charity shows at weekends.

After the Tuesday matinee we left the stage door and in a cafe I met Dave Woods, or Woodie, as we called him, for the first time. Dark curly hair, chain-smoking and with a tightly belted raincoat around his big tall frame, I think he must have been in his late twenties, though he seemed ancient to me. Woodie told me that he wanted me to take part in one of the shows that he and Chris put on in cinemas for the kids' Saturday matinees. Through plumes of smoke Woodie said that my mum and dad's consent would be needed for it all to be 'above board'. Tipping the ash from an ever-present fag he added that, as an artist's manager, he would be willing to meet my parents. This felt amazing. I had a manager who was interested in me, a manager who carried a big briefcase stuffed with papers, who tipped the waitress when the bill came and who said he knew too many stars to mention.

Woodie came to Poplar to see my parents and explained that he wanted me to be in his shows. My dad wasn't interested but Mum puffed on Woodie's fags and thought it would be a good idea. It was agreed that at the end of my next week off from *Oliver!* I would go to meet him in Hounslow and stay overnight with him, his wife and children. Chris was in the kids' show too and this meant that I would be with him and we'd get closer. As for the charity show, it was easy because it was really a spoof of *Oliver!*, with us singing along to the long-playing record of the musical.

Friday came and I made my way with my pyjama bottoms and overnight things to meet Mr Woods outside the ABC cinema opposite Hounslow West tube station, at the end of the Piccadilly line. It took an age to get there, and it was dark when I came out of the station. Woodie was waiting for me, with a fag hanging out of his mouth, the briefcase in his right hand and his raincoat belted up so tight even the air couldn't get in.

After a meal in a cafe we made our way to his house and his family. He lived in Isleworth, a fifteen-minute walk along poorly lit streets with more trees than I had ever seen. When we reached his house every room seemed lit up. But he didn't put a key in the lock. He rang the doorbell and a woman answered it and welcomed us in.

It was a boarding house and there was no wife or kids to be seen.

Woodie told the landlady that I was very tired and needed to sleep. I stood in the hallway not knowing what to do, what to say or where to go. He took my hand and as we started to go upstairs the landlady wished us a good night. With every step my heart was rising up in my chest like it was going to burst. I didn't know why I felt like it.

I asked him for the bathroom. He pointed to a door and then to another telling me that it was 'our room'. In the bathroom I quietly put on my pyjama bottoms and kept my vest on. I had barely said a word since we arrived. I kept wondering where his wife was. And his kids.

He was waiting at the door of the room. He took the small bag and clothes and closed it behind us.

There were two single beds across from each other; Woodie wore pyjamas and a top which was buttoned all the way up.

'Brushed your teeth?' he asked.

I lied, and nodded. He got into one bed. I got into the other and lay there. My heart was still racing. I stared at the ceiling.

'Good night, son.'

I said goodnight and he turned the bedside lamp out.

Through the thin curtains the street light outside illuminated the room. Somewhere downstairs a radio played. There was a long, long silence and I prayed that I would fall asleep quickly, but my heart was beating so hard I could feel it in my head.

'You cold?'

'No,' I said quickly.

I heard his bed creaking. He was getting up.

'I am. Cold. So I will get in with you.'

And he did. He pulled back the bedclothes and got in beside me. To warm him up, he said.

All I knew was that it was not fair. What he was doing was not fair. He pushed himself around me, put his arms over me, and then his hand undid my pyjama bottoms. He played with me. He was kissing my neck and touching my cock and I couldn't breathe. Then I remembered that man in the docks and I switched my head off from the rest of my body. Like Woodie had switched out the light.

And there was nothing more.

I was okay. I was somewhere else.

He said afterwards that he loved me, loved me like his own son, and that he had been to prison before because people had lied about him, but he was a good man, and just wanted to be good to me. It would be our secret. If I ever told anyone then I would send him to prison.

Over and over again he told me what the police would do, that they would say he had confessed everything, but that it would be a lie, because he would never tell about our secret.

In the morning I asked him about his wife and kids. He said they'd been killed in a car accident, and I felt sad that I had asked him. I'd been brought up to trust the word of adults, especially when they were talking together. My dad used to tell us that children should be seen and not heard. So I didn't ask Woodie any more questions.

After breakfast he asked me to help him shave, and whether I wanted to hold the razor. As the landlady passed us at the scullery sink she said: 'Your dad is very proud of you.'

I didn't know what to say. It felt like I had been hit. It was a lie. He wasn't my dad and she had said he was. I was now in a place I didn't know and I didn't know how to make it stop.

We did his show that day and it was okay. On stage I forgot all about what had happened the night before. He hadn't physically hurt me, he'd just hurt me inside, like there was a big weight inside my chest.

Chris was nicer than he had ever been to me, hugging me and kissing my neck. But I didn't want him to. Not any more.

He kept asking me if I was all right because I was quiet, and for a 'chatterbox' that was unusual.

I told him I was okay.

That afternoon Woodie took me home and thanked my parents for letting me stay with him and his family, and for taking part in the show. He told them he would consider managing me. My mum was charmed by him, and took another of his cigarettes, while my dad took a dislike to him. It was agreed, however, that as I was still in my three weeks off from *Oliver!* I would return to his house next Friday evening, stay with 'the family' and do another show. Then, lighting another cigarette from the one he was finishing, he told me I was a good boy, and left.

Friday came along too soon and I wasn't ready for it. The day before I had taken the day off school for my re-licensing with Mr Langley. This time the medical was bearable because they didn't conduct it in front of my mum, as they had previously. Mr Langley inspected the bank book and suggested that my mum pay in the savings each week rather than whenever she thought about it, reasserting that she was not to withdraw money from it. He looked over my school reports, gave me a nod, then minutes later we were outside headed for the post office so my mum could make a large withdrawal to repay the loan sharks.

On Friday afternoon we were sitting in front of the fire, just me and Mum on the hearth tiles.

'Got yer bag packed?' she asked.

I nodded, unable to find the words that I wanted to say. I wanted to tell her something. I wanted her to help me.

'Mum?' She glanced at me. 'I don't think I should go to Mr Woods'.'

She didn't look at me, she just poked the fire and smoked her fag.

After a short while she asked why. I felt my throat tightening. My heart started beating fast. I looked out of the window.

'Because...'

I didn't know what to say, how to put into words what had happened. I struggled in the silence. Finally, I said: 'Because I think it's going to rain. And I don't want to get wet.'

Mum was still looking into the fire, poking at the embers. She put down the poker, looked at me and said: 'Don't go if you don't want to.'

Then we both sat in the silence that followed and watched the flames dancing in the fire. I waited for her to say something else, for her to tell me that she knew, and that she wanted me to stay with her. But she didn't.

I looked out to the darkening sky, and I went to Hounslow West station where he was waiting for me. Wearing the same tightened raincoat, carrying the same briefcase, still with a cigarette hanging from his mouth.

Smiling, he let out a sigh, then he reached out, took my hand and said: 'All right, my son?' And I started searching for that switch inside me.

10

Living in our new maisonette in Poplar meant that life changed. It was good that we had three bedrooms but deep down my brothers and I missed the fun of sharing beds, even when I was doing nocturnal waterworks. My other two brothers, Stevie and Danny, changed schools when we moved but they didn't seem too bothered; they just got on with making new friends.

With new neighbours I went through the novelty phase of being the boy from *Oliver!* again, but when I refused to sing for them in the pub on a Friday night they soon gave up on me. Mum was still office cleaning, and had started working in a lard factory, but Dad had given up on the docks, where work was becoming harder to find. After a series of jobs including a stint at Lusty's Turtle Soup factory he went to work as a park keeper, and seemed happier than ever. He enjoyed being in the open air, being in charge of the tennis courts, the running tracks, and he loved being around the football teams that played in the park.

Though still relatively close, Garford House, St Vincent's estate, seemed an empire away and there was no reason to go there, not even when I went to visit Nan and Grandad Clayton or Nanny Cashman. By now Grandad Cashman was long passed; we had stood in Cable Street, outside Badgers sweet factory, and watched him go by in a box. Nanny Cashman had said that she had 'given the hospital a man and they had given her a bag of bones'. But then it was well known that our nan loved a fight, as well as a pinch of snuff.

Woodie had become my manager and was now a fixture in our maisonette, sometimes even staying the night, where I would sleep in the same room as him on the top bunk bed. My mum liked him because he was generous with his fags – untipped Player's Weights, the same as she smoked. But he wasn't a man for the pub and this gave my dad another reason to distrust him. If anyone worried about what was going on, his pervasive presence in every step of my life, then no one said anything. Besides, he had a way with words, and he impressed adults. There was always something that he was waiting on, a big deal, or something that he needed to sort out for me. Even though being in those charity versions of *Oliver!* had almost got me sacked from the New Theatre. It soon became clear that they weren't for any charity; they were a lucrative side-business for him and his mates who worked in the cinemas. The theatre producers were furious that their show was being ripped off, parodied, and it was made worse that Chris and I were appearing in the real thing.

So when the shit hit the fan, Woodie wasn't asked to explain, neither were my parents: Chris and I were called in front of the nancy-boy company manager. He gave me a warning to 'steer clear of these shows and these men', then winked and smiled at Chris and asked him to stay.

Woodie never took no for an answer and the shows were changed to rip off other productions that we could sing along to, and I continued to stay at his, though the boarding houses in question changed with alarming regularity. His explanation to landladies as to why he was behind with his payments was that he was waiting for a cheque to clear, or there had been an unexpected robbery. But eventually this strategy stopped working as his excuses dried up and we were booted out, forced to find a new spot to play happy families.

All the time I stood by, being asked nothing, saying nothing, but wanting to shout out that it was all a lie. A fucking big lie. But I never did because I knew no one would believe me and I would wind up in trouble again. I wanted to say that he was a liar and that he 'interfered' with me; my dad never did that. My dad might fight with my mum and argue and get drunk but he left me alone at night. Sometimes I was so angry with Woodie's lies that I would leave him in the street and walk the opposite way, telling him to go away. But he would just stand there with a face like a sad dog, the fag hanging from the corner of his mouth, and I would stop and wait for him to come for me because I knew I could never escape. So I gave up trying.

School was still awful. Twelve and a half years old and surrounded by hundreds of people, I felt alone. I wanted to tell everyone what was going on in my head. I wanted to let it out, so I started being difficult again and wetting the bed, which I hated. Concerns about my school reports were raised by Mr Langley, as well as the frequent raids that took place on my savings.

That's when Woodie decided that I needed a more sympathetic school. A stage school. He brushed aside the costs and said that he would take care of it all. Then passed my mum another cigarette.

Woodie found a new school for me during my last two months in *Oliver!*. It couldn't have been further from the East End or more different. The Gladys Dare School of Stage, Screen and Drama was based over twenty miles away, in Surbiton, Surrey. It had its own theatre, the Romsey, and a resident amateur company, the Romsey Players. Woodie would eventually try to work his non-existent directorial skill on these unsuspecting dullards and he would fail miserably.

Gladys Dare had the look of a retired ballet dancer. Her dark black hair was pulled back in a bun and she held herself with a commanding, upright posture. Gladys met me after one of Woodie's shows at Kingston upon Thames and was impressed. I would start at her school in the autumn.

If going to school by train and bus from Poplar all the way to Surbiton was bad enough, no one mentioned the bright mauve school blazer, with a mauve and silver tie and grey trousers. People could see me coming a mile off. Nor was I told that I would move in with Woodie to be nearer the school. The story of his wife and kids had long since been dropped, and there were various other tales of car accidents or separations. When pressed for details he nervously lit up another fag and alongside billows of smoke blurted that it was all 'too difficult' to talk about. I had given up trying to wrench myself from this world of lies after I shouted at him in the street that he was not my dad and that he should stop saying he was. But like always he just took me by the hand and walked along the street with me. After that any resistance seemed useless.

The Gladys Dare School was so unlike my previous two schools. My mate Richard from the East End joined me there – his family wanted him to be on the stage too. There were only four boys and about forty girls. They were all posh and spoke like they had plums in their mouths.

The school was situated just up the hill from Surbiton station, in a big semi-detached house that had classrooms spread across the ground floor and into an adjoining building. In the basement was a set of storage rooms, a kitchen and school dining room that stank of cabbage and boiled potatoes. Miss Dare's study was at the front and overlooked the street. It was rumoured that an elderly relative lived on the floor above – but she was never seen or spoken of. The main building had a large garden, where we were allowed to play, connecting to Miss Dare's residence at the back, on the Ewell Road. Completing the school units was a purpose-built theatre and dressing-room block, where we would do theatre and dance classes, accompanied by a chain-smoking pianist who never took off her fur hat, coat and gloves.

Because it was like nothing I had ever experienced it was fun. The singing star Petula Clark had been a pupil there, which made us feel special; after all *she* had married a Frenchman. Compared to my secondary school the academic side was like pissing up a wall. We just had two hours of traditional lessons in the morning and then the rest of the day consisted of acting, singing, tap dancing and ballet. Early on the teachers decided their main job was to knock the East End accent out of me and for a while this meant I didn't belong anywhere. When I went home to see my mum and dad kids would knock at the door and ask me to say something. Once I did they would laugh and say I 'spoke funny'. At school in Surbiton they did the same. Then after a few months it stopped.

The bad news for Woodie was that he was no longer my manager. Miss Dare ran an agency attached to the school; she took 10 per cent commission on all work and she wasn't going to split that commission with anyone. Initially she too had been taken in by Woodie and his promises of deals to come but he was quickly relegated when he failed to deliver. Nonetheless the work was rolling in. I starred on Sunday evening TV for the first time in the police drama series *Gideon's Way*, with John Hurt and John Gregson.

Despite his new demotion Woodie spotted an opportunity, tipped off Gladys Dare, and I successfully auditioned for a Christmas show in the West End, *Sooty's Christmas Party*. It starred the glove puppets Sooty, Sweep and Soo, and featured Harry Corbett, who talked for the mutes that he stuck his hands up. The director wanted child variety acts to entertain the audience while the scene changes were under way. So Miss Dare put me with two other lads, choreographed our tap routines and together we became the Dare Boys. The only problem was that I couldn't work because I needed the statutory three months off before I could be relicensed. But Woodie had a plan.

As I was now living with him in Surrey the application was made to Surrey County Council and we got the licence. To my intense relief there was no medical. But towards the end of the run of the show during one of their routine inspections I came to the attention of the London County Council licensing authorities. Their records showed that I should not be working, but resting for the obligatory three months. A blind eye was turned for the remainder of the show, Woodie and Miss Dare were nowhere to be seen, and my mum was left to face the wrath of the licensing authorities.

Towards the end of the year I joined the West End cast of *Peter Pan* as Curly, with Dawn Addams as Peter and Alastair Sim as Captain Hook. They were both big stars but Alastair Sim was famous to me because of the St Trinian's films and the Ealing comedies. Woodie was keen for me to get closer to Alastair Sim, even feeding me lines to say to him while we were waiting in the wings to go on stage, but Mr Sim kept a genial distance and responded to every attempt at conversation with a soft, 'Is that so?' before smiling and looking off wistfully into the distance with his thoughts.

As young as I was, I recognised Alastair Sim's magic, his embracing charisma on stage. His Captain Hook bordered on the cowardly. He adopted a comic effeminacy, cod bravery, blimpish bravado and pathos that just made you smile. I plucked up courage to ask for his autograph. Others had tried and he had refused, but I wouldn't be swayed.

He was applying make-up sticks to his face inside his dressing room; he was wearing a tired and torn old dressing gown and his spectacular Charles I wig sat on the wig block. He wiped his hands on the tea towel across his lap and beckoned me into the room. Looking at me with the face of a tired dog, he gently asked me if I would ask a road builder, baker or bricklayer for their autograph. I told him that of course I wouldn't. They weren't famous, and they weren't actors either.

His response was considered: they did their job just as he did his. It was a job, and he was very lucky because he enjoyed doing it, and so did a lot of other people too.

I was about to interrupt but he gently returned the autograph book and pen, and said: 'We are all just doing our jobs. And people like you and me are very lucky.'

That was it. I left the dressing room without his autograph, but I left it uplifted and happy. I carried that thought with me throughout my career and I still do.

All was not well at Gladys Dare's. I was thirteen years old and I had been there about six months when I was summoned from class. The fierce Miss Dare questioned me about 'Mr Dave Woods' and why my parents were behind with my school fees. She dug into her roll-top oak desk, pulled out some papers and went on to explain that some of the debt had been paid by my professional work, but that definitely didn't cover it, and that I should bring it to the attention of my parents.

My mum dressed up and made the journey to Surbiton where Miss Dare expressed her concerns about Mr Woods as well as the unpaid fees. Ever used to wrestling with unpaid bills, my mum promised to sort it out and a few days later I moved back home, to the room I shared with my brothers, who barely knew the posh-speaking TV upstart who had walked out on them. Woodie refused to walk away, blamed Miss Dare and convinced my mum that it was all a mistake. Then he hung on from a distance. He was working as a holiday-camp entertainer and as the summer approached he suggested that I should do appearances and perform at the weekends too. He said he could get me a summer season on the Isle of Wight, which he did.

That summer, Miss Dare tracked me down to let me know that I was needed back in London for a film audition. Woodie happily boasted to all and sundry and took me to the Wardour Street offices of the film director, and husband of Shirley Bassey, Kenneth Hume. Auditioning for a film was exciting. Wardour Street was the heart of the film industry and all the big companies, like Paramount and Columbia, had their offices there.

Woodie wanted to come into the room with me but he was firmly told to wait outside. In a large smoke-filled office, surrounded by people, I was given a script to read. Kenneth Hume played the other parts, and I made them laugh. They asked me about the other parts and plays that I had been in and then I left, Woodie alongside me.

Miss Dare phoned later to say that I had got the part of 'Peter' in the film *I've Gotta Horse*, and that I had to learn to ride a horse. It would be thirteen weeks on the film at the impressive sum of £15 a week, filming in Great Yarmouth and Shepperton studios.

Woodie was not happy. He was still surly because he hadn't been allowed in the film offices. Now he tried to find ways of stopping me going, even feigning tuberculosis, which had zero effect on me, and anyway, working on a film was too exciting a proposition to miss. Besides, when it came to money, Gladys Dare was not to be meddled with. My mum attended the school to sign the contract while I was seeing out the remaining days on the Isle of Wight. Meanwhile I learned to ride a horse by helping the man who sold donkey rides on the beach and as the date approached I returned home to Poplar to pack.

Miss Dare found me a chaperone, sometime actress Miss Pearl Winkworth, previously a student at her school. Pearl would accompany me on the film and watch over me. Woodie hurried back to London and insisted that he should be my chaperone; Miss Dare dismissed him with a wave of her hand and reminded him that he was not licensed for such 'activities'. Then he pleaded with me. He said they were taking me away from him and that I would never see him again. I remember feeling absolutely nothing.

I've Gotta Horse starred the pop idol Billy Fury. Billy was a rock 'n' roll star women fainted over and men copied. They queued for tickets for his shows and concerts, and his shy countenance and alternative stage presence captivated all.

The film featured other stars of the day: the Irish singing trio the Bachelors, Amanda Barry (who played Billy's girlfriend), Michael Medwin, Jon Pertwee and Fred Emney. As 'Peter' I didn't have much to do in the film except speak up every so often, be cheeky, accompany my 'grandad', who was the trainer of Billy's racehorse Anselmo, and do the odd bit of singing and dancing. And, of course, ride the horse.

What a horse Anselmo was; he stood about four times taller than me and when it came to filming they just shoved me into the saddle, slapped his arse and we went galloping into the distance. But no one had told me how to stop a racehorse. I was terrified, so I did what I did with the donkeys and I jumped off. After that they kept Anselmo well away from me, thank God.

Staying in a four-star hotel overlooking the beach at Great Yarmouth was amazing, as was being chatted up by Brian, the tough, rough lad who accompanied the producer of the film and Billy Fury's manager, Larry Parnes. Brian made me feel special and one night he got Pearl, my minder, drunk and put her to bed so he could take me back to Larry's house along the sea front. But all was not well. When Brian arrived with me Larry hit the roof, and fifteen minutes later I was dispatched by car back to the hotel. Nothing was ever said again and Pearl woke up the next morning none the wiser, merely a little 'fragile'.

When Billy's summer show finished in Great Yarmouth the filming moved to Shepperton studios and I lived at home. Woodie was nowhere to be seen, which was unusual. Every working day a chauffeured car would pick me up early and bring me home at the end of the day. Pearl would always be waiting for me at the studios.

Towards the end of the long schedule there was a big row in the studio. The director, Kenneth Hume, was furious because I had fallen asleep on set. He shouted that it was an unacceptable way to treat a child and insisted that they check me into a hotel for the rest of the filming. No one argued with him; phone calls were made, Pearl was taken to one side and admonished, and then we were both booked into a beautiful hotel on the banks of the Thames, close to the studio.

Tough-lad Brian had long disappeared and there was a new Czech boy who was Kenneth's assistant. The boy was sent out to buy me pyjamas and a toothbrush and Pearl had to take care of herself. He was nice, gentle and quiet. And handsome. He looked about seventeen. As we were leaving the studio for the hotel he whispered that if I wanted he would come to my room after Pearl had gone to bed. I wasn't yet fourteen but I knew what I wanted, and I wanted him. Dinner at the posh hotel couldn't pass fast enough. Pearl was invited to take drinks in the bar, but she insisted that she would put me to bed first.

As she left me in my room I stood and waited for the Czech boy to come. I stared at the door and willed him to arrive. And he did.

The excitement was incredible. He quietly told me to follow him. Then he took me into a room with the biggest four-poster bed in the world and on it was Kenneth Hume. When I looked round the boy had gone.

Kenneth was kind and warm. Not at all like he was on set – a man who shouted and screamed when we were filming. He told me to stop calling him 'sir', that I could call him Kenneth. Then he gave me a whisky and Coke and asked if I would like to sleep

72

with him in the big bed. I nodded. It felt nice that he wanted me to be with him, and he was warm and soft like a boy, not like that man in the docks, or even Woodie. I knew he was famous and he was important and that made me feel good too.

Nothing would happen, he said, he just wanted to take care of me. He liked me because I was cheeky, and I was a good actor. He asked me about the man 'Woodie', who had come with me to the audition. I said he was my manager, but Kenneth gave me one of the serious silences that adults give when they don't believe you.

In the darkness of the bed he put his arms around me from behind and pulled me close. He smelt of perfume and cigarettes, and he was still wearing the white dressing gown with a blue trim around the collar with his initials on it. Because of the Coke and whisky I found I didn't need to use the switch inside me. I felt warm and silly, and I fell asleep.

Night after night it was the same ritual. He would try to put his dick in me but it hurt and because I was growing in confidence I told him that if he did it I would scream. This made him even more excited; he shouted 'Oh Jesus!', shot his arsenal and I returned to my room, unaccompanied.

After about a week in the hotel the car started taking me home, and we finished the film.

I didn't see the Czech boy again until the after-film party in Soho and because I had drunk some beer I told him that I fancied him. We were standing outside the Italian restaurant, La Dolce Vita, where the party was being held. I looked into his eyes and he looked into mine. Someone shouted his name, so he smiled, took my hand and told me to take care of myself. He was wearing a bright silver suit with a blue striped shirt and was so nice to me. Then he turned towards the person who had called him and I never saw him again.

The attention of the men didn't bother me. I was growing sure of myself. Woodie had bombarded me with letters while I was on the film set though he had stayed out of sight. I knew that men, even men married to famous singing stars, fancied me. And I had confidence as an actor because I kept getting every single part or commercial I auditioned for.

With the film finished I got back to the boring routine of the hour-and-a-half journey to school via Waterloo station. Now I was in long trousers and I even managed to ditch the school blazer – when I wore it in the East End I usually got beaten up, or called a queer. So I thought it better not to advertise and got a black blazer instead.

In the early morning rush hour, military music blared across the station as a sea of men marched off the trains with newspapers under their arms, umbrellas and bowler hats, and disappeared into London. Previously Richard, my mate, had travelled with me, but now he had started taking another train, even avoiding me. I had no idea why, so I went alone. I boarded the train for Surbiton and, as always, sought out a single carriage all to myself: I would stop anyone else from getting in by hanging out the window until the train left. Just as the train started to move a man jumped into the carriage and sat on the other side in the opposite corner. I was furious.

The next stop was Wimbledon, about fifteen minutes away. As the train pulled out of the station he spoke. 'Hello, Michael,' he said.

I spun round and looked at him. He was a complete stranger. He spoke in a very quiet, but posh way.

'Don't worry,' he said, 'I'm not going to harm you.'

I just kept looking at him.

'My name is John. Dr John. And I follow you every day. You leave home every day around 7.50. You walk along Bow Common Lane, then you take the back streets to Mile End tube—'

He outlined my complete journey, back and forth, even including the slight deviations on the way home. He then told me that he was going to give me his phone number because he liked me and he wanted me to visit him at his home in Bayswater. As he wrote it on his card he said that he knew I could keep a secret.

I looked at the phone number, which started AMBassador, the first three letters in capitals you had to dial, followed by the four numbers.

'I'm a friend of Kenneth's,' he said. He may even have said that he was his doctor. That made me feel a bit better, knowing that he wasn't a madman after all. I had to promise I would ring him otherwise he would wait for me the next afternoon after school. I promised, and he left me on the station platform at Surbiton.

I slipped the telephone number into my school case knowing that Dr John was right; I would keep this secret. I had already kept a lifetime of them, it was how I knew to survive, how to fit in, and I knew it was a part of being different from other boys.

I left the station and walked up the hill to school. A place where I felt safe, or at least I thought I was.

12

If Gladys Dare's school was in another era, then I was happy there. The teachers despaired and left me to drama and dance, and if we took any exams then they passed me by. I excelled at acting and I was becoming a bit of a know-it-all. I knew some of the other kids at the school didn't like me because I had no hesitation in telling them they were out of step, or out of tune, or just not good enough. I was terrible and showed no concern for their feelings. I had become overconfident, perhaps from the attention of older men, so I was unaware what was coming.

Three boys at the school, including Richard, had suddenly stopped talking to me. They avoided me at break times, and when I'd ask one of them why, they simply ignored me. Then the girls started doing it. No one in the entire school, except the teachers, would talk to me or acknowledge my existence, unless they had to in the class or in an exercise. I had no idea why it was happening or what I had done. I just wanted someone to tell me, then I could apologise, or explain. I liked them, and what was worse I wanted to be liked by them. All of them.

This torture went on for weeks. I kept telling myself it would end one day, that they couldn't keep it up, they'd get tired. But it continued. Then, one morning at assembly, Miss Dare called me to the front of the gathering, while the other teachers stood behind her. She had that stiff, immovable face that she wore when we did ballet class. I wondered if I'd been offered another part and she was about to deliver the good news in front of the entire school. So, beaming, I made my way to the front and stood before her. She told me to face the front then grabbed me firmly by the shoulders and twisted me round to face the school with the words: 'The front, I said.'

There was a long pause and then she stood beside me and said: 'Who do you think you are?'

I didn't understand.

'Pardon, Miss?' I replied.

She repeated it, very loudly. Still I didn't understand, and after a long pause she said she would tell me. I was 'nothing'. 'Nothing'. Who was I to tell other people how good they were? Did I really believe I was *that* good?

Her reprimand went on for what seemed a lifetime. I had no idea it was coming and so I was completely unprepared; I thought she liked me, I thought she protected me. I tried to stop myself from getting upset. She told the school that they were right to 'send me to Coventry', because I was no one and nothing. As much as I tried not to, I cried in front of the whole school. I sobbed, my face smothered with tears and snot running from my nose. I dropped my head and cried in their silence.

After an eternity she told me to go to the toilets and wash my face. I walked slowly from that room to the boys' toilets. And I stayed in there a long time. Never in my life had I felt so hurt. Hurt by someone who I trusted, who I thought liked me, and who I didn't have to do any secret things with. I went home that night and told no one. It was another secret to keep.

After that I changed. I stopped talking so much at school and held back from answering questions or trying to be the best at singing, and dancing, and acting. In the end I believed that I really was bad. That I was a 'nothing' who had got 'too big for his own boots'. And as I changed they all knew that they had won, especially Miss Dare.

When I started making myself smaller they started being different to me. They knew that I couldn't bear the silence, and not being liked. Over the next weeks the boys started talking to me again gradually, one by one, on the basis that I shouldn't tell the others. The girls forgot about it and treated me normally. But what happened that morning in assembly ground its way into my bones.

13

It was 1966 and the world felt like it was spinning upside down. The skiffle groups and Pat Boone had given way to the Beatles, the Dave Clark Five and the Rolling Stones; fashion erupted out of Carnaby Street and onto the King's Road and psychedelic drugs were on the rounds. People in San Francisco were singing about going there and wearing flowers in their hair – and that was just the men.

I left school at the age of fifteen and three months with no academic qualifications. The worlds of chemistry, algebra, physics and even home economics had failed to reach my half-forgotten school. I was qualified to act, sing, dance and mimic, and I had a long CV to prove it.

I exited the school building for the last time and walked down the hill to the station, into a working world that I already knew. I'd appeared four times in the West End before I was fifteen, including in John Barry's musical the *Passion Flower Hotel*, with a young cast of Pauline Collins, Francesca Annis, Jane Birkin and Bill Kenwright. My CV covered three and a half years and ranged across cinema films, television appearances, West End and regional theatre, as well as lucrative commercials and modelling. I went to sign on at the youth labour exchange in Poplar and when they asked me what job I was looking for, I told them. I also confidently said that they wouldn't have to worry about me because I had an agent, a summer season and a job coming up: the UK tour of *Peter Pan*. It felt like the world was opening up at my feet; other avenues, however, were about to be closed off.

One afternoon walking along Bow Common Lane a man swaggered along the street towards me. I knew him instantly, but he had grown and put on muscle. It was Micky from school: my first secret friend. As he approached I grew nervous, but there was something in me that warmed to him.

Strong, blond and blue-eyed, he greeted me with an 'all right' as if we had seen one another only yesterday.

'Yes,' I replied, 'I'm all right. And you, Mick?'

I stood looking at him and for a moment I wished I could go back to another time when everything was complicated but containable, when I could have that friendship and closeness without any judgement, especially my own. But the moment gave way to reality.

'Still doing that acting lark?' he said.

I nodded then asked: 'And you, what are—'

'Docker,' he said. 'In the docks.'

I waited, I didn't know what to say next, but he did.

'Lot of queers in show business,' he said.

In that long look we held I remembered how he had humiliated me and started the laughter with the other boys when I was naked in the showers at Goresbrook, and how I had tried to cover myself from them. I pretended to think about my response but I knew what I wanted to say: 'A lot of queers in the docks as well, Mick.'

Nothing more was said, not even goodbye. As we parted I think we both understood that we had chosen differently, and I knew I was the luckier of the two.

Woodie hadn't let go and, strangely enough, neither had I. Now I was in my mid-teens I was no longer an attraction to him but he encouraged me to visit him at weekends or for longer periods on the Suffolk/Norfolk coast where he now worked. I increasingly noticed that he disliked gay men, especially ones who were open, and tried to dissuade me from the 'wrong sorts of friends'. I, on the other hand, was ardently in search of those friends.

Just after Christmas we went on the tour of *Peter Pan* and I discovered 'theatrical digs' for the first time: boarding houses mainly run by robust landladies. These women were different from those that Woodie had tried to dupe. They were a canny breed and knew every trick in the book; they didn't have a conversation with you so much as talking at you without pausing for breath. 'You'll find me a generous woman when it comes to the breakfast, but I don't do poached, when you've got a pan frying why boil a pot?' On they would chunter: 'Should you enter the scullery, pay no heed to the husband, he doesn't speak. Chooses not to. He's turning to rubber from the neck down. And I'm a woman with needs!'

In the pregnant pause that followed the chest would be puffed up and she'd continue: 'He is about as much use to me as an unstrung piano. And while I'm being candid, if you use the piss pot don't put it back straight away – the steam rusts the springs.'

They gloried in the names of the famous who had stayed with them. Alma Mackay would point to a single divan bed and pronounce: 'Look! Look! I've had them all on that bed: Tommy Trinder, Arthur Askey – small man you daren't put a blanket over 'im – and Frankie Howerd. Ooooh, what a lonely man—'

She'd pause for effect.

'Mind you, as luck would have it on the Wednesday afternoon, he bumped into his nephew from the Portuguese navy.'

The stories were their way of telling you that they had shred good reputations with reports of unacceptable shenanigans and they'd have no hesitation in shredding yours.

The tour rolled into the regional towns and cities and we boasted a full orchestra; I was playing John Darling, film star Julia Lockwood was Peter, Ron Moody was Captain Hook and Mr Darling, and David Jason was the boring but brilliantly funny Gentleman Starkey.

One of the other boys, Ian, had been in the show with me before. He had an ageless quality so got away with playing a young boy for years. He was a couple of years older than me, and a confident brawling queer, as I knew from first-hand experience. We'd once had an argument in the dressing room and he'd brought the proceedings to a swift halt with a well-aimed kick to my balls. A few days after that we became firm friends.

Knowing that I fancied other guys he told me that he was going to open my eyes. On tour he introduced me to pubs where they had separate rooms for 'queers and nancies'. It was totally illegal to be homosexual and you could be arrested just for trying to chat up someone, so separate rooms were safer. When they closed at 10.30 there were all-night cafes where you stirred your tea, popped your pills and sat with over-made-up boys and drag queens, listening to shocking stories of cocks and beatings, or both. The more naive you were, the more gruesome the details became, especially from the prostitutes, who competed with the queers for the most eye-popping tale.

I loved it. I threw myself into this new frontier so readily that I was taken aside by one of the older queer actors and informed in no uncertain terms that we were criminals, that we could be arrested for trying to meet other men, and that I was to desist. But Ian told me to ignore the old queens and to just keep my wits about me. Anyway, it made no sense. How could we be criminal when there were queers on the radio every weekend? And just after lunchtime too!

Every Sunday afternoon Julian and Sandy – Kenneth Williams and Hugh Paddick – gave public life to our secrets. They were as camp as a row of tents and lisped across BBC radio's *Round the Horne* speaking polari, slang used by some gay men, and audiences loved it. It was like being in on an amazing joke that was being played across the whole of the country. And when I clutched my sides at Kenneth William's squeal of 'OOOH Mr Horne, bona to varda your jolly old eek' (nice to see your lovely face), I was also clutching at myself, loving that we belonged. It was amazing that the audience didn't shout at queers, they laughed warmly. And we could laugh with them.

There were plenty of queers who knew how to make you laugh, especially in those pubs where they screamed and ranted at each other, and everyone had a woman's name. But being young and queer had its problems, like being forced into sex on the threat of exposure or blackmail. Luckily, none of that worked with me. I'd been round the block and had my ticket punched to prove it. Another older queen, aptly named John Gay, tried to take it upon himself to protect me from predatory hawks. He asked me to promise that I wouldn't go to 'criminal haunts': the back-room bars. My flagrant two-word disregard for his advice meant that he eventually gave up and warned me that I would be 'locked up' and that it would all end in tears.

Yet under Ian's tutelage I had managed to seduce the assistant stage manager, who was about twenty. It was a drunken one-night stand, but it was a formative experience because finally I was going for the men I desired, rather than the other way round. Apart from that one experience, and the downing of halves of bitter or port and lemon in smoke-filled bars – despite the drinking age being twenty-one – I remained virtually untouched and relatively innocent.

At the end of the tour we returned to London. I had enjoyed the bars and the seedy back rooms and now I wanted more. Ian promised me that he would show me a London that would lift me off my feet, and that he would take me to proper places for poofs. Not like the 'provinces'. No, he insisted, he was going to take me to bars in the West End where you 'could get shagged left, right, and centre, and get a drink bought into the bargain'.

One night I made the excuse at home that I was going 'out'.

Who with, was the response.

'A mate,' I replied.

My parents didn't question me; they had watched me making my way in life in a world so different from theirs, so they accepted my independence and merely said that I was not to be too late back.

As we walked through Soho, along Berwick Street, Ian waved at the women hanging from the windows plying their trade. Further along we turned left into D'Arblay Street and beside the entrance to a dark mews we stopped at a door. Ian pressed the buzzer and someone let us in. We went down a steep flight of steps to a second door where we paid the admission fee of a few shillings and entered. If Gladys Dare's public shaming of me had been the worst moment of my teenage life, this was the best. I could not believe it. There were no 'dirty old men', no one shoving a half pint of stout across a bar to you. It was dark, there was music playing and men as young as me were dancing with one another, holding one another, and no one batted an eyelid. Cheek to cheek, body to body.

Ian dragged me from my stupor towards a bar where you could buy Cokes or coffee, but nothing else, and then disappeared onto the dance floor in the arms of a man.

I had died and gone to heaven and it was only just beginning. Over the next few weeks I met boys there who had gone to the other stage schools and some who I had worked with. We had all previously kept our heads down, even the effeminate ones. As time went on a few of the older, chubbier men tried to hit on us, but if they were too persistent we would enlist the help of the lesbians from the club opposite, the Subway, who loved any excuse to kick a queer. Especially an old one.

Ian kept his promise and I discovered most of the pubs and clubs dotted across Soho, from Shaftesbury Avenue all the way up to Oxford Street. They were often at the top of several flights of steep stairs, 'to keep the old queens out', or tucked away at the end of an alley. You always had to convince the doorkeeper or barman that you would not consume any alcohol, otherwise you weren't getting in. And once I knew about all-night buses the city was mine.

The gay scene was not simply confined to just these bars, it also mingled with mainstream bars and discos, such as the Bear, or Ward's Irish House on Piccadilly Circus. There was also the Speakeasy on Wardour Street, where the music crowd hung out with Long John Baldry, the famous blues singer, who was known to like a boy or two, but who soon brushed off my advances.

We would wander from one bar to another, calling out to the working women with whom we were on first-name terms, knowing the all-night cafes where you could grab a free coffee if the owner fancied you and you knew how to control his wandering hands. This was night life beyond imagining. But it was a life that came to an end when the sun began to rise. What happened the night before stayed with the night before. Exchanged telephone numbers were discreetly hidden away and you had to be careful not to speak to someone in the street unless you really knew them because it could be a trap.

There was always the fear that you might walk into the bar and see someone from your 'other life': someone from your area, or your work. Occasionally a friend would have to dash out of a club or slip into a dark alley to avoid being seen. There were plenty of other places to meet too: cruising areas in cemeteries, parks and river towpaths, or public conveniences for those who liked it rough or dangerous, or who were too terrified to be seen anywhere else. But for the most part it was like a stage perform-ance, all bright lights, make-up and bugger tomorrow. Only the desperate got caught, only the stupid took too many pills. We were young, and London was for the living.

If you wanted to 'get off yer tits' there were purple hearts, Pro Plus, amphetamines and weed. I was too big a coward. I preferred booze, and whisky and Coke was the fashion. Some weekends we'd venture west to Earl's Court and the famous leather and denim pubs, the Coleherne, or Brompton's Hotel. Here the rough boys would threaten you to make you buy them a drink, and the off-duty guardsmen would tell you it'd cost a 'fiver'. Unlike Soho you had to be careful here. There were no lesbians or prostitutes to look after you. It was known that 'pretty policemen', dressed in tight white T-shirts and ripped denim jeans, would lean against the pub walls outside and wait for you to chat them up, then they'd arrest you for 'soliciting for an immoral purpose' or 'pro-curing an act of gross indecency'.

There were some who were blackmailed by the people they had gone back with, or by those who'd picked them up in the public toilets, the 'cottages'. There were the queer-bashers too. And in the corner of every bar was an old queen warning you what your future would be: 'You'll be old and no one will fucking want you either, dear,' they would hiss over a warm gin and tonic. Yet the world they talked about existed elsewhere.

London was at our feet. And as an actor I didn't have to worry. Lots of actors were queer but they kept it to themselves and got on with the job. There were even rumours that singing stars like Johnny Ray were queer. I had found my place, and dangerous though it sometimes seemed, I belonged, especially as the faces and names became familiar.

I celebrated my sixteenth birthday at the end of that year and the world felt warm and wonderful. Living at home was difficult, but I kept my worlds apart from each other. If Ian raised a few eyebrows, or solicited my dad's disapproving laugh, then they would excuse it to the neighbours and family as 'show business'. Even when my dad found a small number of photos of naked men in my room I faced him down, said they were Ian's, and challenged him for going through my personal things. He never responded. He just looked right through me and left my bedroom. If anyone suspected anything they kept it to themselves; there were some things that could never be said.

After a few months of having fun and getting to know the bars, I met Lee, one of Ian's conquests, who was short and muscular, had a voice like gravel, a shy awkward smile and one of the cheekiest grins I had ever seen.

I was putty in his hands and he knew it. He wasn't like the other men on the scene: he treated me as his equal, and he carried himself with confidence. Lee was a successful disc jockey at Tiffany's night club on Shaftesbury Avenue and hung around with Tony Windsor, a famous pirate radio disc jockey, who was blowing apart the BBC's monopoly on pop broadcasting.

I knew Lee was seeing Ian but that didn't stop me. We went to Le Deuce and then to the Rockingham, a posh club for 'single gentlemen' (they never used the word queer at the Rockingham) behind the Windmill Theatre. That night we went back to his one-bedroom flat just up the road from Holloway women's prison and for the first time in my life someone actually made love to me. It didn't hurt, and I didn't have to search for that switch inside me.

I fell in love with him. He was the butchest, straightest man I had ever come across, who loved to laugh and live life at the edge. I saw him for a couple of weeks but then the novelty began to wear off for him. He stopped returning my phone calls. I quickly learnt from the club gossip that he was one of those only interested in 'fresh meat'. But that didn't deter me, I wouldn't give up. When I tracked him down I told him I adored him and I was in love with him. He was petrified. Despite his protests of being a 'single man', and that at twenty-four years of age he was too old for me (I said he should have thought about that before), night after night I waited for him outside Tiffany's or one of the other clubs he went to.

Eventually persistence paid off and after months of pursuing him I moved in with him, even though it was still illegal to have gay sex. 'Gay, not queer, dear,' someone had told me on tour, and it sounded much nicer back then. The term queer would be left to the past and memories of school and the bastards who wanted to beat us, or shout up the street after us. I was learning a new language and embarking on a new life.

14

When I told my mum and dad that I was moving out to share a flat with a mate they breathed a sigh of relief. You could cut the testosterone with a knife in our small maisonette. I would be one less bruised ego to worry about.

Lee ran clubs and discos across London and was also a minor music producer. He had a passion for Jaguar cars and, though I didn't know it at the time, an addiction to speed, amphetamines. Before I moved in he told me what the rules would be: there would always be two bedrooms or two beds. If anyone asked why we were sharing it was because we were cousins. I was also never to show him any affection in public or if his family were around – though in the early years he kept me well away from them. His aunt had once asked him why he had looked into another man's eyes 'like that'. When he asked her what she meant, her reply was that 'he knew'.

Later that year, in July 1967, the law was changed to 'decriminalise consenting sex between two male adults in private, who were above the age of twenty-one'. In the bars there were shouts of 'we're legal now' to which some replied 'yes, but still no man will have you'. Lee merely reminded me that I was only sixteen, below the age of consent. The life we led would have to remain hidden.

Being with Lee, my life felt good. It didn't matter that we had to hide our love from other people, or be careful who we let in on our secret, I finally had someone. Lee was crazier and even more irrational than I had first thought. He had no sense of danger or urgency, physical or mental. He chased business dreams and record deals that ended in nothing and got into incredible money problems without telling me. His discos around London were hugely successful and the venues were always packed, but he thrived on physically fighting unruly clients, or with his bouncers. Adrenalin was his drug, and the amphetamines, and he was mine. I never needed anything other than the life I kept together for us.

When I raised the issue of money problems and unpaid bills he just snapped his fingers in mid-air and said that I should stay away from things that did not concern me. I did, and eventually it all went wrong when we were forced to do a moonlight flit, a dash into obscurity, in a caravan he had bought on hire purchase. That first night we slept in a field.

But as usual he fell on his feet and found a derelict cottage on the outskirts of Hemel Hempstead. He leased it for a peppercorn rent on the undertaking that he would restore it. The deal was done and it was left to me to do the work, which I did with determination. I threw myself at the job while he stood looking on, can of lager in hand, feeling totally useless. Later I discovered the lager can was filled and refilled with whisky and Coke to get him through the day.

In our early years Lee met Woodie; they got on well and did some business together, booking bands and orchestras, when Dave Woods became the general manager of the prestigious Tower Ballroom in Great Yarmouth. They had a scam: paying a band one price but issuing a fake contract to the venue for another, higher fee, which they split between them. The Tower Ballroom put Woodie at the top of his empire. In the summer seasons he rubbed shoulders with the big television variety stars, Morecambe and Wise, Val Doonican, Des O'Connor and many more. Often when Lee had to go there to meet Woodie and check on a band I went with him.

'He is not my dad,' I would always protest as we drove into Great Yarmouth.

The response from Lee was, 'Leave it, Mick. Leave it.'

On one memorable visit one of the older women who worked in the cloakrooms at the ballroom told me how lovely it was to see me and gave me a hug, mentioning that she had met my 'brother' too. I was momentarily shocked, fixed a smile and walked away. After that weekend I never went back. I faced the horrible truth that Woodie was taking advantage of other boys, and it made me feel dirty, cheap and helpless. I couldn't find the words to tell anyone, not even Lee, who loved me.

Throughout this period my career was taking off as I made the successful transition from the curse of being a 'child actor' to a working actor. After the first night of a play at the Leatherhead Theatre, Surrey, I was chased by the international agents William Morris, but I had no idea who they were so I played hard to get and they walked away. I did two movies back to back, the musical *Goodbye Mr Chips* with Petula Clark (how I ached to ask her about Gladys Dare) and Peter O'Toole – a brilliant actor but very unpleasant drunk who loved telling us to get the fuck out of his way – and finally finishing off with *The Virgin Soldiers*, where I worked alongside David Jones, soon to be better known as David Bowie. David was a quiet, thin, sullen boy in his early twenties who would sit alone singing to his guitar in the deserted barracks in Berkshire where we filmed. He knew I was gay and we flirted, but nothing more came of it. Besides, he was too shy for me, I liked a bit of oomph!

When I wasn't acting I worked in Lee's discos, taking the entrance money and cashing up (and stashing a bit aside for the chaotic days that I always knew would appear), or working in a builders' cafe on Westbourne Grove where I would fall into unrequited lust with unsuspecting scaffolders.

We kept our lives private. Lee had mostly straight mates and enjoyed straight bars, where I learnt that he seduced straight men. As an actor I knew there was no need for me to broadcast my sexuality, people advised me to keep quiet and just get on with it. Of course there were still some directors who believed in using the couch for casting, whether you were gay or straight. If you wanted the part then you had to prove how versatile you were, or desperate. That was how I was cast for *The Virgin Soldiers*, though when the director asked me out to dinner he told me that I had the part regardless of my answer.

So I went to dinner, then on to bed. It was common and you opted in, or you opted out. And though the partial decriminalisation of gay sex had changed lives, I was 'jail bait': I still wasn't twenty-one, and some found that attractive.

My mum and dad were struggling along together and I would go home about once a week, unless it was too tense between them. I had learnt by then that they could not live with or without one another. I knew I shouldn't get involved in their fights but I still did – always taking my mum's side – and it never helped. A luxury while visiting them was to disappear off to the steam bath at Poplar Baths. This was a place where I had found naked men to look at from the age of fifteen, and it had been metres away from where we used to go swimming with the school.

I can't remember how I stumbled on the baths but for a young gay man it was a dream, and the older heterosexual, mainly Jewish, men soon included me as a feisty little member of their massage team. We massaged with fury. Old men, young men, fat and thin, all part of the team that recreated the old Eastern European tradition of *shmeissing*. This was the process of soaping up the body and lathering it with a long raffia mop before whisking it just above the skin to open the pores and burn the poor bleeder into submission. Then on hearing their cries, slowly bringing the soft soapy raffia mop crashing down onto the body and rubbing it all over, before repeating the process until they could take no more. The unspoken eroticism and utter peace of watching these dockers and workmen stark naked and without a single inhibition – their bodies sweating and toned – was breath-taking. It never lost its lustre, not even as it and the clientele faded over the years. I knew too that there was a smaller steam room, not as hot, but steamier in a different way. Nicknamed the 'blue room' it was where gays and bisexuals and the dubious would gather for a massage and a 'touch up'. I steered clear of that room for years until I no longer cared what people thought or said about me and eventually I had the courage to migrate between the two.

Over time my relationship with Lee changed, even though I was still crazy about him.

I suspected he was playing around, so one day, instead of going away for the night as I had led him to believe, I decided to lie in wait. My suspicions were confirmed when I caught him in the arms of a sweet teenager – actually I jumped out of the built-in wardrobe at the moment of climax and challenged his indiscretion with the words: 'If you excuse me I think I'll go to bed now.' Never a man to surrender easily, he locked me out of the bedroom and went back to his young conquest. I responded with the strength of an ox and throughout the night comprehensively emptied the lounge of all its furniture, dragging it from the ground-floor flat to the garage over 100 metres away.

So I, too, began to look elsewhere for sexual attention. At the steam baths I met Brian and his wandering hands. He was married with a wife and kids, and I lusted after him. He was like a bigger version of Lee, twenty-six years old, over six feet tall and athletic, but he frightened me too. There was something unpredictable about him, and his eyes were ice blue and cold. He was also a small-time criminal, working street scams on tourists and other unsuspecting souls.

Once he came to the flat I shared with Lee, but I got very scared and I panicked, rebuffing his sexual advances. He was having none of it. He grabbed me by the neck and started slapping me. I thought quickly. I said we should go out and find someone for him, a friend, at a pub nearby. For a moment we moved towards the front door, then he dragged me by my hair and pulled me back into the bedroom. I shoved him towards the wall. He pushed me back. I was no match for his strength, and he was clearly turned on by the struggle. He pulled me to him and started undoing his trousers. I yanked myself away, he grabbed my hair once more, and then it went black.

I came to on the bed as he tried to rape me. Pleas streamed out of my mouth. I promised him money, I promised anything he wanted. And with words, words incessantly pouring out, I managed to talk him out of penetrative sex. I talked him to orgasm. When it was over he took all the money I had, and some of my belongings.

The next day I didn't need to tell Lee; the bruising said it all. We both knew that we couldn't go to the police because of my age and our relationship, and we knew they would never believe two queers against a married man. Instead Lee wanted Brian's name and address. He and a few mates would sort it out, he said. But I refused. In the end we forgot it, because you just had to. Worse had happened to others. It was a lucky escape and I convinced myself that I had provoked him. He had wanted sex, he had wanted to use me, and I should have just reached for that switch inside my head. I should have accepted that was what happened to gay men, but I had decided to stick up for myself, I had decided that I deserved better. Nonetheless I still wasn't going to the police.

Over our years together, primarily due to his ill-health, Lee let me get close to his family. I was acceptable as the novelty, 'the actor that they saw on telly', but I was just 'a friend' and that was enough for me. It didn't matter because I felt so secure in our relationship. I had escaped the excesses of the swinging, drug-fuelled sixties, and we had survived so much together. Mad times, good times, drunken brawling times. Despite it all, I still had him.

When I worked alongside his mother in her garden nursery in Hertfordshire I was always 'our Leon's friend, Mick'. Over the nine years we were together they saw that I 'looked out' for him, maybe they noticed that I cared. 'You're like a brother to him, Mick,' his mother would say quietly and unasked. We grew into men together. We were just boys when we met.

But his incessant drinking, mood swings, the fights and eventually the suicide attempts drove me away. The closer I got to him, the more I supported him, the weaker and more useless

I made him feel. And when I backed away I felt helpless too. It was impossible. Just him touching me made me feel wanted, alive, sensual and sexual, and because of that he couldn't bear to rely on me or want me.

Finally it got too much. One day at the house in Hemel Hempstead I quietly packed a suitcase and walked to the station. It was the saddest I had ever been but I knew that if I stayed it would eventually destroy me too. No shouting, no drama, just burdened down with pain. His reaction, he said, was that he understood and he wondered why I hadn't left years ago. But in the years that followed he never gave up caring about me, nor me him.

Lee died many years after we'd parted. He told his mother he was going to bed early because he had one of his migraines. The next morning she found him dead. He had tried to commit suicide on many occasions when I was with him. Once, after a weekend's indiscretion, I returned home to find him unconscious from an overdose. Only his beloved dog lying beside him had prevented him from dying from hypothermia. He tried again with pills, and when I brought him round he begged me not to call an ambulance, though eventually I had to. His final attempt before I left him had been to try to blow his head off with a shotgun: his friends in the local police force cleaned up the place afterwards and disguised it as an 'accident'. It was a miracle he lived: the gun had jerked, blowing away half his lung and part of his guts.

Strangely enough even these events would shape my future. Visiting Lee in hospital I saw two doctors trying to bring a woman back to life, and the image etched itself onto my brain. I watched in seeming slow motion as they took total control of the situation and of her life: there was not a moment's hesitation about what they should do, or who should do it. It was only a few minutes but they had taken chaos, and in their unbroken silence, restored life. It was mesmerising.

I went to Lee's funeral and to my surprise I was put in the first car with his mother, a place reserved for the closest relatives. I protested and said it wasn't necessary. But the family were adamant. Gladys pointed to her son's coffin in the hearse ahead of us, and said: 'I put your flowers on Leon's coffin.'

I nodded.

'It is what he would have wanted,' she added.

I quietly thanked her and nothing more was said. It was her way of telling me that she knew. She had probably always known, but some things did not need to be said.

As they closed the curtains at the end of his service of commitment I smiled and thought of him at Tiffany's on Shaftesbury Avenue. His tired, gravelly voice announcing the last dance, 'You're My World' by Cilla Black. Me at the far end of the dance floor, a sixteen-year-old boy on the verge of a new life, not knowing where I was going, or where I wanted to go, but understanding for the first time in my life that I belonged. And looking back at me across the hundreds of heterosexual couples dancing to a public proclamation of love was Lee, that shy, cheeky grin creeping across his face.

15

Once I took the hard decision to leave Lee I felt stronger, but I hadn't given any thought as to where I should go.

So I found myself turning up at Kenny Parry's basement flat in Myddelton Square, Islington. Kenny was a formidable character actor, born and bred in Wigan and with a very pronounced Northern accent that he used to great effect. Especially when cussing. His career as a character actor was second to none, having worked alongside Dick Emery, Benny Hill, the legendary Kenneth Horne, Franco Zeffirelli, Richard Burton and Elizabeth Taylor.

Balding, toothless when it suited him – and it often did – Kenny would describe himself as an 'egg on legs, dear, but overflowing with talent. Talent, dear', and finish it off with a flourish of hands waving in the air. He was also a gifted clairvoyant and 'mother' to many a male actor, especially northerners like Tom Courtenay, Nicol Williamson, (honorary northerner) John Thaw and Albert Finney. Indeed 'Mother Parry' had given many of them a home when they got to London, and food and laundry facilities until they found their feet, or 'even worse, a woman'. I'd worked with him in *The Tempest* and he'd taken a shine to me, and to Lee. 'I do threesomes too you know,' he once generously offered, but we studiously ignored it. I ignored too his fervent attempts during the play to grab at the 'porcelain tea service' between my legs.

As an admirer of his camp and his talent, I was allowed into his hallowed halls. I rang the buzzer, the front door of the building was electronically released and, case in hand, I made my way down the stairs to his flat. At the foot of the stairs I saw the bottom half of his voluminous figure.

'Is that you Alice?'

I replied that it was. (All of his 'daughters' were called Alice at some point in their incarnation with him.) He didn't wait for me, but turned into the flat with a statement trailing behind him: 'Spirit has sent you here for a reason. A reason, dear.'

I closed the door behind me.

'Don't put the bolt on. I'm expecting trade,' came the instruction from the living room.

'Trade' was the term used for casual male sex. It being market day he expected one of his many callers.

I stood in the sitting room, in which photos of Kenny with the famous and the infamous bedecked the walls.

'Spirit tells me you're on a journey, Alice. A journey.'

Spirit had obviously noticed the suitcase hanging from my right arm, too. Before I had time to reply he was on his feet: 'Right, get that case in that spare bedroom, and get that place fettled and firked. You'll need somewhere to stay. Somewhere to stay, Alice. And come Monday you'll need to get down that labour exchange. Bills don't pay themselves, you know.'

And that was it. I became his new live-in daughter, Miss Cashman – Alice. There was no use arguing. That was my title.

With Kenny there were no shades of grey. Life was full of certainty or clairvoyance. Despite some failed attempts, he did have an uncanny gift for clairvoyance, sometimes predicting what would happen and offering evidence from the spirit world, something known only to you and a departed one. The actress Dame Eileen Atkins was one of his fond admirers, as was Dame Siân Phillips. A casual phone call to Kenny would produce amazing news of a love affair, a devious agent or a new contract. If you thanked him he scolded you that it was nothing to do with him; it was spirit, it was his guide. And he meant it.

In a trance he would often argue with said guide, White Owl, begging the spirit to let him 'get a word in edgeways', only for a full-scale row to break out between them. Except on this side we could only hear Kenny and the air turn blue. If it all became too much and he crossed the line with White Owl, then his head would toss and jerk and he would boom: 'Cover your stomach, dear. Cover your stomach. He's drawing the power. He's drawing the power.' Another time he jumped his hefty frame up from his throne of an armchair, ran to the kitchen and threw a bowl of water over the invisible guide, shouting: 'Now find your way back to the fucking reservation.'

It was hilarious and frightening at the same time but you could not laugh. If you did, that was the end of your clairvoyance and the curse would be placed upon you. A famous actor once questioned Kenny's powers. When the actor failed to appear on stage due to laryngitis, Kenny announced to London that this was God's punishment for all the years of over-acting, and for doubting spirit.

Yet as spiritual as he was, Kenny could be vicious. One evening a young woman knocked at his door rattling her tin: 'A little something, Mr Parry? For charity.' He looked her up and down and beckoned her closer: 'Charity, dear? Charity?' Then he paused: 'This is what I think of charity, dear. If Nurse Edith Cavell were to come back from the grave and knock on my door selling poppies, I'd kick her in the cunt and tell her to fuck off.' Then he gently closed the door on the ashen-faced woman and carried on with whatever he was doing.

Life was hectic and crazy at Kenny's. The flat was never without a guest, or a man turning up from the aptly named Smithfield meat market at six in the morning. Once, after a man left and Kenny had finished his 'dolphin act' (his daily bath), I was commanded to help him strip out the rubbish from his bedroom wardrobe. In reality I did the work as he watched and provided the commentary.

'Open that envelope Miss, there might be money in it.'

It was a pair of teeth.

'And much fucking use they were. That was Miss Courtenay [Tom Courtenay]. Private teeth! My gums were covered in fucking ulcers, Alice. And then he cursed me with that cat!'

I learnt that it was sometimes better not to enquire further.

While I was staying with Kenny I had several meetings for a film series based on the 'Confessions' books, starting with *Confessions of a Window Cleaner*. I was first in line to play the randy title part. I had interviews with the producers, Norman Cohen, Michael Klinger and the young and gorgeous Greg Smith. It was co-written and directed by the renowned Val Guest who had directed *Casino Royale* and the *Quatermass* films. After several interviews I was invited to have afternoon drinks at Val's house in St John's Wood. I hadn't thought much about playing the part. It was just a tongue-in-cheek comedy role and I knew I could get away with it, but I certainly hadn't connected it to my private life.

'I've worked with her,' Mother Parry had said to me before the meeting.

'With who?' I asked.

'Her. That sexy Greg. Send her my love.'

So I did. Suddenly the atmosphere of the drinks party changed. A look flashed between the men.

'How do you know Ken?' asked Greg, a hint of concern in his voice.

I explained that I shared a flat with him.

There was a tiny pause, then smiles and nods all round. They said that he was a funny actor. Very funny. There might even be something in the film for him. Then the subject was dropped.

As I was leaving Greg asked if I had a girlfriend, to which I replied that I didn't.

'Playing hard to get,' he smiled.

I laughed and nodded.

I never heard from them again. Robin Askwith, with whom I had worked when I was younger, got the part and was perfect. According to Mother Parry I had been saved from a fate worse than death, but it was clear to me they didn't want a gay man near the role.

Despite not getting the series of *Confessions* films my career was still going well, and I was about to star in a one-off play for ITV.

A couple of years earlier I'd had a fantastic break in the thriller *Unman, Wittering and Zigo*, directed by John Mackenzie, and starring David Hemmings. The film was set in a public school and Hemmings played the new teacher who comes under threat from his students. I played a leading role, Terhew, one of his threatening pupils. David was one of the great icons of the cinema in the 1960s, but by this stage he was going through a difficult time. It looked as though his marriage to Gayle Hunnicutt was on the rocks and he was often to be found with a brandy at the hotel in Llandudno where we were filming.

For the most part he kept a discreet, star-like distance from the younger men, but one day he invited me to dinner. His driver picked me up and I was surprised to discover that I was the only other actor there. It was largely a family affair, with Gayle, his in-laws and the film's executive producer, Gareth Wigan. I had no idea why I'd been invited; he had hardly spoken to me except on the set. Out of the blue during the meal he leant across the table and told me that his agents thought I was good.

I thanked him.

'Very good,' he added.

After this he just stared at me for a while and then went back to sketching something on the paper in front of him.

Eventually the evening began to wind down and we all stood up to go. As we were leaving David grabbed my arm and held me back. 'Stay,' he said, 'have a brandy.'

I shook my head and reminded him that I had an early call.

He didn't reply, he just kept looking at me.

'Can I see the sketch?' I asked.

He gave it to me. It was the assembled dinner party with the title 'Bored Meeting'. I smiled. Then he closed in on me and gently pressed me against the wall.

'I am going to have you,' he said quietly.

I stared into his eyes. I thought he was taking the piss, that he was winding me up, that he wanted to reveal to everyone that I was gay. I'd had that experience before on a film set and it wasn't pleasant. I shook my head and tried to speak, then lowered my gaze. On the other side of the door there was laughter. After a while he stepped back and turned away from me and I left the room silently.

On set David and I had a few scenes together. There was one where I had to challenge him and frighten him off in his study at the school. We started filming in the early morning. The director, John Mackenzie, was very relaxed as we rehearsed for the main camera angle but David was edgy and he was visibly sweating. We did a couple of passable takes for the camera, but David and John wanted to do the scene again. John gave me a few notes to improve the performance then, as they were resetting, David took me to one side and we left the room, shutting the door behind us. He produced a bottle of brandy, took a long swig from it then pushed it to me. I took the bottle without encouragement and swallowed a generous gulp before we went back inside to redo the scene. We knocked the shit out of each other. It was the way he liked to work: raw, edgy.

Another film quickly followed, *X, Y and Zee* (aka *Zee and Co.*), starring Elizabeth Taylor, Michael Caine and Susannah York. I played Gavin, the shop assistant. It was just three scenes, one of which was with Elizabeth. There were rumours about Elizabeth Taylor being unreliable to work with and spending endless days in her trailer until she felt ready to do her scenes. My experience was the opposite. She was invariably on time, or only fashionably late, always polite and she knew the lines – in the right order.

I rehearsed the scene with her stand-in, and when the crazy Hollywood director Brian G. Hutton decided the time and I were right, Elizabeth was called to the set. Announcements preceded her. 'Elizabeth is coming. Elizabeth is coming!' echoed across the studio. She virtually wafted onto the set, her entourage of make-up artists and minders, dressers and hairdressers peeling away until there was an image in front of me of a small woman in purple hot pants and with the most amazing, piercing, violet-coloured eyes.

'Ready to go?' asked Brian.

'No,' she said, and came towards me. 'Hello, you must be Michael. I'm Elizabeth.' She held out her hand and smiled.

I mumbled hello and said it was nice to meet her.

'Nice to be working with you.'

Then she looked at Brian, her smile dropping away: 'Now I am ready.'

Apart from our scene, shot from several angles over a few days, there was no other communication, except on the final day. Control of photographs and publicity was rigid. Everything had to be approved by someone two steps removed, and I had requested a photo with Elizabeth. 'Not possible,' came the response.

I was not to be deterred. As the studio lights began to fade and we finished the last scene, I grabbed my courage with both hands and asked Elizabeth directly. She said that a photo with her was fine and asked when I was finishing on the film. I told her this was my last day. She nodded, gently tousled her hair and shouted: 'Let's have some lights on around here!'

'What's going on?' demanded the first assistant director.

'It's Michael's last day and we are gonna have some photos together.'

The echo reverberated and someone else called out: 'What's going on? Who wants the lights back on?'

'I do!' she boomed.

Up went the call: 'Put the lights on. Get the goddamn lights on.' And we stood there as Gianni, her photographer, snapped away. Then she disappeared, having cost the studio untold sums in overtime as we stretched past the working day. Only Elizabeth Taylor could do that, and with style.

I was riding the crest of a wave, and John Mackenzie offered me another film with Carole White. Yet the success, the films, the interest from international agents felt like it was happening to someone else; all the time there was an undertow. Ever since I'd visited Lee in hospital after he had tried to kill himself with a shotgun, the image of the two doctors trying to bring that woman back to life had been replaying in my head. I was nearly twenty-five years old. I knew I had to make a decision.

16

I sat down one Friday afternoon and explained it all to Kenny. I hadn't discussed it with anyone.

'It's meant, daughter. It's why spirit sent you here, dear,' was all he said.

Once again I packed my case, and left. I knew I didn't have the time to hang about if I wanted to become a qualified doctor. I phoned University College London and learned that to study medicine you needed at least four O levels in sciences and English language, and three A levels, preferably in chemistry, physics and biology. The problem was that these qualifications were usually obtained over a period of four years. I knew no medical school would take me at the age of thirty and that even now I was on the edge of inadmissibility. I searched around for possibilities: adult day classes, night school and correspondence courses, before I hit on the crammers.

Crammers existed primarily for public school kids who had failed their exams or hadn't achieved the required grades for university. I made some phone calls and found a cram school on London's City Road, just north of the financial district. The place was called Borlands. It was possible to cram four O levels into four months, and the subsequent three A-level sciences in six months. I then saw how much it would cost, and the amount was dizzying, but I knew I had to take a risk and the education would be worth the money. I'd just starred in the TV drama, *The Jesse James Story*, and had enough money to pay for the first term, so I went to see Borlands to meet the secretary.

It was like stepping back 100 years: the institution was Dickensian, decidedly impoverished, upper class, and run by four men who ranged from the academic (Mr Baldwin), to the military (Mr Butler), the detached (Mr Bennett) and the comic (Mr Griffiths). The interview both depressed and galvanised me. I was told that I had a mountain to climb as I had no basic education on which to build, but if I was determined they would not hold me back (slight pause), so long as I was able to pay the fee for the first term up front. Never happy talking about money, I waved the subject aside.

The secretary took me on a tour of the ancient establishment, which stank of a mixture of pear drops and rotten eggs (ethanol and hydrogen sulphide). The building ranged over two imposing double-fronted floors and a basement where the chemistry and physics labs were housed. If it was to work financially I decided I had to move back home and rely on the stretched resources of my mum and dad.

When I told my agent, Jeremy Conway, that I was leaving show business to study medicine he hit the roof. It was understandable. He had built my career up over the years, and the word of mouth about the TV drama I'd made had been very good. But despite his pleas, I had become evangelical about retraining; I wanted to have a sense of purpose. No amount of common sense would change my mind and I threw myself at the task of cramming to get the necessary qualifications. For months I knew nothing but studying and studying, I even fell asleep studying. I shut myself away from my previous life and I did what I did best: I learnt the 'lines'. Repetition, repetition, repetition. In a play you have a director to guide you, whereas here they presumed you knew how to get to where you were going. My school education, apart from inspiring a love of words and imparting a free imagination, had produced nothing of any academic consequence in me. But I would not be deterred. What I didn't know, I had to learn how to understand, and how to apply it.

Mathematics eluded me, algebra was unknown to me and trigonometry sounded like something they did to you. Using the repetition process, I passed the O levels without any problems. However, physics was something I couldn't come to terms with, nor the teacher. The other subjects I began to enjoy: the predictable logic of chemistry and the sheer artistry of biology captivated me, as did the tutors, who loved their subjects and who were real performers. These tutors, with the exception of the physics teacher, suddenly had real confidence in me, and they were not frightened to show it. With my acceptable O-level grades what had seemed impossible now seemed within reach, but I had to earn the money for the six-month A-level course. It was going to be tough, as I had just a few weeks to do it in.

I got in touch with a few casting directors who liked my work and called my agent. There was nothing. I scoured the papers for work and eventually took a job on a building site at Snaresbrook Crown Court. During the second week doing labouring work – which was hilarious, sex-fuelled and macho – I got a call from Jeremy. He'd got me an audition, and it was a big job: ITV was planning a prime-time compendium of J. B. Priestley's plays and prose to celebrate his eightieth birthday and all the parts were to be played by just eight actors.

The next day I went to the building site with my suit, shirt and tie in a dry cleaners' polythene bag. As the day finished I nipped into the toilets and came out washed, suited and booted. Ignoring the whistles and innuendos from my fellow labourers, who I was already fond of, and vice versa, I headed to Green Park. There, Corinne Rodriguez, a casting director who was an old friend, took me into her office to meet the director and the producer. She said that she could hardly believe I was available to do it, that she loved my work, and then they pushed the script towards me so I could read a couple of scenes for them.

When I was finished Corinne showed me out and promised to be in touch. By the time I got back to my parents' place there was already a message to ring Jeremy. I thought it must be another audition, it was too early to hear about the Priestley. But no, when I rang him, he told me I had got the job! Rehearsals would start in a week's time, and then he told me the fee. It was exactly what I needed to pay for the next six months at Borlands. I should have been excited about starring in ITV's celebration of

J. B. Priestley – the great man himself was to take part – but all I could think of were the months of chemistry and biology and the interminable challenge of physics that would follow. Nonetheless I beamed at the prospect. It should have dawned on me that I was bordering on the psychotic.

I said goodbye to the wonderful workmen at Snaresbrook Crown Court, who assured me that one way or another I would be appearing there again, and started rehearsing in Kensington, later recording over five days at Yorkshire Television's studios in Leeds.

Jack Priestley was a powerful force, and he knew it. During a pause in the studio he lit up his pipe, and with a satisfied glow, told one of the actresses that she looked particularly pretty in her long frock, before adding: 'But you could do with lifting that hemline and showing a bit of leg. I still have influence, you know.' Once the recording was completed the director and the cast, which included a young Marcia Warren and Robert Stevens, headed out to the best restaurant in Leeds to celebrate. Priestley, his wife, Jacquetta Hawkes, and the head of drama, David Cunliffe, were dining there too. At the end of the evening Priestley made his slow, determined way towards our table, still puffing on his pipe. 'You did me proud,' he said, 'but what I find incredible is that you like one another. Just like my "Good Companions".'

This ITV show was a great opportunity for any actor, and superb roles for me. I should have listened to the people around me and realised where my vocation really lay, but all I could think of was getting back to Borlands for the final push, and filling out the applications to medical schools.

My age and my lack of formal education were formidable barriers to obtaining a place at medical school, but then luck played a hand.

One night at a gay bar near Hyde Park an American guy asked if he could sit with me because he was being pestered by another man. I smiled and told him that was what gay bars were for.

His eyes nearly popped out of his head as he mouthed the word 'gay?'. I nodded and smiled; he was nice. Sweet and nice: precisely the type I never went for, so it was easy to chat. It transpired that he was a vice president of a major American pharmaceutical company and was in London on business.

As I was a budding medical student he made me feel important and offered to help with contacts in the medical profession. I was charmed and flattered. Later that night, after more than a few drinks, we ended up in bed. It was disastrous.

As I dressed to make a hasty exit from the Hilton on Park Lane he told me he needed to see me again. He was married with children but admitted that he was bisexual. A week after he left, an airmail letter arrived telling me that he was in love with me and wanted me to move to the States where he would put me through medical school. Gently I got him to understand that it was a one-sided love affair and that we should just be friends. He reluctantly agreed, and friends we became. I knew I had done the right thing. I needed to do this for me.

When he was in London I often saw him and at the pivotal stage of my trying to get into a medical school I asked for his help. University College London was engaged in a major research and drugs trial with his company. He said he would have a word with a colleague who was the Dean of the Medical School but made clear that it would be nothing more than a meeting so that she could advise me about my application.

Late one afternoon I left Borlands and made my way to Gower Street and the university. The dean met me in her basement office; she was kind, gentle and interested in my previous life as an actor as well as why I wanted to study medicine.

'What is your ambition?' she asked.

'My ambition?'

'Yes. Your ambition. As a doctor.'

She waited. It was a question I hadn't thought about.

'My ambition,' I said, 'is to be woken up in the middle of the night to be told I've got to go down to Casualty to stitch up a woman, and to swear about it.'

She smiled and said: 'Good. You know what it's all about,' and then added, 'All I can promise is that you will get an interview.'

I walked out on air.

Yet in the end it wasn't the awful, hostile, classist interview – 'Well, no one in your family's done medicine. Have they?' – by the new Dean Professor Hall Craggs that sealed my fate. It was physics. My grades in chemistry and biology were excellent, but with an E in physics I was advised to retake the exam, even though no medical school had offered me a place. My money was running out and so was time. I decided to get a job where I could study alongside.

That was how I ended up at the old Westminster Hospital in Horseferry Road working as a theatre porter. After an initial queasiness I became fascinated by the surgery being carried out in front of me, and I would talk to the patients and put them at their ease before they met the rest of the operating team. The formidable Sister Rock decided that I was her man to single-handedly run the cardiothoracic and gynaecological theatre across the road in Page Street. There I worked with the heart pioneer Charles Drew, and luck upon luck, Dr Wyman, the Dean of Westminster Medical School, who was his anaesthetist.

I also had the experience of meeting Father Murphy. A man was being kept alive on the operating table so he could be given the last rites. Father Murphy presented himself at the operating theatre. He was large of personality and of girth; I decked him out in theatre whites, and ignoring his comments about my 'gorgeous blue eyes that a soul could get lost in', I took him to theatre. I watched as he half closed his eyes, made the sign of the cross on the man's head, and anointed him with the oils; I was instantly back among the rituals, fears and hopes of my childhood. A junior registrar waited impatiently to sew up the dying man's chest. Father Murphy nodded to the surgical observers and followed me back out: 'Are you from Ireland?' – he was a man who didn't wait for an answer – 'You've piercing Irish blue eyes … and no wedding ring either.'

Back in the changing room he slipped the holy oils into a velvet pouch and came straight to the point: 'Would you be free for a spot of dinner, and a few drinks, later?' I agreed to meet him for drinks; it seemed like a safe bet given his position. In fact, the evening finished at Church House, Westminster Cathedral, with me being chased around a vast circular table having rebuffed the 'holy man's' advances the entire night. 'No, Father,' I pleaded, 'No!'

Deeply out of breath he suddenly stopped, placed two hands on the table to support himself and said: 'For God's sake will you give up and let me at yer? The sky's the limit.'

Amused, I asked: 'Don't you mean Heaven?'

'Don't play semantics with me,' he said and lunged at me.

I rushed for the door, fled down the steep flight of stairs and into the street. I'd come within inches of seeing not only the colour of his vestments but the size of his communion wafer too.

Studying in snatched moments at the hospital and at night, and with the help of a correspondence course from an Oxford college, I retook the physics exam. But I just couldn't get the logic of physics, and despite the hard work I only increased my pass to a D. I was totally deflated, I felt useless – there was nothing more I could do with this unintelligible subject.

Charles Drew helped and encouraged me: he had brought me to the attention of Dr Wyman, who told me to let him know when I received my results. I knew this was my very last hope. I dropped him a note and he replied that, though he wasn't confident, he 'would have a word'.

I waited desperately every day for news hoping upon hope that he would be able to pull a few strings and get me a place. Finally a letter arrived at home from Westminster Medical School. Unfortunately, even with Dr Wyman's degree of influence, there was no place for me to do medicine.

Over the following weeks Dr Wyman asked me if I was interested in studying dentistry at the school. I knew without hesitating I only wanted to study medicine, nothing else, so I politely declined, but I was devastated. All the hard work, the sacrifices, the chasing of my dream had just ended. I had let myself down. Once again I thought of Gladys Dare's dressing-down; I had got above myself, and I would have to face the disappointment of colleagues and friends, and of course, my mum and dad.

17

It was time to start again and so I handed in my notice at Westminster Hospital and called Jeremy Conway.

Poor old Jeremy didn't know how to react. I'd been so fixed on this idea that I don't think he ever expected to hear from me again, but he was his usual kind self. 'It's good you are back,' he purred down the phone. 'Very good. But people have got used to you not being available.'

It was true. You are only as good as your last job and mine had been a while ago. His advice was clear. I hadn't capitalised on the successes of the TV drama nor the Priestley; people would not take me seriously unless I had the guts to graft and, if necessary, start afresh.

The casting director Corinne Rodriguez came up trumps again and after a very brief audition I was cast in *For King and Country* at the Mermaid Theatre, run by the eccentric Sir (later, Lord) Bernard Miles. It was a tiny part, and I would have to understudy the lead role too, but I was back in business. I scurried around playing small parts on TV and gradually began to re-establish myself. Jeremy proved to be spot on. The success, the movies, the TV drama and the Priestley had all been wasted. They were in the distant past.

So, following his advice, I auditioned for the Royal Shakespeare Company's 1976 season. Jeremy felt that a break into the classics and the rigours of Shakespeare was just what my career needed, and he represented some key people there. The format for the audition was religious: one modern piece and one verse, expected to be Shakespeare, in which you displayed your expertise with the iambic pentameter. Iambic pentameter sounded like a branch of trigonometry. I'd been to a kids' stage school, not a drama school, and I lacked confidence with Shakespeare because I didn't understand it, certainly not the way it was performed, or rather 'sung'. It was like a foreign language. I agonised about what to do for my 'verse'. Then I thought of something unexpected: I would blind them with cheek – and hopefully a laugh.

I was ushered into the hallowed rooms of the Royal Shakespeare Company and told to take a pew. The casting director and three directors asked me what my two pieces were. I said my modern piece would be by Priestley (good old JB), set in the trenches of the First World War, but that I would rather not announce my second piece. They nodded, lifted up their pens and waited.

I finished the Priestley with his sombre words: 'I did not discover any deeper reality in war,' paused long enough and then, adopting a broad Yorkshire accent, launched into the comedy monologue 'The Lion and Albert', with the opening lines setting the tone:

There's a famous seaside place called Blackpool,
    That's noted for fresh air and fun,
    And Mr and Mrs Ramsbottom
    Went there with young Albert, their son.

It was outrageous. No one did modern comedy verse; you did either Shakespeare or Jacobean. But switching from one character to another in the monologue was sufficient to keep them from stopping me midway.

When I did stop they were silent but smiling. It had obviously been a boring afternoon. 'Never had that before,' muttered one.

They all agreed.

'And you're with Jeremy?' said the casting director, raising an eyebrow.

Later that day Jeremy called me at home.

'You've got it. Well done. You're going to Stratford. And don't forget to remember me to Judi and Ian McKellen.' I had done it and I was chuffed.

Off I went, along with Alfred Molina, recently out of drama school but who would rise to become a movie star, to join Trevor Nunn's production of *King Lear*. I would also be in *Destiny*, a play about the rise of the National Front, by David Edgar. It was the usual practice, playing a small part (the classical phrase was 'spear carrying') and understudying major roles, in case the actor got hit by the same bus that Oliver had dodged all those years ago. But, as Fred Molina reminded us, there were no small parts, 'only small actors'.

After three weeks rehearsing us into the company we headed to the London home of the RSC, the Aldwych Theatre, and opened there. Donald Sinden as Lear and Michael Williams as his Fool wowed London audiences. On our opening night, Judi Dench waited outside our dressing room, congratulated us and welcomed each of us to the company. She wasn't in our production; she and Ian McKellen were in an acclaimed production of *Macbeth*, but she made it her business to include us.

I knew, however, that Shakespeare was not my forte. After an understudy rehearsal the assistant director had me called every day for one-to-one 'corrective' rehearsals. On the backstage notice board were the dreaded words: 'Mr Cashman. Solus'. It felt like I was on my own, in a sea in which everybody else knew how to swim. Time and again I was told it was not for me to interpret the part of Edgar but to fit in with the production and Michael Pennington's interpretation. Unable to hold back anymore I blurted out that I did not like Michael's interpretation.

When my six-month contract came to an end it was not renewed, which was unusual. Once again I had over-reached myself. Instead of accepting the help that I needed from the assistant director I kicked it away because I was terrified. I was embarrassed for a while but then shrugged my shoulders and just got on with it. Following the RSC season I had some financial security and I moved out of my parents' home into a tiny one-bedroom flat in a Victorian terrace overlooking Victoria Park in Bow. It was bliss.

There was no one in my life sexually or emotionally during this time, apart from the odd fumble at the steam baths. Then one Saturday at the baths I saw the most amazing man and my heart skipped a beat. I offered him a massage, and he quietly accepted. He lay there as my hands luxuriated and made sensuous love to his magnificent body. It wasn't crude or sexual, it was adoring. As we stood by the showers he spoke.

'You don't remember me, do you?' smiling through blue eyes.

It was the boy who had let me sit and watch him getting slowly dressed in the gym changing rooms at school.

We saw each other at the baths often after that, and we'd meet for a drink. Then one evening we ended up in bed together, and despite the amount of alcohol he'd consumed, we made love.

So it continued. No commitment, nothing pre-arranged, just a phone call out of the blue, and generally when he was drunk. Emotionally I wanted more, but it complicated his life, and so he moved away and soon afterwards married. I knew from my own experience how hard it was to run outside of the pack and I had wanted him to join me in our tiny struggle to be free. I think he couldn't look forwards, he could only look back and see his family and his background with all their expectations rooting him firmly to the same spot.

The absence of a relationship didn't worry me. I got on with work, with my career, my friends. I starred alongside Roy Marsden and Ray Lonnen in the ITV Cold War spy series *The Sandbaggers*. The series ran for two years and provided me with a good profile and reputation on television. For the first time since quitting acting for Borlands I felt like my career was on the rise again. And certainly my confidence was growing since my RSC season. I had got my mojo back.

Sandbaggers finished on a high, and I decided to return to theatre in order to cash in on my newly acquired public profile.

Then my love life took an unexpected turn one Saturday night in the West End: I met a young director who I fell in love with and who I soon realised could not fall in love with me.

During our two plus years together, Andrew helped me to find a real sense of confidence in my talent as an actor, and in that respect he was incredibly kind and generous. He took me to his hometown in Northern Ireland, where his parents still lived, and showed me the divisions of communities and people. The country was being torn apart by the Troubles then, by sectarian violence and bombings. In the late sixties the British Army had been brought in to restore order. Terrorism and murder were carried out by extremists on both sides of the religious divide and by the late seventies there seemed no end in sight. There were no-go areas for Catholics, and for Protestants – or even people who were suspected of being either.

On a visit to see his friends and family I became fascinated by this divide and told him I wanted to experience it at first hand: *Destiny*, the production I had been in at the RSC, had the Troubles at its centre. Against his protests about his safety and mine ('Michael, you look like a British soldier') I insisted on him sneaking me into the renowned republican Divis Flats in West Belfast and then onto the nearby Falls Road.

As we approached the flats a man came out of a second-hand furniture shop and stared at me as we walked by. A young child was dispatched on his bike to ask my name, where was I from, and why was I there. Andrew, emphasising his Northern Irish Catholic accent, answered for me. As the boy cycled back to the waiting man we made a fast exit.

In London, where he also lived, Andrew introduced me to my first Gay Pride march, in 1979. Nearly 500-people strong, we gathered at Marble Arch and set off towards the University of London Students' Union. We were a mixed group of women and men, of various ages and appearances, and we were escorted on either side by a phalanx of police – there, presumably, to protect us or prevent us from devouring the bemused and baffled onlookers.

With a sense of daring, and adrenalin coursing through my veins, we marched along Oxford Street as the chanting started to rise: 'Two, four, six, eight, is that copper really straight?'

Not waiting for an answer, up rose another defiant shout.

'We're here, we're queer, and we're not going shopping.' (Though quite a few did peel off as we went past Selfridges.)

The Pride march ended in a party at the Students' Union which went on into the evening. I sensed real strength being with strangers on that celebration of who we were and I was ready to do it again.

Andrew was a good, driven, passionate man, but the relationship was disastrous for me. Physically, the sexual chemistry was perfect, it was magnetic. However, if I had been insecure in relationships before then this was the drowning point. Intellectually I thought he was beyond me, and so emotionally detached that it threatened me. In answer to my declarations of love, he replied that he loved me, but was not in love with me. To my self-destructive masochistic mentality that meant he would never be mine and that he would fall in love with someone else and leave.

What compounded this was that he loved anonymous sex, in places like Hampstead Heath, and I didn't. At the baths it suited me: it was furtive, hidden, momentary. But doing it brazenly in public, with others joining in or watching, was my idea of hell. Even when I kept the promise to myself to visit New York before I was thirty (I beat the deadline by two weeks) I fought shy of the easy sex available in bath houses and back-room bars. Staying at the YMCA, which was all I could afford, I must have been the only man in the gay universe that never knew it was a 'knocking shop'; towels hung over doors not to dry out, as I thought, but to signal that the occupant was ready, willing and eager to entertain all comers. I had hoped the visit would adjust me to the different life with Andrew but it failed miserably.

Some mornings I would wake early and watch him sleeping. Seeing how handsome he was I felt that it could never last, and I wondered how long it would be before he left me. On other occasions I would punish myself by waiting in his flat throughout the night, not knowing where he was, who he was with, or when he would come back.

After two and a half years, I left. By then I was good at leaving. There was no blame, but I realised I was tearing us apart with my jealousy. We had had the good sense to keep our own apartments, as well as our own friends, so, difficult and painful though the separation was for us both, I gradually acclimatised through what I knew best: work.

In the midst of this relationship breakdown my youngest brother, Danny, was injured, yards from our parents' home, in a hit-and-run motor accident. Initially his injuries seemed superficial and he was kept in for observation. However, only hours later a blood clot blocked oxygen to his brain and he was transferred to the Royal London Hospital at Whitechapel where he underwent major surgery. Tensions were high and, in an angry exchange in a side room, defending my brother Danny, I finally came out to my dad. My other relatives fell silent, my dad pierced me with his confused blue eyes, told me that he was old-fashioned and he did not want to know, then turned and left the room. I started to go after him but my Aunt Eileen held me back. I went home and told my mum what I had told my dad; her reaction was that she had always known, then added that she had a boyfriend, too, though there was nothing 'funny' going on.

'No,' I said softly, and thought of Alec and her and the bus rides home.

Nothing more was said between my father and me: the issue would find its own time to resurface. I had taken another public step to be myself and I felt liberated.

Danny, twenty-four years old, physically recovered but the injury changed his life for ever. It altered our lives too, particularly my mum and dad's. At a time in their life with their sons now adults, and two married, it should have been an easy coast through retirement but they would take up the burden and, sadly, their divisions would continue.

As the relationship with Andrew ended I was cast in a musical, *Layers*, ironically about a gay ménage à trois, which played at the ICA in London. It was directed by Drew Griffiths, who was one of the founders of Gay Sweatshop Theatre, and who was tragically murdered a few years later when he picked up the wrong man.

The show was written by Alex Harding and Alan Pope, and the music was sublime, sitting perfectly with my voice. If I had failed to make a huge impression with the critics with *The Sandbaggers*, then this grabbed them, and we played to capacity, despite the Falklands War, which had an adverse impact on London theatres.

After one performance I received a message to call Peggy Ramsay, the infamous and hugely successful agent. Her secretary told me that Peggy wanted me to have tea with her at her offices in Goodwin's Court, just off my old stomping ground St Martin's Lane. Two things you always noticed about Peggy's office were the smell of coffee beans being roasted in the shop below, and the worn chaise longue over which she draped herself. Elegant, flirty and slim, with an expensive silk dress shimmering off her shoulders, she leant back on the chaise, took off her glasses and fixed me with her gaze.

'I enjoyed your performance in the play. You have obviously suffered in love,' she purred.

I didn't tell her I had just ended a disastrous long-term affair; she already knew it. She knew everything that happened in London.

'Yes,' I replied.

'It's a charming piece, the musical, but it won't go anywhere.'

I told her that the producer Michael Codron, who was gay but discreet, was coming to see it, so there might be a chance.

'Him, dear? At a gay musical? He wouldn't be seen inside that theatre outside of a yashmak,' and then she leant forward and picked up the programme of *Layers*.

'It says here you are a writer. That you've written plays.'

I had tried my hand at writing and had had two plays produced on commercial radio. I'd decided to put it in my CV to make me look more interesting.

'Do you write like anyone? Pity if you do.'

'I don't think so,' I replied.

'Well, let me be the judge of that.'

I left Peggy's office promising that I would drop a play in for her to read. I didn't know then that she had represented literary giants like Samuel Beckett, Eugene Ionesco, David Hare, Robert Bolt, Joe Orton and the hugely successful master of British theatre Alan Ayckbourn, among many others.

I quickly delivered the play, and she warned me 'not to wait by the phone' because she was very busy.

The next day Peggy was on the phone. She had stayed awake to read my play, she said, a black comedy set in a Blackpool boarding house and based loosely on Kenny Parry. She said it was 'good' and she wanted to see me as soon as possible so asked if I could I bring her something else? I pulled out my only other typewritten play, based on the relationship between my mum and dad. It was dark, but there was humour too.

It was early evening and we were in her office as her dipso-maniac bookkeeper toiled away in another room. She waved my Blackpool play at me, which I had had professionally bound: 'Congratulations! You can write.'

I glowed and thanked her.

'If ever a play like this comes back into fashion it might get done,' and she put it on the small round table in front of her. 'I shall send it around of course, to Codron, not for HM Tenents, maybe Hampstead, but I don't have much hope. Not for this one.'

My heart sank. I thought it was a funny play with a good twist at the end.

She looked at me and smiled and said: 'But you are a writer dear. A writer.'

The sheer force and weight that she gave those last two words immediately made me feel taller.

'Really?' I asked.

'But you have got to be shaken up. I want to turn your world upside down. I want you to be daring, and different.' She thrust a glass of wine towards me. 'I am going to take you to the theatre, to art galleries – what are you doing tonight?'

Hours later I was walking home through the City of London having just been to the National Theatre with Peggy. I felt like

I was on a cloud. She had the most extraordinary charm and energy, and she swore like a docker. But most of all her enthusiasm was contagious, and she believed in me. She believed in me and she wanted nothing in return.

For the next few months I saw Peggy twice or three times a week, often following a phone call telling me to be at the British Museum, a theatre or an art exhibition (Picasso, Braque, Pollock).

As for the play about my mum and dad, she declared it was well written but she needed 'a lie down' after reading it. I had to be lighter or bolder, one or the other. Then she announced that I should go and work with Alan Ayckbourn at his theatre in Scarborough.

What Peggy said, Peggy delivered, and after auditioning for Alan, I joined him in 1982 for the autumn season on the east Yorkshire coast.

Life was taking a new turn and I was ready for it. But the past was about to rear its ugly head, and speak.

18

We were rehearsing Ayckbourn's musical *Making Tracks*, set in a run-down recording studio, while another of his plays, *Intimate Exchanges*, was in performance. This was a tour de force of multi-roling, with two actors playing all the roles in sixteen plays, each with two different endings. It was rumoured that Alan had been so pissed off the previous season about actors always wanting their 'tea breaks' and paid overtime that he had decided to take his revenge by reducing the acting pool to two! The first night of the play he threw a lavish party at Scarborough's posh Royal Hotel.

'Peggy tells me you can write,' he said.

I shouted above the din that I thought I could.

'Well, she tells me she has to have a lie down after she reads anything you write,' (he quoted Peggy to the syllable) 'but if you write something lighter, six actors, then I'll do it,' he said.

Peggy! I felt overjoyed, got rather drunk, and about an hour later made my way back to the holiday flat I was renting. It was early winter, cold and it was pitch black, as I made my way along the road under 'Suicide Bridge'. I had no idea why but my attention was suddenly drawn to a man with a dog on the far side of the road. I looked across but I couldn't see much in the darkness and continued walking. The man stopped. I took no notice until he called out.

'Micky?'

I turned. I knew that voice but I couldn't believe it. Not here in Scarborough, not after all these years. He crossed the road and came towards me.

'It's me. Dave. Dave Woods.'

I froze. Woodie.

In the dark we conducted a short, stilted conversation during which I promised to go and see him the next day. He was living in a ground-floor flat that adjoined the garden of the house I was staying in, literally no more than twenty yards from where I was living. He dropped into the short conversation that life was not so kind to him any more.

That night I lay awake thinking about him and what he was after, and how he could try and ruin things for me. Panic rose in my chest. I told myself I was a thirty-one-year-old man, I wasn't a child any more. But I kept hearing his voice.

When I woke I dealt with my hangover by taking a long sea walk and pondered what to do about Woodie. I then popped into the theatre. It was early and the post hadn't arrived but in my pigeon-hole was a note. Nervously I took it out and opened it. It was okay, it wasn't from Woodie, it was from Alan: 'Dear Cash, you may not remember our conversation last night, but I do. So, to repeat, if you could write a light piece for us, no more than six actors, then I would love to direct it for you. Love Alan.'

It was an incredibly generous offer. I soon learnt that Alan and his future wife, the actress Heather Stoney, enjoyed helping aspiring writers and actors. It was how Alan had begun when he first worked in the theatre as a 'not very good actor, and even worse assistant stage manager'. Stephen Joseph, who introduced theatre-in-the-round to the UK, advised Alan to write and the rest was history.

My mood soared and I went out for a bacon sandwich. Woodie could wait for another day, though, as he had said to me the night before, he now knew where I lived.

I hadn't seen Woodie for over a decade before this. I believe that by hanging on to his boys he convinced himself that his behaviour wasn't abuse, he had been helping us. He had stayed in my life as long as he could, well after I lost my sexual attraction for him, always passing me off as his son, despite my protests.

I despised the lies, but no matter how much I objected he just carried on, wearing me down into abject silence.

How my parents never found out is a mystery to me. Maybe they did, and it was just another part of their son's world that they didn't understand. The fact that I was a successful child actor was the icing on the cake for Woodie. Other families wanted their children to succeed too and he could use me to a second advantage. Though I know he had served time in prison, probably for fraud and confidence tricks, I don't think they ever caught him with his hands inside another pair of trousers; he was too wily an operator for that.

In the daylight of his Scarborough flat Woodie looked what he was: a sad old man. His clothes were worn and threadbare but I reminded myself that you never knew with him; he was the consummate trickster: it occurred to me that he might have put them on for effect. He shuffled around his garden flat, which eerily looked onto mine, making coffee and telling me we mustn't disturb his 'son'. The words smashed into my head: another boy was living under his roof. I wanted to get out but I didn't know how. It was utter madness, and he acted as if I had no idea of who he was or that his life consisted of lies and abuse. He continued with his narrative and said he had been following my career and was proud of all the things I had achieved. Times were hard for him, he couldn't do his 'act' any more and bookings were drying up. He sounded like Mama Rose from *Gypsy* when he lamented that 'Variety is not what it was' and held up a copy of *The Stage* newspaper to prove it. I wanted to tell him that he had always had a crap act, except when he was robbing kids of their fucking childhood. But I didn't. I just sat there in the depressing sadness.

Of course he tried to guilt-trip me, a classic survival tactic, by telling me that all the sacrifices he had made for me had been worth it and that he did not 'begrudge me one penny of it'. Especially now I was successful; with *The Sandbaggers*, the films, and now I was here working for – the question hung in the air like an unbroken fart –

'Alan Ayckbourn,' I said.

He sniffed and started to tell the story of how he had come to Scarborough to manage one of the theatres, but stopped abruptly when a young blond guy in his twenties came from one of the adjoining rooms.

'Did we wake you, son?' he asked.

Son!

This man knew no shame.

Then he said he would make the 'boy's' breakfast.

'You Michael?' the guy asked, throwing me a smile, and he told me his name. I stood up to shake his hand and we chatted amiably as Woodie busied himself in the kitchen.

'I often use the name Cashman,' he said.

'Why?' and I feigned a smile.

'Well, in a way, I suppose we are brothers.'

The utter sadness: I realised that he too had been ensnared into a world of lies, had been robbed of his childhood, become Woodie's 'son' and, heartbreakingly, he still believed it. I wanted to find the words. For me. For him. For what had happened to us both. But my stomach churned. I couldn't think of anything to say.

I didn't have to because Woodie filled the silence. A short while after I left, never to return.

Woodie persisted. The letters came, week after week, never directly asking for money, but full of stories of how he had fallen on 'hard times'. He wrote that he was on his own, and repeated that he had always tried to be a 'good man'. I recently found some of those letters, and also the ones he wrote to me when I was twelve, thirteen, fourteen. They seem so sad and patently artificial. Over the years I rarely replied, and his letters finally stopped.

I don't know what became of him. And I don't care. Maybe it is 'Stockholm syndrome', but I felt my life with him wasn't all bad. For a while I became 'special', and he introduced me to theatres, museums, and a life lived on the edge that I would keep with me for ever. However, I only know for certain what I gained; I will never know what I lost. I survived.

19

I settled into the routine of the rehearsals for *Making Tracks* and then the performances. It was a clever musical with the usual Ayckbourn twists and middle-class aspirations; the reviews were mixed, yet the box office was healthy.

Alan was keen for the production to head to London, as all his shows did. But this one was proving harder than most. One evening his regular producer, Michael Codron, came to see the show. After the performance, at Alan's insistence, the entire cast was called into the auditorium. Alan introduced Michael and asked him to repeat what he had said to him immediately after the show. There was a lot of coughing and spluttering, then Michael said that he loved the show but actually he would need an all-star cast in order to produce it in the West End. Everyone went home glum, I think even Michael Codron.

Regardless of Michael's scepticism, Alan persisted with other producers and we opened *Making Tracks* at the Greenwich Theatre in south-east London. Greenwich had a great reputation and productions there often transferred to London's West End. But again the critics didn't warm to us, nor the play, and they disliked the music. They said Ayckbourn was 'not at his best'. It hurt Alan, but he never expressed any regrets. He headed back to Scarborough, where daily reports about the performance and the audience reactions were faxed to keep him in touch, and from where he sent notes down to us in response. The audiences always turned out for a new Ayckbourn and this was no exception. Directors, producers and casting directors made the trip, so for actors it had huge potential.

With no rehearsals in the day, just evening performances and two matinees, I pulled out my portable Olivetti typewriter and started to flesh out my ideas for a new play. On bank holiday Saturday I had asked Paul Todd, who was performing in the show and who had written the music, if he would deliver the bulky envelope to Alan that weekend when he returned to Scarborough. When I arrived at the theatre on Monday, Toddy was already there. 'I gave your envelope to Al,' he said.

'And?'

'It's upstairs on your dressing-room table.'

I leapt up the stairs. There was no way he could have read it so quickly. My mind was racing to conclusions: maybe he had changed his mind, perhaps there was no longer a slot in the summer season? There, on the table, was the same envelope I had sent Alan. His name had been crossed out and 'Cash' (his nickname for me) was scrawled above it. Inside was my play, *Before Your Very Eyes*, with a handwritten note attached to it: 'Dear Cash, When I read the first stage directions my heart sank…'

My own heart was in my mouth; it was true the play started in a circus, after all it was theatre-in-the-round, with someone on a trapeze wire across the auditorium. The letter made me aware that this was the theme most commonly adopted by writers who sent Alan unsolicited manuscripts. Despite this he went on to discuss the material and how I should develop it, offering ideas, theatrical devices and advice. When I finished reading the letter I sat down. He wanted to see the next draft. And he had finished his note with 'Congratulations'.

On cue, Toddy popped his head round the door, grinning from ear to ear.

'Well done, Cash. Al says it's good.'

Over the remaining period at Greenwich I spent every day writing and rewriting the play, sending draft after draft up to Scarborough with Toddy at weekends. The letters I received in response were model essays on how to write a play from a master playwright.

On our last Friday, Alan and Heather arrived in London and after the show they took the cast for dinner. Alan thanked us all, said he was immensely proud of us, and proud too that we had kept 'faith' with him. It was Alan Ayckbourn at his understated best: the reality was the complete opposite. He had stuck with us and had refused a star-studded cast that probably would have handed him a commercial success.

As we left the restaurant he took me to one side. He told me my play still needed some work but he was going to send me a commissioning contract, and he would put it into the summer season. For days afterwards I grinned like a Cheshire cat! Peggy negotiated the deal with Alan's famously tight general manager, Ken Boden. 'I can't make them budge,' she told me. 'They will only go to three thousand.'

It was a fortune – more than I ever expected. I told her I would let them do it for nothing.

'Absolutely not dear. You are a writer. They want to do your play, so they have to pay. Besides, should it transfer into the West End or get done elsewhere, they get a slice of the royalties.'

I put the phone down in my wonderful little one-bedroom housing association flat overlooking Victoria Park, and wanted for nothing. On Shakespeare's birthday, as predicted by Kenny Parry, the contract arrived, and I signed it and sent the three copies back.

Then the doubts started to rise: would what I had written on the page be funny, or interesting, or thrilling on the stage? It was after all a 'comedy thriller'. I read the play again. Then again, and again. By the end of the day I believed in it. And because of Alan's guidance I was able to add some new twists. Rehearsals would begin in Scarborough in June: Alan would cast his assembled company and he suggested that I return as a performer in his yet unwritten musical revue, *Incidental Music*, and also act in the Terence Rattigan play, *The Winslow Boy*. That way I would be on hand for rehearsals and the rewrites that 'are always necessary with a new play'.

Peggy hadn't read it yet. She insisted that she wanted to read the final draft, but she told me that Alan was 'no fool'. When

I saw the promotional material for the new season my heart skipped a beat. The second play of the season, playing for three weeks in repertoire, was the 'world premiere of *Before Your Very Eyes* by Michael Cashman'.

The company in Scarborough consisted of a few familiar faces and some new ones. I managed to book myself back in with my old landlady, and studiously avoided Woodie. The season was under way, the musical revue had opened to rave reviews, and then Alan told me who he intended to cast in my play. For the most part he had cast it perfectly but I had one reservation: I thought that one of the actors was too young and might struggle to carry the demands of the part. But as a new playwright I was deeply grateful that the play was being done at all and so I didn't say anything. Alan said that during rehearsals we should resist any request by the actors for rewrites, as actors could be the most positive force imaginable but also the most destructive, adding 'believe me, you cannot write a play by committee'.

The cast list was announced and placed up on the backstage notice board alongside the 'Rehearsal Call' for the first day, which always started with a read-through of the play, attended by backstage technicians, front-of-house teams and various others.

With the exception of the opening night, the read-through is the most nerve-racking occasion when putting on a play. I was about to experience it from the writer's perspective for the very first time, which was terrifying. Jokes that don't get a laugh, hearing it spoken aloud for the first time, the rhythm of the dialogue not flowing, the stage directions – which sometimes made sense of the dialogue – being totally ignored, all of this combines to make a playwright doubt their skill, and their sanity.

Alan had distributed the play on the Friday night so that the actors could read it beforehand. I had tried to keep myself away from the other actors over the weekend. My worry was that I would hear someone discussing my play, as I had become hypersensitive and overly protective. My plan failed and I ran into Matyelok (Puck) Gibbs, whose partner, Ursula Jones, was playing the lead.

'Cash! Cash! I read your play last night. Hope you don't mind. It's brilliant. Fucking brilliant. I couldn't stop turning the pages.'

I blushed and thanked her, but thought she was being kind. Francis Lynch, the technical stage manager, known infamously as Miss Lynch, told me it was a 'fucking nightmare and I needed locking up' – which from him was quite a compliment. Others were equally kind and the weekend went quickly.

On Monday I met Alan backstage in his office. He presented me with a mug of coffee, told me it was all going to be okay, then he stood up and said: 'Ready?' I gulped and nodded. He opened the door and, armed with my script, a notepad and pencils, we walked into the rehearsal room. The atmosphere was electric, chatter and smoke filled the air, actors and technicians congregated around the free biscuits, and Isabel, the company stage manager, shouted that we were about to start.

As the silence descended the butterflies in my stomach started fluttering, and the urgent need to pee or run from the room and get a proper job sweeping floors overtook me. Then the swishing noise of pages turning and throats being cleared.

'Okay?' asked Alan as he looked around the room. No one said a word. And with a nod from him, we began.

The read-through went well, the jokes got their laughs, the characters came to life (apart from one), and there was a satisfied hush as the last line was delivered. I was chuffed, but now it was time for the difficult bit, to let go and walk away. I knew it would be better if I kept my distance so that the actors and Alan would not feel inhibited and could develop their relationship without the zealous presence of the playwright hanging over them.

I still kept an ear to the ground, and about a week later the gossip that I'd heard in the theatre bar was confirmed by Alan. He was having a problem with one of the actors. We discussed it and together managed to accommodate the problem in our final rehearsals. Overall the rehearsals were fun; nearly all the actors loved their characters, they enjoyed the thriller elements, and they revelled in doing the magician's tricks – sawing the lady in half and the disappearing cabinet – so we approached the first performance with confidence.

If I thought a read-through was terrifying, then I hadn't anticipated the horror of a first night. The audience assembled, packed into their seats, the lights dimmed and a collective expectant hush descended over the theatre. All the writing, the planning, the problem-solving and flashes of sheer genius vanished in that moment. We were in the arms of the actors, the technicians and the audience. We had done all that could be done. I felt impotent.

But I had Alan and Heather beside me, who had been through this experience so many times, and they totally protected me, and fed me gin.

The local reviews were mixed, but Scarborough audiences loved the play and the theatre was full every performance. Peggy sent a letter saying that she had finally read the play and would be making the four-hour journey to see it. She did, however, issue a warning that she thought 'the play reads better than it will play'. I shot an unusually assertive postcard straight back saying that 'on the contrary it plays better than it reads'.

When Peggy arrived I took her to the Royal Hotel where she gave excuses why she was unable to have dinner with me afterwards, even just a sandwich, because of an early train the next morning. I knew she was expecting a dull night and was trying to manage the fallout. I knew too that she never held back on her opinion, once famously holding up a newly written play to the author, saying 'you are a wonderful writer, a wonderful writer, but you'd never know it from this pile of shit' before dropping it into the bin.

I was nervous, she was nervous, and Alan and Heather were like cats on a hot tin roof. Miss Lynch was overjoyed that Peggy was here and that the 'shit was finally going to hit the fucking fan' – adding, in case I hadn't realised it, that Peggy would 'tell it like it fucking is'.

At the interval she came out for a drink. I was terrified and she sensed I was desperate to hear her thoughts, but she looked at me and arched her left eyebrow: 'I'm saying nothing,' she said, 'I'm saying nothing.' Alan did the talking, she gossiped about the latest disaster in London, and then went back in.

When the show finished and the animated audience left the auditorium there was no sign of Peggy. Minutes passed, and still she didn't appear. Alan, Heather and I shared concerned looks and my face started to turn crimson as I thought, 'she's found the emergency exit and bolted', so I decided to go in search of her. Suddenly there she was. We faced one another in the long corridor. She stopped in her tracks, placed her hand on the wall, fixed me with her amazing eyes and said words I will never forget: 'Coup de théâtre, dear. Coup de théâtre.'

Ideas of sandwiches were thrust aside and we had a delightful dinner at the hotel. Far from the dull night she had anticipated she finally went off to her room in the early hours of the morning, having convinced the night staff to open another bottle for her and her 'playwright', and encouraged the critic from the *Telegraph* to give me a good review. Despite her enthusiasm Peggy couldn't get the producers to make the journey to Scarborough. She conceded that I was correct in my assessment that the play 'played better than it read' and suggested that this might be part of the problem. However, she assured me that she had not given up, and added that I should now start thinking about my next play.

Top left: Aunt Ivy, Nanny Clayton, Johnny, me and the Treumanns

Top right: A good hair day at the Gladys Dare School of Stage, Screen and Drama, aged 12

Bottom left: 1963 and the journey begins – practising my autograph

Bottom right: Giving a public appearance at a cinema in the mauve blazer of Gladys Dare's stage school

Following pages: If you can't change character, change clothes

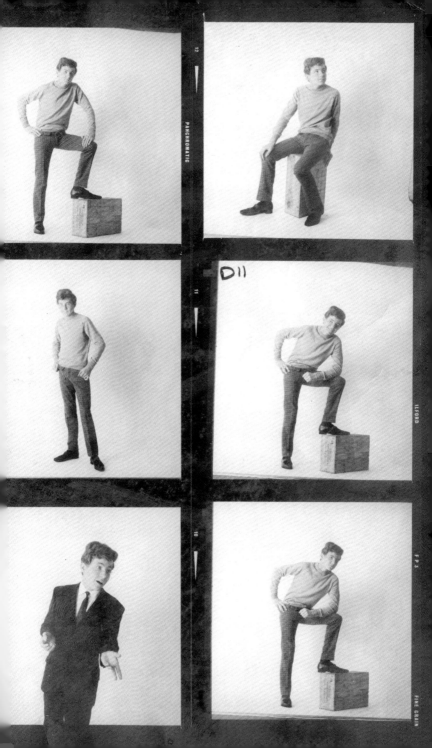

PANCHROMATIC

ILFORD

FP3

FINE GRAIN

D11

Above: The photograph that cost the studio thousands! With Elizabeth Taylor on the film *X, Y and Zee*

Left: As Jesse James in ITV's *Armchair 30*

Below: The exterior set of *EastEnders*; June Brown, me and little Willy in the foreground

Above: The cast of *EastEnders* strutting their stuff in the Royal Variety Show

Below: Just a kiss, 1989

SCRAP EASTENDERS CALL OVER GAY KISS

Cashman . . . hit back

By PIERS MORGAN

FURIOUS MPs last night demanded a ban on EastEnders after the BBC soap showed two gay men kissing full on the lips.

The homosexual love scene between yuppie poofs Colin and Guido was screened in the early evening, when millons of children were watching.

Tory Terry Dicks stormed: "It is absolutely disgraceful that this revolting scene went out at 7.30pm.

"If the BBC can't stop showing these perverted practices during family viewing time then it is time EastEnders was screened after 11pm or scrapped altogether."

And Tory Geoffrey Dickens, added: "I think the time has come to reconsider the whole future of EastEnders."

But the decision to show Tuesday's scene was defended by Michael Cashman, the homosexual actor who plays Colin.

Gay rights campaigner Cashman — who lives with his real-life boy-friend — hit back:

"We showed two people in a loving relationship who just kissed. It was NOT a sexual kiss."

YOU THE JURY

DO you think TV should show scenes of men kissing each other? Ring one of the following numbers today with your verdict.

YES: 0898 555448

NO: 0898 555449

An 8 second call costs 5p.

Screen shocker . . . the gay kiss between EastEnders Colin and Guido

Above left: Pam St Clement and Kathryn Apanowicz from *EastEnders* proudly join the fight against Clause 28 (Section 28)

Above right: The road to equality and the battle against Clause 28

Below: Artists rally against the hateful Clause 28 at the Playhouse Theatre, London

Above: Before Ian and I had our heads shaved for our roles in *Bent*, raising money for Stonewall UK

Left: The transfer from the Royal National Theatre to the West End, 1990

Above: Paul, 1985: every picture tells a story. Stunning

Below: Oh, I do like to be beside the seaside! Scarborough 1983

20

The season was mad and wondrously chaotic. Work had gone amazingly well and being a bona fide, produced playwright felt good. I never got over the thrill of having my play performed on stage, the words and images that I had put to paper being played out for real. Repeatedly I would creep into the theatre to watch the play and wait for the audience's reaction. It was a real joy when they leapt from their seats at the thriller bits, silently lapped up the pathos and rocked with laughter at the gags.

Thanks to Alan it was an easy season for me. My routine consisted of very late nights and then lying in until about midday, at which time I would get up and stroll along the seafront, from South Cliff to North Cliff. And then there was the sea. The grey, challenging North Sea, smashing onto the rocks, sending holidaymakers scurrying in all directions, and the summer mists that hung over the harbour for most of the day as cold water hit warm air. Always in the background, rising above the sound of waves crashing and falling, was fairground music from the pleasure beach. Night would give way to the electric sounds of arcades and fruit machines, and the smell of beer, fish, vinegar on chips, and sweet sickly candy floss.

Day after day I walked the same routes but never with the same experience. It didn't matter that I was always alone. I had become a bit of a loner, and as a playwright who cared about his work I had made a few enemies. Miss Lynch, also a bit of a loner, befriended me as, 'No other fucker wants you', so too had Alan and Heather, and two of the actors. But because I lived alone in London I wasn't yearning for company. And like the end of a stay anywhere, I started to look at things through different eyes, as if seeing things for the last time, capturing the images and the experiences.

It was widely known that I did not like the actor who played the lead in my play. But instead of realising that he was miscast and should never have had to play the part, or indeed that he was deeply unhappy playing a role he wasn't suited for, I took it personally. Some of the actors would complain to me, and we would moan together. Then I would complain to Alan. Finally Alan sat me down and gave me a sensible talking-to: 'Cash, I never believe someone walks out onto my stage to give a bad performance. Never.' Instead of seeing the enormous depth of understanding and generosity in that, I merely sulked.

During my time in Scarborough, I became intrigued by the Grand Hotel, the huge V-shaped, Victorian granite building that sat on the edge of South Cliff looking out to sea. It was made famous by the Brontës, who had holidayed there, along with thousands of others who rushed to the spa town in the 1800s. Now it was owned by Butlin's, which specialised in all-inclusive weekly holidays – without the booze – and its entertainers, the Butlin's Redcoats.

In my last weeks in the town I decided to have a good look. Climbing up the steps I entered a small reception room that opened onto a massive hall with stairs sweeping upwards into the building. Carpets had been replaced by a red vinyl floor, a few holidaymakers hovered near reception and in the background was music coming from a bar off to the left. I walked slightly further in and stood on the brink of the big hallway. It seemed like a different era, the 1950s or '60s, and it took me straight back to my days in the holiday camps as an entertainer – when I was Woodie's straight alibi. It was time to leave.

I skipped down the steps and outside into the fresh air, leaving the smell of stale food and beer behind me. Passing the front of the building I paused at a cabinet attached to the wall displaying photographs of Redcoats. There were equal numbers of men and women, boys and girls; some were caught mid-performance or mid-dance with a proud holidaymaker beaming at the cameras.

It all brought a smile to my face, especially those of ballroom dancing, which I had picked up in the holiday camps. I turned my head away and then quickly looked back. A photo caught my eye. The Redcoats in close-up. One of them was gorgeous: blond, blue-eyed and with a smile that went from ear to ear. I gazed a while, had a momentary thought about going back in, but turned my back on Butlin's and headed to the shared flat that I had recently moved into above the baker's in Aberdeen Walk.

The end of my season was approaching, once I finished *The Winslow Boy*, and I was ready to get back to London. I couldn't wait.

21

With the final week in Scarborough looming I decided to change
my daily routine and to get into the theatre early, using it like
a little office where I could write. Backstage was the basement
of the technical college, and was typically pokey. There were just
two dressing rooms, an overflow room that doubled as a rehearsal
room, and a couple of offices and workshops. The communal area
was used as the green room, where we would gather for rehearsal
breaks, intervals, or just to get out of the crowded dressing rooms.

Late one morning the backstage phone rang: it was Joan from
the box office telling me there were two people waiting front of
house who had party invitations for the actors and that I must go
to greet them. Intrigued, I wandered out from the green room and
came face to face with two Butlin's Redcoats.

'Here's your "actor",' said Joan dismissively. The young female
Redcoat did not have my undivided attention. For, if he had been
gorgeous in the photo, he was even more so in the flesh. Incredibly
blue eyes, and that lovely smile.

'Hello,' he said warmly. 'Barbara Windsor sent us.'

He smiled again and then went off looking at the photographs
of past productions dotted along the walls. My eyes followed him,
and then darted back to his colleague. She gave me a knowing
glance, her eyebrows raising faintly, and then the invitations for
'Miss Barbara Windsor's end of Season Party'. The young man
didn't even give me so much as a backwards glance as they left.
The bright orange card announced that we were invited to 'Miss
Barbara Windsor's Soirée' to be held in the Empress Ballroom of
the Grand Hotel from 11.30 p.m. onwards on 9 September. The
only other instructions were to RSVP, and that there would be a

'Buffet'. It made me grin. And I made my mind up that I would go, after my late-night revue.

When the night in question came around I was on the verge of going home after my show, but Eddie Lipscombe, our gifted theatre designer, said he would go with me to the party. Eddie and I had had a little fling the previous winter season and he was lovely, a real change from my usual butch, slightly aggressive types.

We had a couple of drinks for Dutch courage and then walked the short distance to the Grand Hotel. Outside a huge banner declared 'Welcome Stars of Scarborough Shows to Barbara Windsor's Soirée'. It was about 11.45 p.m. and there were holidaymakers hovering with their cameras. As we mounted the stairs one of them called out: 'You've missed the red carpet!'

Indeed, the Redcoats had formed a guard of honour, and just inside the doorway tossed in the corner was the red carpet.

A Redcoat checked our invitation and directed us to the ballroom where we posed for a photo with Barbara as she stood meeting and greeting like a true professional. The place was packed and the atmosphere was fantastic. A live band was playing, the dance floor was full, and so were the bars. The stars of the summer season had all turned out for Barbara; it was clear she was dearly loved.

Eddie went to get a couple of pints of lager for us. I stood there on my own, in my crazy jumper that looked like a deckchair cover; the mood was infectious, people were happy and just having a good time. I noticed someone at my elbow and turned.

'Hi, how are you? You're the actor from the theatre.'

It was the gorgeous Redcoat. He told me his name was Paul. I was flattered that he had remembered me, very flattered, and we started talking.

Eddie came back, gave me the lager and then politely excused himself to join some other friends, and I didn't try to dissuade him. He drifted away, giving me a knowing look.

There was a silence but it didn't seem to matter. I filled it by asking Paul if he wanted a drink, a beer. He told me he would have a drink a bit later and started telling me about the cabaret that was coming up, but I wasn't listening properly: I was captivated by his amazing charm, it was effortless. His dazzling blue eyes kept pulling me back and they were offset by long, dark eyelashes. He had a funny, lopsided smile and when he grinned he had a nice habit of placing the tip of his tongue between his teeth. The face was warm and open and he laughed like a gurgling drain. He was about my height, had a good physique that a young man carries well and a real sense of confidence. His red coat clung tightly to him, the white trousers even tighter, and the red bow tie protruded out from his crisp white shirt. As he spoke, his voice was warmed with a hint of a northern accent. He had a lovely way of looking right into my eyes, as if he knew me, and then he would look around the room and focus straight back onto me. For some inexplicable reason he made me want to smile. There was an easy spontaneity about him and an openness as he greeted people who passed. And he completely occupied his space, as if he had nothing to prove. It was so attractive – I was like a moth to a beckoning flame.

After a while someone came and whispered to him and he apologised to me, explaining that he had to go and do the cabaret but that he would be back.

I drank the last of my beer and made my way to the adjacent bar. I was suddenly very chirpy and said a cheery hello to the two barmaids, who glared back. Eventually they deigned to serve me, threw the change onto the counter, and, confused, I retreated back to my spot and waited for the gorgeous Paul to appear on stage.

'He's nice. Nice. But straight.'

I turned to see Eddie.

'I know,' I replied.

'Don't get hurt,' he said.

Did he mean as I had hurt him, when I had brought an end to our brief affair? I liked Eddie enormously, he was very attractive, but sexually it never worked. We were like two wheels in search of a different bike, so we never really got anywhere.

A short while later there was a drum roll as the lights in the ball-room went down and a compere announced that the cabaret was about to begin. He told a few well-worn jokes and asked for a big warm welcome for 'a group that had won the regional heat of *Search for a Star*, the fabulous "Kontract"'. Three young guys walked onto the stage, Paul among them. Out of his red coat he looked even sexier, like a young Paul McCartney. They launched into their songs. Paul was the lead singer of the close harmony group, and the crowd loved them. When it was over the audience roared for more, but a comedian took to the stage and the entertainment came to an abrupt end.

A few minutes later I spotted him going towards the bar, where he had shared a few congratulatory words with some guests and picked up a pint from one of the barmaids. I stood back, waiting and discreetly watching. He then came straight over to me. I quietly sighed with relief; he hadn't forgotten me.

'Well done,' I said. It was so nice to have him in front of me.

He thanked me, sipped his beer and fixed me softly with his eyes. We talked about his singing – he liked that – and my acting and writing. He asked me if I had been on TV and I told him about the *Sandbaggers* series. He said he knew of it, that he and his mum used to turn over to another channel every time it was on. That put me in my place, and it made me laugh. It was easy chatting to him, there was no tension.

Then in the middle of our conversation a woman in her late thirties threw herself at us like a thing possessed, grabbed Paul by the arm and shouted in my face: 'This is MY Redcoat' as she dragged him off to the dance floor. Eventually he came back minus his beer and the woman.

'I didn't know you belonged to someone,' I said sarcastically.

'I don't. And certainly not her. Her husband's a copper.'

I went off to get him another pint, but I couldn't get served, or rather the two women behind the bar would not serve me. After a while Paul appeared at my shoulder and asked if there was a problem. I told him and he eased forward to the bar, waving to one of the women. She rushed towards him and served quicker than I thought possible. He turned to me with a cheeky grin and we walked back to our spot against the wall, as the ice maidens went into a huddle. I dropped into our conversation that I had a flat not far from the hotel and wondered whether he would like to come back for a drink.

He nodded but said nothing.

I looked at my watch: it was gone two in the morning.

'In a rush?' he asked.

I shook my head, then he passed me the pint and told me he would be back. Within minutes he reappeared and explained that now he'd been given permission to finish work he was free.

'The offer still stands,' I said, hopefully.

'I need to get changed. Meet you in reception in five minutes.'

With that he downed the pint and rushed away. I couldn't believe my luck and I glimmered like the crystal ball over the dance floor. He'd accepted the offer without question, he was coming back! I looked around the room and noticed there were very few people left.

I saw Barbara in the distance and went over to thank her for a lovely evening. She smiled and said: 'It wasn't lovely. It was naff.'

I laughed and insisted it had been good.

'Nah,' she giggled, then added quietly, 'it was naff. But camp.'

I kissed her on the cheek and started to leave. 'Here, you a cockney?' she called.

I nodded and told her I had watched her when I was a kid filming *Sparrows Can't Sing* in Limehouse.

'*Sparrers Can't Sing*! That was a bleedin' long time ago,' she laughed as we waved goodbye.

At reception there was no sign of Paul but the icy bar staff were positioned in chairs either side of the door. 'Here he comes,' said one of the women looking me up and down; the other laughed nervously and chewed her lip. I sensed a bit of discreet homophobia and moved towards them. From nowhere Paul appeared in front of me dressed in a T-shirt and the tightest of white jeans.

'Ready?' he asked.

I nodded, dismissed them with a look, and he led me out of the hotel. As he said goodnight to the women one of them burst into tears.

'Okay?' I asked

He just shrugged his shoulders and looked behind to see if anyone was watching.

At the flat everyone had gone off to bed, so we went to the kitchen. Out of his natural habitat Paul was quieter, waiting for me to take the lead.

'Tea?' I asked.

He nearly choked. He was expecting alcohol, but I didn't have any. There was a charged silence as we both looked at each other. I was about to ask him if he would like to go into the living room when he leant forward unexpectedly and kissed me. Surprised, I flinched, but didn't move away. I felt the gentle pressure of his lips on mine, then his soft mouth gently opening. His arm wrapped around my waist and he pulled me towards him. I started to resist but he held on to me and my arm reached out to embrace him.

I was not in control.

This wasn't how it was supposed to happen with a straight man, not even after six or more pints of lager. He was undoubtedly taking the lead. I broke our embrace and gestured towards the door and silently we went upstairs to my bedroom. We didn't even have time to switch on the light. We grabbed at each other, trying to get deeper, closer, as we stripped. We didn't make it to the bed. I was learning fast. This wasn't just sex, it was intimate, not just animal but soft, gentle, exploring, needing, wanting each other, wanting to go further and further.

I didn't really sleep, I just drifted in and out, waking briefly to check that he was still sleeping soundly and happy to see that he was. Outside the seagulls were at their loudest, the dawn light coming through the open window. I looked at him in the bed with me and felt unsure what to do. I nuzzled closer and he didn't pull away.

I quietly asked if he was awake, if he was okay, to which he nodded. It was the embarrassment of the morning after the night before, but he had stayed, he hadn't rushed away, chased himself down the street trying to avoid a memory of what he had done or where he had been. I offered the tea we never drank the previous night, but he shook his head.

In the daylight he looked younger and shy as he tried to hide his body. His skin was so white, dotted with a few freckles, his body soft and muscled. His hair fell forward over his face as he sat trying to get dressed and maintain his composure. Then minutes later he was gone, leaving the phone number of the hotel by the side of the bed. I was tired but too excited to sleep. I just lay on the bed remembering the events of the night before so that I would never forget.

Drifting into the morning's haze I silently thanked Miss Barbara Windsor for her 'Grand Soirée'.

22

Over the next few days I saw quite a bit of Paul. We managed to work around his different shifts at the hotel and my performance times. My season was coming to a close, but Butlin's would continue for longer, then after a three-week break resume for the Christmas and New Year. Work was hectic with me performing in both lunchtime and late-night revue as well as *The Winslow Boy*. But I always had energy for him. He was easy to be with and, for a nineteen-year-old, he was mature and seductive beyond his years – though green when it came to show business. He seemed to think that a good voice and talent got you through, so I gently tried to shake him up to the harsh reality.

My life felt invigorated. I had forgotten what it was like to look forward to seeing someone, to spending time together. It felt so much better than the faux independence of being alone.

Trusting my instinct that Paul was not going to be a flash in the pan, I asked Alan if I could return for the Christmas show, *Seven Deadly Virtues*. He said he'd love to have me back, and asked me to write another play for next summer. Then, as suddenly as I had got used to my new life in Scarborough of bars, discos, romantic walks and restaurants, Paul vanished. I heard nothing for three days. It was unnerving. I felt lost. I couldn't stop thinking about him: that smile, his laugh and his optimism that lit up a room. I barely knew him, yet I missed him.

I found a saucy kiss-me-quick postcard, slipped it into an envelope and dropped it by the Grand Hotel, reminding him that I was leaving town soon. He called the theatre, without a hint of remorse or excuse, and we met up. It was like nothing had happened, but it dented my confidence.

Scarborough was a small town, and the gay scene minuscule. So too the late-night bars and discos that Paul liked to frequent. There were eyes everywhere, and they weren't always friendly. He lived in the rampantly heterosexual family environment of Butlin's, the *Sun*, *Daily Star* and pay bingo. I had the theatre, and the gay scene, and some envy. He was more relaxed in my world, he was open, warm and totally disarming. He wasn't phased by anyone, meeting strangers like he was deferring to very old friends, and he loved nothing better than getting drunk, and talking sport, and his passion, Nottingham Forest FC. We had the same wicked sense of humour: we both came from fairly big working-class families and he loathed Margaret Thatcher, which was a relief. When he'd left school he'd faced the mass unemployment created by her policies. He'd worked hard as a teenager to get through sixth form college, but he had been lucky too. He was here by chance; on the insistence of a friend he had auditioned for Butlin's and was shocked to get in. Like me he had escaped to another world.

It was all going so smoothly, so easily, then one night as we walked to the flat he told me that he was deeply confused about me and that he had never felt like this about anyone. Then, in the silence and the darkness he said, 'I love you.' I panicked and, not knowing what to say, pretended I hadn't heard. It was a relief that he didn't repeat it. I didn't need this, and I wasn't ready for love. Besides, before now it had always been me that uttered those words first.

My evasive tactics didn't work for long and two days later he, the nineteen-year-old, sat me down to talk about it. I told him that it was very hard for me to believe that he loved me, but he ploughed on and repeated that he had never experienced anything like this before. As I listened I kept hearing the voice in my head saying I didn't want a relationship, that he was too young, that the thirteen years between us would be impossible to overcome. I had been hurt too many times and I just wanted to keep my life simple. But I didn't say any of that. Instead I bought some time by saying that we should just wait and see.

After about ten days of seeing each other he asked me to the end-of-season disco – there seemed to be no end to the end-of-season socials – but as I wasn't working that night, I decided to go and see Barbara in her play instead. On my way home my curiosity, and my desire, got the better of me, and I turned up at the party.

Everyone was in fancy dress except of course me. I looked around the disco for Paul. He was on the dance floor, dressed as Robin Hood, in a smooch with an attractive young woman. As soon as I saw this it confirmed to me that the relationship was going nowhere. I hadn't been away for more than a few hours, and here he was in full heterosexual throttle.

I stood on the edge of the dance floor watching them and actually enjoying the pain I was going through. Then he saw me, his smile broadened and when the dance finished he came over, ignored everyone else and made me feel that he only wanted to be with me. Like putty in his agile hands I relented, loving the attention.

Later, after more alcohol, with him still dressed as Robin Hood, we went back to our version of Sherwood Forest above the baker's shop and made love. But I was confused. Was he straight, gay or bisexual? Or was he pretending?

This question was still bouncing around in my head when one night, on a walk home in the dark, it all came pouring out: he had only had sex with three other guys before me, and all in the last three months. Two of them at the same time. As for women, it was clear that they were very attracted to him and he wasn't refusing the attention. He was more confused than me and he didn't want to label himself.

Yet when we were alone I had no doubts about us. No one had ever made me feel so needed, or so wanted. Our relationship was tender, loving, passionate and addictive. He would tell me 'I love you,' but I would only reply 'I know. I know.'

One Sunday lunchtime I was summoned to a bar for a drink with Jackie, Paul's immediate boss at Butlin's. After several glasses of white wine she began to lecture me, telling me that Paul was in love with me and I should take him seriously and consider myself fucking lucky because he could have the pick of Scarborough. I stuttered excuses and gave a brief outline of the incomprehensible agonies of my past affairs, but she dismissed them with a wave of the hand, and beckoned for another glass from the bar. About an hour later, she gingerly rose to her feet, teetered towards the door and left shouting, 'The actor's paying, the fucking actor.' So I did.

Walking along the seafront later, I asked Paul why he'd got Jackie to say it. He replied that if I didn't believe him then maybe I would believe somebody else, and she was his only friend who knew. Yet still I doubted. How could a beautiful nineteen-year-old love me, I kept asking myself? I could find no answer.

After my final show at the theatre, we all said brief goodbyes and went our separate ways as if we had never spent all that time, sweat and tears together. One or two of our company I thought would remain friends but most of us knew we wouldn't. It was the reality of the business that we worked in; intense, close bonds were formed while working together but were rarely sustained afterwards.

I spent the final weekend with Paul. We had only known one another for just over a fortnight, but it felt like much longer. He was a party animal and loved nothing better than drinking and dancing the night away. On our last night we had champagne in the Butlin's bar, and then disappeared off to a staff 'Malibu party', which just meant taking a bottle of Malibu and drinking it. As we walked in a drama ensued: the barmaid who had refused to serve me back at Barbara Windsor's soiree screamed, burst into tears (again) and ran into the kitchen, followed by her friends. Paul ignored the whole thing and went in search of drinks, but

I was now even more curious. I walked into the kitchen where, on my appearance, the young woman started sobbing hysterically. I asked if I could help but was shoved back by someone, then Paul rushed in, grabbed me by the arm and we left.

As we walked along the deserted streets he confided in me that he'd been having an affair with the woman, whose name was Andrea, and also with her friend. He told me that both women were in love with him. Immediately I felt deeply jealous. I asked if he was in love with them too, but he said no, that it was just sex and added that he'd had plenty of sex with women, especially in his home town.

My head was swimming; I was confused and hurt. We walked to the foreshore where, alone on the beach and in the safety of darkness, we cuddled and held each other. I had felt so vulnerable but now I felt safe. There under the stars, and the influence of alcohol, we kissed without a care. Back at the flat we made love and he said again how much I meant to him. In the morning we went out and I very discreetly bought him a ring. In the privacy of a shop doorway, I slipped it onto his finger. We mouthed our goodbyes and he turned and left. I stood and watched as he walked away, up the hill to Butlin's.

In the station, as I waited for the delayed train to London, I looked out at the technical college where the theatre was housed, and the rooftops lining the rise to the Grand Hotel. I thought of the amazing changes in my life since I had first arrived in Scarborough, and I thought of Paul: the fun, the happiness and the spontaneity that he had brought into my life. And I was suddenly lonely for him. I wrote him a letter, and for the first time admitted how much I loved him, how much I missed him before I had even left, and how I wanted us to belong together. I had promised to phone and write every day and I was keeping my promise.

23

Back in London I was quickly back to my old routines: seeing my friends at the steam baths, the gay bars, the LA, Benjy's disco and a few West End haunts, but constantly thinking about Paul, too.

Work was picking up, and I was getting on with the new play for Alan. Peggy asked me to see her. She wanted news of Scarborough and anything that might have been hiding in the closets there. She said they needed more copies of my play as there were enquiries from three German companies, and that the producer, Michael Codron, had liked my play and sent it to Peter Wood, who was famous for directing Joe Orton and others. Draped across her chaise longue, she said it was good to have me back 'from the provinces'. She waspishly waved into the air that Codron had asked Alan to direct it in London, but 'selfishly he had fucking refused'.

I had no time to interrupt, she was on a roll. She was at her best delivering unexpected news – good or bad.

Ray Cooney had his own Theatre of Comedy in the West End and had 'liked the writing' but ultimately didn't think the play was for him. However, he wanted to see me about writing something else. My work had created some interest in the right quarters and Peggy was thrilled. She also liked the two new ideas I had for farces. 'Go and see Cooney and tell him about your ideas. He can have one – not both.' The thing I loved about her was her total certainty about anything and everything. Even if she didn't like something, it was absolute, never half-hearted.

I left her office but she hadn't given me a chance to tell her about Paul. I wanted her to know that someone wonderful was in my life, and that I felt different, almost contented. She had buoyed me with her energy and I walked home to the East End elated, and ready to tell Paul when he rang me that night from the phone box on the street outside the Grand. How strange it must have been hearing my news from London, when there he was in Scarborough where we had met, surrounded by memories, and separated by distance.

Over the next few days the conversations started to get difficult. When we did speak it was strained. Paul would get upset and tetchy if he rang and I wasn't home to answer the call, even though I told him it wasn't intentional. When I did phone he was either not in the office or he couldn't talk because people were around. And finding a bloody phone that worked in the West End, or one that wasn't awash with piss, was nigh on impossible.

I wanted to share everything that was going on in my life – and there was so much. The excitement I felt about the house that I had bought in Mile End before the summer, a house that we could move into together, that my brother, Johnny, had started rebuilding for me. On my second day back in London I'd visited Johnny there and been amazed at the progress. Now he wanted me to help him completely strip and replace the roof. I scampered to the top of the scaffolding, looked down to the street below and my courage evaporated. I said that we would get someone else to do it, that I would pay. Anything, but I was not going to do it myself. Besides, there was nothing at the back to protect you from a sheer drop three floors down. Johnny ignored me, ripped up a huge ridge tile from the apex of the roof and threw it at me. 'Catch,' he said, which I did.

That night I arrived home knackered but happy. The physical work felt good. I waited for Paul's call. Again I had so much to tell him, but he shocked me.

'I can come to London, tomorrow,' he said.

I was thrown. I didn't know what to say and my head filled up. I wanted to be with him, I said, but I had to work on the house. It would be difficult to fit him in, so I could only see him for an hour or so. We then hung up.

The enormity of what I had just said hit me; I rang back immediately and waited for him to come to the phone. When I heard his voice I told him in no uncertain terms that the house didn't matter, he should come. There was a silence then he quietly explained he had already informed his boss he wouldn't be going to London, so someone else could have the day off instead. I was ashamed, I knew I had hurt him and I was angry with myself. I slowly replaced the handset on the phone and wished I'd never answered it earlier.

The next weekend I went up to Scarborough. It was a relief to see Paul. In the short absence I had forgotten the effect of his charisma, the charm, the cheeky grin. Standing together with others in the Butlin's bar I snatched moments when I could just gaze at him, forever aware that he and I could not even hint at our affection for one another in that setting. He was being cool, slightly detached, and I wondered if this was for his mates or because I had so badly hurt him. As the night went on he relaxed and whispered that it was good to see me and that it was better than all those phone calls. I breathed out and said that I couldn't agree more.

After the disco, as we walked back to my B&B, he suddenly mentioned he enjoyed 'group sex', and that if I hadn't turned up at the end-of-season disco he would have gone off with the girl dancer. My stomach turned and tightened; it was his turn to hurt me. I coldly reminded him that he said he was gay, but he just replied that he was still seeing women up until the day before he met me.

We walked on in silence and finally I asked: 'And since?' He did not reply and the thought of him being with other people dug deep into my gut as the pain made me realise how much I needed him. He was right to hurt me, I had treated him like someone I wanted to be with when it suited me and rejected him when it didn't.

Over the weekend I tried my hardest to make amends, to relax, to fit in with his work schedule and to just be in the moment. And for the most part, if I didn't try too hard, it worked. It was better when we were alone, away from the prying gaze of others, where we could touch and hold one another. Physically and emotionally we clicked, and we laughed, a lot.

I went back to London happier than I had been in a long time, and I was determined to treat him better, and commit to someone who was good for me.

The letters and the cards continued, and I started work on a BBC series, *Birds of Prey*, starring Richard Griffiths. But again the long distance took its toll; the phone calls were fraught with extended silences, and 'no, I didn't mean...', or 'I have to go, someone wants to use the phone...'.

Then he told me he was going home for the weekend, to Newark, and he might not be able to speak to me for a couple of days. So I tried to forget him as I disappeared into bars and discos clutching pints of lager, drunkenly convincing myself we would never survive the distance or the moods.

I was woken by the phone. It was late, very late, and the call was quick. He asked if it was okay to ring me back. I sat in the darkened room and waited, the street light casting sodium shadows, and when the phone rang I grabbed it. He sounded happy, he had been out with his mates in Newark, he was having fun and I could tell he'd had a good drink.

Within seconds the conversation altered, and probably because of the alcohol, his tone changed and I heard the sadness, the cry for help, in his voice. It all came pouring out and finally the grown man in me woke up. I understood every word he said because I had experienced the same thoughts and the same feelings. He talked about the difficulties of our relationship – he worried what people would say, how they might treat him, and he didn't want his Butlin's room-mate to find out, in case he wouldn't share with him any longer. And he hated the word 'gay'. He said: 'I just love someone who happens to be the same sex. And I really love you. I love you and miss you very much.'

We talked openly and I was moved by his honesty. I recognised too that through my obsession with loving and losing I had totally ignored what he was going through, and I thought how mean and self-centred I had been. He was from a small market town in the Midlands, had a close family and friends, and his first gay sexual experience had been just a few short months ago. Starting a gay relationship while living and working in an ostensibly hetero-sexual environment was challenging, and it was all so new to him. It was like he'd walked into a car crash and I had left him in the wreckage and gone to London.

When I put the phone down I sighed deeply and sat in the glow of the lamplight for ages knowing instinctively that we had changed.

I delivered my new play to Peggy and, while I waited impatiently for the response, I continued working on the house with Johnny. The place was taking shape and I felt a real sense of achievement. I loved the fun and the banter, especially between Johnny and Cass, the Jamaican plasterer, which reminded me of my days working on the building site at Snaresbrook.

Then the long-anticipated call came from Peggy. She 'didn't like it at all'. It was her at her critical best, but it was depressing as she launched into a lecture about my 'having too many ideas and needing to get away from my background, which was a com-fort zone'. So I did what I do best, and took refuge in more work, and, unusually, I took refuge in Paul too. It was over three weeks since we had last been together, and he was coming to stay with me for the weekend. Friday could not come fast enough.

Nervously I waited at King's Cross for his arrival. It was just before five and commuters were rushing in every direction. His train slowly came to a halt and I scanned the horizon, straining to spot him. There he was, with that lovely slight swagger, making his way towards me. He saw me, and his smile got bigger and bigger the closer he came. Surrounded by people, our hands touched momentarily as I took his bag. To the rest of the world we were just two ordinary men meeting one another, but, in that one slight touch, so much more was said.

I nodded in the direction of the underground and we descended with the crowds towards the West End, to see *Evita*.

It was his first time in London, apart from as a young kid when he'd travelled with other Notts Forest fans to watch his team play at Wembley, and he took to the capital naturally. The tube, the buses, cheap restaurants, Theatreland and everything else that was so workaday to me seemed wonderful to him. I saw the city through his eyes and I grew ten feet taller; I wanted it to be perfect for him.

That night we eventually fell into bed. Together at last in my home: easy, natural and comfortable. In the morning I woke before him and watched him sleeping. I gently wrapped my arms around him and caressed him. I kissed the soft down on the back of his neck, curled around him and traced a finger over his dark eyelashes, and he woke up. Later I watched him pad about the living room, opening cupboards and the doors of the huge armoire that separated the kitchen area from the sitting room with its two armchairs, dining table and oak chairs and side table. I stood behind him and held him as he ironed his shirt and white jeans. After watching a matinee of *Cats* I showed him the lights of the West End and we chanced our arm with a new musical called *Little Shop of Horrors*, which was so wacky that as soon as the overture started we fell in love with it. We took the number 8 bus home through the City, all the while talking incessantly as I pointed out the sights.

I learned more about his family, his three sisters, Janet, Karen and Sharon, and his mum, Mary and stepdad, Dick. He told me about the grammar school that he went to, and how he hated having to queue up with one other boy in front of the entire school for his free lunch vouchers, and about his mates working in the coal mines or the power stations. It started to dawn on me how hard he had worked to change his life.

The more he drank the easier we talked: the romance of his childhood in Liverpool and the fact that his mum named him after her favourite Beatle. I said he was lucky it wasn't Ringo; 'Cheeky fucker,' he replied, and we laughed. There was a quiet sadness in his voice as he briefly mentioned his dad, a Londoner, who he hadn't seen since he was six.

Because it was the weekend Paul needed to get the football results and see how it affected his beloved Forest. 'Where's your telly?' he asked.

I pointed to a cupboard; he thought I was completely insane when he found the television set put away because I wasn't using it.

'You're daft,' he said and grinned.

And I thought: you've summed me up perfectly.

I smiled at his world that I didn't really understand, and my world that he was so willing to embrace. I was entranced by his maturity.

After watching three West End shows in two days, we got up late on Sunday, managed to keep our hands off each other for thirty seconds and headed off to a pub in (then) unfashionable, dodgy Old Street, at Shoreditch. With its windows boarded up the pub looked run down. We left the daylight outside and entered Paul's very first gay bar – a land of half-naked men, guys with moustaches more suited to Mexican cowboys and tight denim jeans with designer rips in just the right places. Added to all this, in a corner was a sprinkling of men dressed top to toe in clinging black leather, some of it barely able to restrain the pounds of flesh fighting to get out. His eyes popped out of his head and he roared with laughter. After a few slurps of lager he relaxed more. The music swamped the crowded bar as the DJ pandered to his Sunday afternoon punters.

'Like Butlin's,' I joked.

'Especially that lot,' he replied, looking in the direction of a chorus of multicoloured drag queens in the corner. He was at home and loving the lust-driven looks he was getting. At the bar he got me a drink and I watched him soak it all up from afar. By the afternoon he could hardly keep away from me. For the very first time he was in a public place where he could kiss me without hesitation or fear.

We made our way home for a sleep, to rest, to make love. Then another bar in the evening. We danced with my friends, male bodies in a heave, pushing back against the music, pushing back against one another like ballerinas in bovver boots, balancing bottles of poppers and expectations. We shouted above the music, and we laughed and laughed with the excitement. We could be ourselves and we didn't have to give a flying fuck. At the bar two drag queens, encouraged by onlookers, came to blows but the bouncers ignored them. We staggered out onto the Mile End Road and headed for home.

For one blissful night I didn't get dark and argumentative, or look for inconsistencies and challenges. I took the relationship as it was. I watched as Paul unflinchingly entered a new landscape, a place where he could be himself, and maybe – terrifyingly – where he would grow away from me. That last thought I pushed away like one drink too many. I took his arm and we walked the twenty minutes to my place, where we fell asleep in each other's embrace.

On Monday morning there was a gentle silence, both of us knowing that he had to leave. I busied myself to conceal my sadness and realised that I hadn't once tried to escape him by immersing myself in work. I had just enjoyed the experience. It felt strange and it felt new. I checked the clock and announced that we should head for King's Cross, to give ourselves plenty of time. The station seemed empty, yet people were all around us.

I stood looking at the huge clock and mentally urged it not to move forward. Standing as close to him as I could, I tried to feel the touch of his hair on my face as he turned to look at me. He was going. Going away. So much had happened in just one weekend, we had shared so much and I wanted us to share more. It felt like we fitted together. I kept looking at him so that I could vividly recall his features when he was gone; the turn of his lips as he smiled, the flash of his teeth, the blue of his eyes with that unique hazel fleck in the left. We stood there saying nothing. I thought about jumping on the train with him, but what would happen when I got to the other end? What of my commitments in London? We had tea in the station buffet and I tried to force a

Mars bar down – but I had little appetite. The clock on the wall called time on us; the train was waiting.

And then it happened. Without any warning he grabbed me and kissed me. As he pulled away I sat there stunned. Neither of us looked around the buffet to see if anyone had witnessed it. It was as if they didn't exist, no one else did. He had kissed me in broad daylight. We smiled like idiots. Bliss-fed idiots.

At five minutes to two we walked to the point of separation – an invisible line stretched between us – and again we kissed. Then I stepped back, we looked at each other and, mouthing 'goodbye', he turned and walked away. I wanted to call him back. I wanted to shout 'I love you Paul Cottingham' but I just stood there watching him making his way along the platform. He faded from sight and climbed into a carriage at the far end of the train.

I waited as all the doors were closed, the exhaust rose above the engines of the InterCity 125 and the ticket inspector removed the departure board, and held my vigil as the train slowly heaved itself out of the station. As if in slow motion, I turned and walked away.

24

Since Paul's visit to London our relationship was on a more even keel. The phone calls were easier, less demanding; Paul was more focused on work too. The problems hadn't gone away: his fear of family and friends knowing he was gay, what people would say, still haunted him but talking about these problems made them less toxic. I made another couple of trips to see him and eventually I settled back in Scarborough to rehearse and get the Christmas show open.

Now that we were physically together in the same town a lot of the nagging issues faded away and so did the tensions. We slipped into a routine of work, nights out and work again. Paul completely surprised me when he told Kevin, his Butlin's roommate, that he was gay and was having a relationship with me. Eventually his friends and mine welcomed us both. By including people, rather than excluding them, we both began to recognise that we were making commitments to a future, maybe even our future.

Both of us working through the holiday season meant that Christmas and New Year's Eve were soon out of the way. Paul's season finished a week before mine so he moved in with me to my attic bedroom that I'd taken from my old landlady, Sandra. We started to think about what would come next; I knew it was crunch time, and though we didn't say it, he did too. When I finished my run at the theatre we would both be leaving Scarborough but would we be heading to the same place? He had to think about his career too, either with Butlin's – he'd been promoted to chief Redcoat, the youngest in their history – or as a performer.

One night, walking back from the chippy, he told me that he wanted to move to London when I returned there at the end of January. I was delighted, but shocked. He had previously said that if he ever moved to London he would have to 'prepare' his family, that he would have to think of something. So, in the afterglow of his decision, we thought of something. Paul was to become my lodger – which seemed rather apt, as lodgers had a reputation for sleeping with their landladies. In his diary he simply wrote: 'Sunday, February 5. Move to London. The East End.'

He made it appear so simple, but it wasn't.

On our last day in Scarborough I said my silent goodbyes to the town, and to all that it had given me. I knew I would come back, that Alan and Heather would always welcome us, but it would be different. They had been good friends to me, and to Paul – welcoming him in without hesitation. I needed to go back to London because of my career, and for us. If we had any chance of surviving it would not be in a small town that knew both of us too well, a town in which we occupied both separate and intertwining worlds. I had arrived two and a half years earlier at Peggy's command, escaping a failed and miserable relationship, and now I was leaving with someone who said he loved me. Someone who I loved and wanted to be with. It seemed unbelievable.

In that tiny attic room, I mouthed a silent farewell to the version of myself that had appeared here years before. In the street below, the taxi announced its arrival; Paul and I kissed and hugged in the room where we had made love in the eaves, and finally, with landlady Sandra waving us off, we left for the station to begin our journey.

25

We had been back in London only one day but I was eager to get to work with Johnny on the house. I was obsessed with getting the place finished for us to move into, so I crept off while Paul was still sleeping, leaving him a note with instructions for meeting.

A few hours later Cass, the Jamaican plasterer, announced Paul's arrival with a 'Pretty blond boy at the door!' Paul peered down through the hole in the floor. There was a look of horror on his face.

'What?' I asked and smiled.

'You said you'd bought a house. It's a hole in the ground.'

'Fucking right there,' said Johnny, and off we all went to Bruno's cafe in Mile End for mid-morning breakfast and the start of Johnny and Paul's friendship.

Paul wasn't in a job so he started to help out at the house. It was good to be working together, but when we got home there was no time for us, and it was driving him mad: I would shut myself away in the bedroom tapping away on the typewriter. Alan wanted the play about the building site, *Bricks 'n Mortar*, and I was working to a tight deadline. Some evenings we broke the ritual and went to the pub with Johnny. And the first weekend at home I took him to the steam baths: he hated it, and he didn't like my friends there either.

But at the weekends Paul came alive; especially when we went out to the bars and gay clubs in the East End. Unlike at the baths he got on really well with my few close friends from that scene, and it helped that we all loved dancing and getting laden with drink. We would meet at my mate Alan's for a few lagers, then trot off to Pigeons, the gay disco on the Romford Road, Stratford.

It was one of the venues run by 'Tricky Dickie', who operated gay nights in different pub rooms on different days across London.

Pigeon's was a huge pub and the disco was on the first floor. You paid an entrance fee for your supper ticket, after which you could drink until two in the morning and dance like a maniac. Often they had a cabaret, a drag act or a male stripper. But it was the dance music that drove us wild. The sounds of Gloria Gaynor, Donna Summer, Abba, Erasure, Culture Club, the Communards and the East End Boys and West End Girls of the Pet Shop Boys, threw us into a mass of infinitely corruptible energy. We were like a huge wave, growing, swirling and thrashing at the command of Trickie Dickie's vinyl army and his two-console disco. Stripped to the waist and sometimes armed with a bottle of poppers we danced and danced, only leaving the floor in search of lager, before rushing back to the seductive frenzy. When it came to closing time they literally threw us out onto the streets, where Paul and I headed for the night bus, or walked the forty-five-minute journey home.

Sundays were for recovering, and if we bounced back quickly enough then we headed for the LA in Old Street at lunchtime to drink through the afternoon. Although the licensing laws were strict, if the venue applied for a dance or a meal licence, they could serve extended hours. Alternatively, if you were a friend of the publican you would be 'locked in' for illegal drinking. In the evening we headed to a drag act in Hackney and then finished up at Benjy's disco at Mile End, which was only gay on Thursday and Sunday nights.

Soon Paul and I became known as a couple, and we were equals both on and off the dance floor. I loved it that people visibly lusted after him and he loved it too – that smile and the tip of the tongue between his teeth. The gay scene in the East End was thriving and it was a young crowd; the older queens gravitated to bars where you could collect dust and cobwebs. Here there was no time for the dust to settle. We steered clear of the posh places in the West End, but made an occasional trip to the appropriately named Bang in Tottenham Court Road, which was gay on Mondays. But as a group of friends we preferred the East End scene. Very few here took themselves seriously, the fag hags were fairly glamorous, and when it came to gay it was either so butch they could hardly walk or so camp they could barely stand up.

There were real characters there, like Rusty, who wore football strip regardless of the weather, only spoke in Jamaican patois and called all the men 'Virgin' because he knew none of them were. Or the young actress, who later became famous, and used the word cunt so much that she became known as 'Queen Vag'.

When the weekends were so good, and they often were, it made the weekdays with me continuously working bearable for Paul, and so it made it bearable for me. I could work away without feeling guilty. Moving into the house three months after he'd come to London was liberating. We had space, we had a joint identity and because we needed more furniture he could put his mark on the place. In came a 'proper' television and sound system for long-players and cassettes; the kitchen was decorated how he wanted it, as was the bathroom. We chose things together, and we appreciated what we had because money was tight. The house-warming party was from both of us, and included all the new neighbours and my friends, who were fast becoming his friends, and my mum, dad and brothers. And now we had the second bedroom his 'family alibi' as my lodger was complete. We put a few of his things in there and then forgot about it. The age difference, even its illegality, didn't concern us, unlike the constant reminders in those early years with Lee.

Living openly was no problem for us and it felt ordinary. His family were over 100 miles away in Nottinghamshire so posed no immediate worries. Besides, he kept in close contact with them by phone so would be alerted if they wanted to make a trip. But families can be surprising and one Saturday afternoon we returned from the local Roman Road market to find his sister and brother-in-law on our doorstep. 'We were just passing,' said his sister Karen.

We tried to disguise our panic. I took them downstairs to the basement living area, made them a cup of tea, and kept them distracted while Paul grabbed a few things and threw them into 'his room'. Karen and her husband Paul had a good look round, nodded their approval and finally drove back home to Newark. It had been a close call.

26

Paul had settled into London life, but couldn't get a job as a singer, or even as a TV extra. The problem wasn't so much that he didn't have an agent: it was that he couldn't join Equity, the actors' union. Equity ruled showbiz: no Equity card, no job. But you needed to have had jobs to get an Equity card. It was a closed shop, and it was legal.

Through a friend Paul got a job as an usher at the Lyric Theatre on Shaftesbury Avenue. He loved being in the theatre, any theatre; he loved the buzz, the darkness, the ice-cream selling at the interval and seeing the show night after night. I encouraged him to apply for membership of Equity, but he was rejected without explanation, even though he had worked his stints in variety and had the contracts to prove it. It was grossly unfair, but there was no appeal. It then dawned on me that Miriam Karlin, who was a staunch trade unionist and Labour Party supporter, was starring at the Lyric in *Pack of Lies*. We hatched a plan and Paul slipped a letter, explaining his Equity situation, under Miriam's dressing-room door, just before a matinee performance.

She read the letter at the theatre and immediately went in search of him. A few days later we were sitting in front of a solicitor in Regent Street. In 1984 Paul Stanley had represented and defended the Kent miners in the early months of the miners' strike. He was incensed at the unfairness of someone being prevented from joining a union and told us that he would seek a judicial review of Paul's case in the High Court, at no cost to us. Meanwhile Mim Karlin and I campaigned to change the union's rules so that no one else would be turned down without an explanation. The suggested amendment to the rules would have to be taken to the union's annual conference. Mim would propose it and I would second. At least that was the plan until work intervened and I could no longer attend. Undeterred, Mim found another actor to speak in support and in her passionate way explained to the conference the reasoning behind the rule change, finally adding, after a dramatic pause: 'This has happened to a recent variety applicant. But sadly I can say no more as this matter is now about to go before the High Court.' Heads swivelled, officials choked and Paul's membership card arrived a few days later. Paul Stanley and his wife Caroline became friends for life. And we and Mim would plot greater changes later.

With time on his own Paul was making his own friends: Steve, a chef from the Savoy who was just a few years older than him, a guy that he went to football with and a couple of others who we'd met on the gay scene. At the theatre he was promoted to daytime stage-door man, as well as his other work. He had his own friends there too. The space between us meant I no longer felt under pressure. On the work front Alan was happy with the writing of *Bricks 'n Mortar* and I worked to finish the final draft. I was also contracted for a new television series for ITV, *The Winning Streak*, to be made by Yorkshire Television, which was a great bonus.

Our life had developed a nice feel, a rhythm. Paul wasn't so dependent on me, so intensely close. And surprisingly I even went home with him to Newark for his Nan's ninetieth birthday. I think Karen must have reported back from her visit that all was above board in London, and they breathed a sigh of relief when they realised that I wasn't eccentric or out of the ordinary, I just acted for my living. His family was open and warm and funny. Dick, his stepdad, and I shared the same politics; we passionately disliked Mrs Thatcher and held the same opinions about the miners' strike. The destruction and divisions of mining communities and families was heightened in Nottinghamshire where a breakaway union (the Democratic Union of Mineworkers) had formed and continued to work through the strike. His mum, Mary, had had a tough life, but she had a great laugh, an outrageous sense of humour and she idolised Paul. But we still weren't open about our relationship. I didn't think we could be; it was still illegal. So that night I took Paul's bedroom and he slept on the sofa downstairs.

Back home in the East End my mum and dad gradually got to know Paul too. My mum said that he wasn't afraid of work, which was one of the biggest compliments she could pay anyone. It was going so well, it felt like nothing could go wrong.

27

It was our usual routine. Saturday at Pigeon's disco. I was at the bar with my mate Alan when a friend came up and whispered something in my ear.

'Can't hear you,' I shouted.

He shouted back, 'I think you should take a look in the loo.'

The blood drained from Alan's face.

I turned to see Paul leaving the toilet with Steve, his friend from the Savoy.

'What did you say?' I asked.

The friend just shook his head and said: 'Not my place to say.'

I looked at other people staring at me. I felt flushed and embarrassed. Paul joined us and picked up his drink as Steve passed behind me. Instinctively I went to follow him but Alan grabbed me and Steve slipped away into the crowd.

'What's going on?' asked Paul.

'Leave it,' said Alan looking straight into my eyes. 'I'm fucking warning you. Leave it.'

The atmosphere was awful. We stood there drinking, saying nothing. Anger and jealousy, nurtured and cosseted over the years of my life, started welling up inside me.

'C'mon, let's go back to mine,' said Alan, who led the way.

Once outside I grabbed Paul and shouted that I wanted to know what was going on between him and Steve. 'Nothing! Nothing. He's a friend.'

I insisted that something had happened in the toilet. Paul denied it. We got in the car but my anger was uncontrollable and I grabbed him by the neck. Alan threw his arm back and wrenched me away. He drove us home where, after a tortured argument and sustained, tearful denial, we eventually went to bed. But the 'friend' at the bar had watered the seed. The seed of doubt that I had wrestled with from the moment Paul had told me he loved me. The masochistic part of me was finally having its revenge for my utter stupidity in thinking that someone could love me.

Despite this, the next morning things felt brighter; the row was quickly forgotten and I decided to shut the 'friend' out of our social circle. I'd overreacted because I wanted to believe it was true. It fitted the story that I had at the back of my mind, that Paul was waiting for an opportunity to leave me. Nonetheless, I encouraged him to have other friends, to go out with them to the bars and discos; I had to remind myself that this mature man was actually thirteen years younger than me and he wanted to experience life in London.

After all, Paul was infinitely more sociable than me. He had been brought up on pub life and working men's clubs. I'd been brought up sitting outside pubs and seeing the wreckage caused by them: he'd witnessed family fights too, the break-up of his parents' marriage, but he had decided that if you couldn't beat them then you might as well join them. His social life revolved around having a good drink, going to the football, or both. My social life was work and going out dancing on a Saturday or Sunday night. Alcohol was part of the scene, but it wasn't what I went for, and I rarely drank at home.

Rehearsals were due to start for the new series for ITV but at the very last minute the series was postponed. ITV were unhappy with the scripts and would be commissioning others, but I was assured that my character would remain. The bonus was that contracts had been signed so I could sit at home and still be paid. Meanwhile rehearsals of my play started in Scarborough and I went up for the first few days. The tables were turned and it was now me calling Paul from phone boxes late at night, not getting any answer.

'Where were you?' I'd ask.

He'd explain that he'd gone for a drink with people from the theatre: Bev, Shirley and Irish David, or that he'd been to the disco. So, like he had done months before, I hung up and walked the streets with just my thoughts for company. And rough company they could be.

It felt strange being in Scarborough and not being part of the acting company. All I could do was observe rehearsals and feel useless. I went for long walks and returned to looks of 'oh we thought you'd gone' at the theatre. So I would go for another one. I spoiled myself and stayed in the posh Royal Hotel; from my window, across the way, I could see the room that Paul had occupied when I first met him. I gazed endlessly at that room in the Grand Hotel, wanting to hear the thoughts and whispers that originated there and that were so formative to the young man I was living with.

One night I went into the hotel but could stay no longer than for one pint of lager. I felt lost without Paul there. The excitement had gone, and for the first time I realised that my life was empty because he wasn't in it. I decided there and then that I would go back home to London and return for the last few days of rehearsal, unless Alan needed me before.

When I got home it was wonderful to see him and I was brilliantly unsettled by how much I had missed him, and him me.

28

'Why don't you take me to the football?' I said. He asked if I remembered the last time he took me. It was a 'Boxing Day derby' between Arsenal and West Ham at Highbury.

I had asked him to explain it all as it went along. But he was far too excited, the crowd too noisy and I was too cold. At half time, which I insisted on calling 'the interval', we went for a pint and a hot dog. The bars were packed and there were queues for everything, especially the toilets.

I was still waiting for the toilet when he said we had to get back as the second half was about to kick off. I laughed, pointed to the crowds and said: 'Are you joking? The house manager would never let them start with half the audience still here!'

He mumbled something about 'arsehole' as he put the pint in my hand and we returned to our seats. I protested throughout the second half about how they'd started without everyone being seated and how the house manager needed to be horsewhipped. The man next to me told me to shut it and to 'watch the fucking game'. Thereafter Paul never offered to take me again.

'But I enjoyed it,' I said.

'Yeah,' he replied with a smile, 'but you made sure no else did.'

And I couldn't argue with that. So most Saturdays I'd go to the baths and he'd go to football with his mate, Eric, whom I'd never met.

At the baths there were three distinct tribes: straights, gays and floating in-betweeners. Because I was a local I could migrate between them. I had a set of friends from my childhood that I only ever saw at the baths, and another group that included my first literary agent, Eric Wright, his friend Irish Norman, Bert the bisexual docker and African Henry, who had the sneaking admiration of every man there.

Overseeing everything was the short, round, bespectacled Mr Johnson. Johnny Johnson ran the place like a ship and invoked the unwritten, unspoken rules of the establishment. The first rule was that before you left the place you had to tip Mr Johnson. As long as you tipped well and behaved with discretion then everything was okay. What went on in the steam, stayed in the steam, especially in the 'blue room'. Occasionally there was the odd fracas where signals had been misread or friendliness misinterpreted, but for the most part it ran well. Primarily we all went there to relax and forget; anything else was an unexpected bonus, or burden.

One Saturday, Irish Norman asked me where Paul was. 'At the football,' I replied.

'Is he?' he said with a knowing look. He then asked me if I knew Eric.

'Eric?'

'Who your Paul goes to the football with.'

I shook my head.

'You shouldn't let him go out you know.'

'What?'

'Your Paul. You shouldn't let him go out on his own. He's a good-looking fella.'

He pulled a face, like he'd just eaten a marshmallow with a shit filling.

I told Norman that I trusted Paul, and in any event I didn't own him.

'I was only saying that if he was with me...' and he took the end of his sentence into the steam room.

The following week I went back to Scarborough for the technical and dress rehearsals of *Bricks 'n Mortar*, followed by the previews. It was going well, the comedy worked and the audiences loved the characters, especially the brilliant Russell Dixon as a myopic bricklayer who was too vain to wear his glasses. Once again Alan had made me stretch the physical boundaries of theatre and in every performance we built a house on stage.

After the last preview I was approached in the bar by a handsome dancer who was appearing at the Spa. He had been to see the dress rehearsal of my play and had loved it. I was always a sucker for a compliment, particularly from an Essex boy, and after a few drinks we ended up in bed. When he left in the early hours of the morning it was clear he thought he was engaging in something more than a one-night stand and asked if we could meet the next day. Paul was arriving the next day for the opening night performance, so I mumbled about it being the press night and that I had a lot to do and maybe we could meet another night. His face dropped and he challenged me to be honest with him, adding: 'I don't do one-night stands and you said you didn't either.' I couldn't remember what I had said. He walked away and I called after him that he should ring me at the theatre.

When I shut the door I breathed a deep sigh of relief. But I had been stupid, I had cheated on Paul and I felt guilty. I had also behaved recklessly; Scarborough was a small town and even smaller if you were in the theatre community. Anyone could have seen me with him, and there would be plenty who would like to impart the news to Paul. I went to my bed with a heavy conscience and deep regrets.

The press night went like a dream, the audience roared their approval at the curtain call and we all went off for the first night party.

Paul looked fabulous, and sexy, and he was so proud. We even danced together at the disco, like old times. Then, both drunk and very happy, we laughed our way to the flat, fell on one another and made love.

Later as we lay on the floor I heard something at the ground-floor window. It was a gentle tapping, and it persisted. Without waking Paul, I got up to see what it was. I teased back the curtain and there was the dancer at the window. My head swivelled to check Paul, then back to the window.

'Fuck you,' he shouted, then turned and left angrily.

Suddenly stone-cold sober I shut the curtains, turned the lights off and when I thought it was safe to wake Paul, got us both into bed. The train back to London could not come quick enough.

On the way home I read the reviews. Most were good, especially the local and regional, which were important, but the one from the *Guardian* was a stinker, so bad in fact that I suggested we put it outside the theatre across the title: '"Morally bankrupt, outrageously sentimental and written with a cavalier disregard for any sort of reality", the *Guardian*.' The critic had also taken offence that I had only used one omission apostrophe in the play's title. However, despite that review, the play sold out and there was talk of a transfer to the West End. I was already dreaming up new ideas for Alan's next season.

If my career was going well, Paul's couldn't get started. He had an agent, but didn't get any of the castings he went for. He had a great voice, but they said he was too young, too old, too tall, or just not quite right. It was the usual bullshit, which he wasn't programmed to deal with. His confidence was badly knocked and he wondered why he had gone to all the trouble to get his Equity card. I talked him up, telling him that I had experienced terrible times out of work, but that eventually it would be okay. We invested in good photographs, full length and close-ups, got him into the casting director's bible, *Spotlight*, and I asked a few mates to think of him if anything came along. Finally things started to click. He was cast in a few small TV roles, and people enjoyed working with him. But it was musical theatre he ached to do.

When the Scarborough season came to an end we went to see the final performance and thank the cast. They had been brilliant and had never stopped believing in me, so too Heather and Alan. At the end of the evening I broached the subject of a new play with Alan and he took me to one side.

'Cash, let me think about it. But I think you need a change of scenery. It will do you both good.' Peggy had said this too, that I was getting comfortable, so I agreed and thanked him.

I looked across at Paul who was standing with the resident ballet mistress, Edna Davies, 'spinster of the parish'. Edna took us for movement and physical warm-up classes in the mornings, and she had allowed me to take part even though I wasn't in the acting company any more. Edna loved telling a story, in her lovely Yorkshire accent, and she was mid-yarn as Alan and I approached: 'I'm just telling Paul about when Dame Ninette de Valois – at the corps de ballet, she came to class and commented on my work. She actually spoke to me.' Edna took up a pose as if she were at the ballet bar, her legs spread wide like a duck. She did a series of quick, sharp movements with her feet.

'She looked at me,' Edna beamed with pride, 'and said, "Filthy work. Filthy work".' Edna then picked up her wine, gave a loud laugh, knocked it back and said to Alan that it was very nice of him to offer and yes she would have the same again.

'You have to shame him,' she whispered.

Alan ignored the proffered glass and moved away.

Back in London the new scripts of the TV series *The Winning Streak* arrived. My character had changed completely; I had gone from being a fay shop assistant to a butch rally driver called Frank, who would battle it out with his rival for supremacy over a woman and the racing track. Clearly they had great faith in my acting skills or delusional casting had taken hold. Paul giggled at the thought of me doing the love scenes and suggested that he had better give me some lessons. Cheeky git, was my response.

I had had a female love interest when I appeared in a television series about the German occupation of Guernsey. We did take after take of me jumping off my horse and rushing into her clutching embrace. The director was a little embarrassed when he took me to one side and said that 'it wasn't working' between me and the girlfriend. I asked him to explain but he said it would be easier to show me. As he replayed the last video take I saw the issue: there we were in a clinched embrace but my arse was trying to pull my crotch as far away from my inamorata as was physically possible. I nodded and so did he. We did another take, the groins met and art was satisfied.

On the strength of the forthcoming series Paul said we should go on holiday. I nearly died. Holidays! Actors never went on holidays. I never went on holidays. I worked. Or pined because I was out of work, and then I wrote. He came home armed with brochures and it was clear he wasn't going to give up. His persistence eventually wore me down; we agreed that he would find something exotic, though I quietly gulped at the spending of money on luxuries. We pored over China and South America (too expensive), or Europe. Then he hit on a brilliant idea. The Trans-Siberian Express ending in Ulaanbaatar, Mongolia. It looked amazing.

We were about to book the holiday when Paul realised there wouldn't be a disco on board the train, probably not even a bar. That put paid to the Trans-Siberian and instead we scoured around and found a three-week escorted holiday in the Soviet Union. It was decided, and our mate Alan was coming with us.

In May we celebrated Paul's twenty-first birthday – and barely noticed that suddenly our relationship was now partially legal. In our usual fashion of separated lives, he went home to Newark to celebrate his coming-of-age and I stayed in London. Everything was ticking along between us, a couple getting used to one another, and he kept me young; we were always out dancing, clubbing and falling asleep on the night bus home.

One night Paul rang from the Lyric Theatre. He was going out after work with Irish David and wouldn't be back until late. I went to bed, where he climbed in beside me much later. The following morning, he left around eight to clean the theatre where he was now doing three jobs. On the floor was his pocket diary that he'd left behind, and I picked it up. I knew I shouldn't. My heart was racing as I opened the diary. I looked at phone numbers of men he had never mentioned, and asterisks on certain days. He had recorded times of how bad his asthma was for our homeopath and I wondered if the asterisks were related to that. I felt my pulse start to quicken. Something didn't fit.

I phoned Irish David and asked if Paul was with him. I lied, saying Paul hadn't come home the previous night. David said he hadn't gone out last night. Paul hadn't been with him.

Jealousy started to work inside my brain – but at no time did I recall my own sexual indiscretion in Scarborough. From the diary I convinced myself that things had been going on with someone else or others for some time. Asterisks and names told a story that only a jealousy junkie could understand.

I needed to speak to someone. The obvious choice was my mate Alan but he was at work where he wasn't able to take calls. I looked across the road to see if our neighbours Mike and Marie were at home. I rang the doorbell several times but there was no answer. My head started inventing scenarios: I recalled faces at Benjy's and Pigeon's. I questioned new friendships that I hadn't been a part of. Most of them followed a pattern: attractive men of roughly the same age. Then I remembered the well-wisher in Pigeon's, and Norman from the baths. All telling me, all warning me, and I was so stupid I couldn't see it.

I arrived at the stage door of the Lyric. He was surprised to see me and although I tried to contain my anger, it came out in a flash. I accused him of having affairs, lying that I knew for certain, and pretending that I had evidence. I held up his diary and I told him I had spoken to Irish David.

'I can explain.'

'I want you to go. I want you to leave.' I shut out my hurt and my stupidity as I turned and left. I expected him to call after me, but he didn't. So I kept walking.

As I made my way through the West End a strange feeling came over me. I felt elated, as if I was walking on air. I realised I was on my own again and there would be no more dreaming, no more happy couples, it was over. It was never meant to be; I had been vindicated.

Later that day I told our neighbour, Marie, what I suspected, and she said to talk it over with him, but I was having none of that. I wanted to play the hurt, trodden-on, lied-to partner; even then I still ignored my own misdemeanour in Scarborough.

Other friends turned up unannounced and we sat in the half-finished patch of garden drinking their champagne. In the end we convinced me that it was the age difference and the temptation in London. Paul didn't come home and I never expected him to.

That night I slept alone in our bed. And with the help of the champagne and the beer I slept well. The following day I started to clean the house from top to bottom. It was early afternoon and the spring sunshine was beginning to dip. I was in my element, stinking of bleach and scrubbing away at the bath. Downstairs the stereo was blaring out some well-worn musical and I sang along. Then I heard the front door bang shut. I rushed into the upstairs hall and looked down. Paul stood at the foot of the stairs staring up at me, a long, silent, open look. I didn't know how to react. I wanted to be angry, but I wasn't. I actually felt lost. Very lost.

'I've come to collect some things.'

I nodded. Then, as if it needed explaining, I said I was doing some cleaning. Paul looked anxious. Very slowly he climbed the stairs towards our bedroom. As he passed me our eyes met ever so briefly and I heard myself saying: 'Don't go.'

He turned.

'Please don't go.'

He started to cry. I started to cry. 'Why do you do this to me?' he pleaded.

I had no answer that I could put into words. But I wanted to tell him that I asked myself why I did it to *me* all the time. But I didn't, I didn't say anything. I reached out and embraced him, pulling him into me, the two of us trying to make ourselves one, our tears mingling and burning into our faces. 'Don't go,' I repeated in a whisper. 'Don't go.'

We held that embrace saying nothing for a long time. Then we went downstairs, where we stood in silence on opposite sides of the kitchen. I was looking at the floor, hoping that he was looking at me.

'You stink of bleach,' he said, playfully.

'Make me happy,' I said.

'If only it was that easy,' he replied and the cheekiness had gone. We agreed that we needed to sort things out, to clear the air, and he apologised.

'I'm sorry, too.'

He nodded.

'Where did you stay last night?'

'Mike's. The electrician from the theatre.'

It was my turn to nod.

'He's helped me to find a bedsit. North London.'

Panic and need rose in my chest.

'Things have got to change,' he said.

On Roman Road the tiny cafe was packed with builders and market traders. We sat at a small table against the wall, ignored everybody else and whispered away about our life. 'What is it you want?' he asked.

'You.'

There was a pause.

'I want you too.'

I told him to come back home and forget all this stuff about north London bedsits. But he shook his head.

I stared at my mug of tea. I heard the people all around us but I couldn't make out any words. My mind rushed back over the last few months, then the last few hours. The only thing I knew with any certainty was that what had happened, I had designed from day one. I had pushed him away from me and I had never fully committed. We came to London together but I left him to get on with it while I pursued my life. Paul had changed his life to be here and I had changed nothing. I was ashamed and I had a deep sense of guilt; it satisfied me that I could feel so bad about myself.

'It might be better if I moved out,' he said.

I said nothing, just stared at the bubbles disappearing on my tea. Our silence in the midst of all the noise. Two men at a table. Trying desperately to keep our lives together but pretending to the world at large that we were not together.

'I will come back,' he said, 'but on certain conditions.'

I started slightly shaking my head. In disbelief, at myself. The smell of bleach wafted up from my red hands.

'There have to be changes. I don't want a monogamous sexual relationship. I want more.'

I looked up at him, and I knew there was nothing I could say.

29

Paul continued working at the theatre and had his occasional nights out with his friends. But he always came home. In the post-crisis discussion we had conveniently ignored the diary; I accepted that he'd had sex with other men and I decided I did not need explanations. Nonetheless, I felt I had to come clean and confess my own indiscretions.

He was angry. Angry that I had put him through pain and yet behind his back I had done exactly the same thing. We agreed we needed to have some simple rules to get us through.

The first was that if we went out together, we returned home together and that if we had sex with other guys we did it together. When we were out alone we could do as we wished but would always return home the same night. The rules were non-negotiable. But we knew that things would change, including the rules.

Paul was adamant that we had to be honest with one another. And I knew that was going to be my biggest challenge. I had been reared on duplicity. Lies had been woven right the way through the fabric of my sexual experiences. From that docker onwards, through Woodie's systematic abuse, the secrecy of Lee, even Andrew and his denial of commitment. I knew what he was saying made sense but I had got used to getting off on the secret. It was my default position. But finally I admitted to myself that I didn't want to lose him. I loved him. He made me feel safe, and wanted, so I would try whatever it took to have him in my life. I knew the difference between love and sex, but because of my barren emotional experiences I got confused by the two.

In bars and clubs I was much more relaxed with him after that, and it was lovely seeing guys chatting up Paul. The new arrangement created a sexual frisson between us and it was great telling one another who we fancied, or trashing the other one's taste. He would often say when I pointed a guy out to him: 'You're weird you are. Awful taste.' Which made me laugh, especially when I replied that he, on the other hand, had exquisite taste in men.

Gradually the rules changed, but we always went home together and that felt good. Really good. We were open about the nature of the relationship, but we didn't go around boasting either. And it did mean that when the 'well-wishers' whispered their news into my ear they could be swiftly dispatched with 'Yes I know. Now fuck off and ruin your own life.'

The response to our open relationship was not always positive. Our commitment to each other was constantly questioned by others, but Paul taught me the difference between love and sex, and I now unquestionably knew that you could not own another human being. And you certainly cannot own love, it can only be given.

If the gay scene was sniffy about open relationships, the straight world was deeply perplexed; it reassured some of them of our moral depravity while others secretly admired and desired it. Even when our families knew about our relationship, it did not stop either of our mothers (conveniently both named Mary) from trying to interfere.

Many years after the start of our open relationship, Paul went on a holiday with my mum and one drunken night when she saw Paul chatting to a very friendly Spaniard she verbally attacked him and told him that he was not welcome in her villa (it was actually a two-up-two-down semi-detached). He stood up to my mum, which took some guts, especially with alcohol around, telling her it was none of her business and that she should keep her mouth shut. The next morning – as with all drunken exchanges – she regretted it and apologised.

Equally Paul's mum, 'in the drink', once fixed me with her famous stare and told me she 'didn't understand about me and Paul'. Dick, her husband, quietly told her to 'leave it'.

'What don't you understand, Mary?' I asked.

Paul winced. He had seen Liverpudlian brawls in his time – and a few at home.

'Well, if you love him—'

'I do,' I said, but she was undeterred.

'If you love him, Mike, then how come you and him go off with other fellas?'

'Because Mary, I love him, and he loves me. And it's nothing to do with you.'

There was a pause while everyone but the two of us seemed to cease breathing. She nodded and then added that she hoped I didn't mind her asking. Neither of the two Marys nor any of the family would ever raise it with us again. They could see we were happy.

Of course there were enormous challenges that came with an open relationship. Some said it was better to have a short period of monogamy rather than the danger of constantly exposing yourself to the possibility of falling in love with somebody else. I had thought that too, before Paul.

Andrew's forays onto Hampstead Heath for anonymous sex had made me feel like someone was holding my head under water and I never knew if they would let me up in time. With Paul it was different, though; it felt natural; I wasn't grappling to belong. Of course it was often baffling for a person sexually involved with us. Invariably they would question why I – in particular – wasn't jealous. It was so simple: I totally trusted him. I felt the certainty that he loved me.

For him it was more difficult. He was still, at times, uncertain about my feelings for him, and this would make him push the boundaries on occasions, to gauge my reaction.

30

The holiday we had booked when we were that idealistic little couple arrived, and we knew that the new reality of our life could pose a challenge. There were increasing reports in the gay press of a new epidemic among gay and bisexual men that seemed resistant to treatment and was transmitted sexually. Life started to get more complex and our rules would have to be revisited.

We arrived in Leningrad, as it then was, in the summer of 1985. It was July and the sun never set, it just dipped and lay low on the horizon. Waiting for us at the airport was our Intourist guide, Olga. In the Soviet Union tourism was tightly controlled; travellers had to be vetted before they could visit and even then they were accompanied throughout. After Leningrad, Paul, Alan and I would be going to Kiev, Yalta and finally Moscow.

Olga was in her mid twenties, she was very attractive, charming, had a great command of English, possessed a fantastic sense of humour and from the start was fascinated by the situation of three men travelling together.

In the eternal daylight Leningrad was impressive. Its architecture was rich and baroque, there was row after row of squares and boulevards built in the grandest style, but when we got to the hotel our faces dropped. Dumped on the edge of the city, and horribly modern, it epitomised the Cold War welcome. If Paul and I had any ideas about sneaking back a friendly Russian or two that was scotched by the presence of 'Babushkas'; fierce, often large, female security guards perched in chairs by the lift and stairs on each floor, waiting to pounce.

Olga told us that even though we had been delayed from London she had arranged for a late dinner, but we had to be in the dining room sharpish. Paul, Alan and I found an empty table laid for six and took our places. From nowhere three elderly women marched towards us and asked if the empty chairs were free.

This wasn't what we had in mind, but I gulped and almost inaudibly replied that they were unoccupied. Polite conversation followed about three men travelling together, as they were three 'old girls'. Two of the women had thick Austrian accents but they assured us they were all from London. One was more talkative than the others; she introduced herself as Claire then said: 'And this is Gretl, also an old bird, and this is Ruth, who can be a bit of a stick-in-the-mud.'

They all chortled, even Ruth.

I decided to spice things up with two words that always flushed out strong opinions: Margaret Thatcher.

'Don't talk to me about that bitch!' said Claire, and she began a tirade about Thatcher's treatment of the miners, the workers and everyone else, while the other two voiced their approval.

'We love you,' I shouted, and we had our friends for the rest of the holiday.

Ruth was the quietest, she was born in London and lived with her sister in Russell Square. Claire and Gretl were both Austrian Jews and had been sent to the UK by their parents prior to the outbreak of the Second World War. Their stories were life-affirming.

They arrived as young teenagers and were sent off to do live-in jobs, where they worked like skivvies, in awful circumstances. Cut off from their families back home they came together with other Austrians and émigrés, and were supported by the Jewish communities in Britain. They told their stories without regret or bitterness, they had 'survived to tell the tale'. These women had faced the reality of Hitler and the Nazis, and their families had sent them abroad while they remained in Austria to suffer or be killed by anti-Semitism. Aged seventeen, Claire learnt that her mother was dying of cancer and returned to Vienna to see her for the last time. As the Nazis rolled into Vienna, Claire made her way back to the UK, being passed across Europe from community to community. She never saw her parents again. Claire and Gretl told their stories in a matter-of-fact way, devoid of emotion or drama. It was the story, as they said, of so many others too.

That first night it didn't take Claire long to ask: 'Are any of you three married?'

'We're gay,' I said.

'And are you all single gays, or you live in a threesome?'

Claire had lived.

After that night we were known as the 'boys' and they were the 'girls'. Paul and I would keep our friendship going with them until the last and eldest, Claire, died in 2013, at the age of ninety-two, a few months after we had visited her in Australia. Our get-togethers in London were uplifting, always political, always laughter-filled and totally unforgettable. Eventually, we got to meet the other formidable left-wing women in their north London network.

After Leningrad, Olga got the measure of us and allowed us some slack, letting us go off on our own to discover the city, and of course to get ripped off.

Watching Paul on the holiday was a revelation. I realised why he had been made the youngest ever chief Redcoat at Butlin's. He charmed this thrown-together group of tourists, even the 'miseries' from Birmingham for whom everything was 'another big disappointment'. He was able to navigate his way around any city with ease and always found the gay quarter. In Moscow his organisational skills would really come to the fore.

In Kiev we got the lie of the city and then took off on a mission. We had been asked to deliver some baby clothes from Israeli friends in London. With Paul in charge, we took a tram followed by a metro and then walked onto a vast housing estate. People stopped and stared; it wasn't normal for 'Westerners' to be seen here and certainly not unsupervised.

We persevered, eventually finding the flat we wanted, but there was no one at home. Trudging away we heard a man call from a window, and turned back. We gave him the letter from our mutual friend, written in Russian; he signalled for us to wait, shut the door, then minutes later returned and invited us in.

The three of us sat in the kitchen as he unpacked the baby clothes and cried. We sat there and said nothing, this simple gift obviously meant so much to him. He made us some black tea, opened the fridge and took everything out, which was hardly anything: some bread, a bit of cheese. He found a bottle of vodka. We spoke no common language, but with gestures he conveyed to us that he had no money for food, though there was money for planes and bombs. We refused to eat his food, but drank some vodka, kissed and hugged our way out of the apartment and then made our way back to the hotel, quietly staggered by the poverty and his hospitality.

On the approach to our hotel we spotted a gorgeous blond Russian. His girlfriend noticed us staring, whispered something to him and they stopped. In perfect English he asked if we were American. His name was Sasha, short for Alexander, and he was engaged to be married.

'What is your girlfriend's name?' I asked.

She remained silent, he smiled and said that it was 'not important', and then asked whether we would have dinner with him that night. 'Yes,' said Paul, a twinkle in his eye. We met him later outside the hotel, Olga lurking in the background to make sure we were not being kidnapped or ripped off again.

Compared to where we had been that morning, this restaurant was on another planet. The place was buzzing, there was a surfeit of food everywhere and the wine, vodka and red champagne flowed. As more alcohol was consumed Sasha became fascinated by the relationship between Paul and me, and by the fact that we were living 'openly' as a couple. I looked at his girlfriend, who said nothing, just nodded and smiled; it probably didn't help that she spoke no English.

At the end of the meal he asked if we would meet him in the morning for coffee at his apartment before we left Kiev. We agreed, and then I said that we would like to pay the bill. He dismissively waved his hand at that suggestion and stood up. The waiters jumped to attention and lined our way towards the door.

'But the bill,' I said.

'*Niet. Niet*,' he responded.

And that was it. We were outside, where he pointed us in the direction of the hotel.

'Cute,' said Paul.

'But straight,' said I.

The next day we promised Olga we would be back in time for the bus to the airport, and off we went to meet Sasha who was loitering nearby. He was alone, and we followed him to a smart, low-level apartment block, as he pointed out some historical landmarks. 'This my parents' apartment,' he said, and asked for our coats.

It was then that I spotted a military cap on the hat stand: 'Sasha, you didn't tell me you're in the military,' I said.

He laughed.

'No. No. Is my father. He is officer. KGB.'

I gulped. That was why we hadn't paid the bill. There hadn't been one. He took us into the small sitting room.

'KGB?'

He nodded, smiling.

'Problem?' I asked.

He came very close and, almost whispering, said: 'Anti-Soviet, problem KGB. Anti-British, problem MI5?' And then he kissed us. On the lips. He closed the curtains and locked the door. Paul Cottingham!

We arrived at the hotel in time to get our cases onto the bus and then the plane to Simferopol for Yalta. As usual we went on the orientation tour with Olga after which she left us to our own devices.

It was refreshing to be on the Black Sea coast but other than that Yalta passed without any great excitement. We were accosted on the streets to sell our jeans, or shoes, or to change money on the black market, and that was about all.

On our last day we made our way up from the harbour and passed a gorgeous dark Yaltan probably in his late twenties.

He saw Paul and they both stopped to look at one another. I stood back cautiously watching. He eventually said in broken English that he wanted us to go to a bar with him. I stepped in, declined, and reluctantly Paul followed me up the hill leaving the disappointed man behind.

After dinner we went to the hotel disco with the rest of our group and there was the gorgeous man again, but plainly drunk. He grabbed Paul, who offered no resistance, grabbed a bottle of Russian champagne and hurtled off to a dark corner. Finally I joined them, but it was as if I didn't exist. And he kept saying to Paul, in Russian, something that sounded to me like '*yellow blue vase*'. I asked Olga what it meant. 'I love you,' she replied and sidled away onto the dance floor with a wry smile.

When the disco closed the man wanted to come to our room but it was impossible. Despite my protests of an early flight the next day, we found ourselves hailing a taxi outside and driving into darkest Crimea in the early hours of the morning.

After about thirty minutes the taxi stopped on a deserted road, we disembarked and it drove off. No money changed hands. The stranger started walking down a small path and we had no option but to follow. I'd had my share of drink but now my anxiety began to sober me up. A few minutes later a small house came into view. We went inside, where the man produced a bottle of vodka and two porn magazines. After a lot of talk in broken English and fractured Russian he crossed the room and lay on a bed, gesturing for Paul to join him.

In the short, stilted conversation that proceeded we learned that he was divorced, had a daughter and now he was on his own. He seemed kind and genuinely wanted us to be in his home.

Paul was almost unbearable. He loved this excitement but I was unnerved and worried about getting back to the hotel in Yalta and the morning flight. I raised the subject of 'taxi' but he pointed to his watch and signalled that one would come at six o'clock. Our coach was leaving at 7.30 and we weren't even packed. Paul could see that I was pissed off, my mood turning ever darker.

The man was now drunk enough to try and seduce us. He opened the magazines and showed the naked women and gestured that I should sit with them on the bed. 'Paul, I'm worried about getting back,' I said, which was an understatement. I was bloody petrified.

'So am I,' he said to my utter relief.

I knew that he revelled in these situations: the frisson, the excitement of unexpected sex, and on those occasions he had the capacity to shut out everything and be solely in the moment. But thankfully not this time.

'What shall we do?' he asked.

The man started saying: 'Girls. Girls. Like girls.'

This was crazy, we were going round in slow-moving circles, so finally in Russian I said: 'No girls. Gay. Gay.'

The man's eyes popped out on stalks and he went perfectly still before stuttering: 'Gay? Gay? Gay?'

He wasn't aggressive, he seemed genuinely confused, but I knew I had to take control. I stood up and whispered to Paul that we were leaving.

The lovely man got up, held open the porn, and started pointing to it, then to us and then the bed. I waved my arms and insisted on leaving, and minutes later we headed along a road without any idea of which direction we were going. Paul wanted to discuss what we should do but I just wanted to take some decisive action, even if it was wrong.

On the deserted road a car approached and I jumped out and waved it down. It was a taxi! I kept saying the name of our hotel to the driver. His passenger in the back started shouting at him, and he shouted back. We were in the middle of a brawl. The woman passenger got out of the car; she put me into the front seat while Paul was invited into the back seat with her, and then off we drove at speed. We tried to make some sense out of the situation but the woman just kept saying 'Da. Da' as we continued.

About fifteen minutes later we stopped, she paid the driver and got out of the car. In broken English she said: 'Your hotel. Now.

Going', then barked orders at the driver in Russian. She watched as he reversed and took us on our way.

We arrived at the hotel as our group was having an early breakfast before boarding the coach; Olga and Alan were waiting with our bags. Alan raised an eyebrow, inquisitively. 'Don't ask,' I said, 'Don't ask.'

At Simferopol airport we were severely delayed due to heavy rain in Moscow, but eventually we boarded the huge Airbus. Olga kept a close eye on us all and said that when we reached Moscow we must all wait at the bottom of the steps of the aircraft. We agreed, except when we arrived the airport was in chaos. En route the storm had worsened and we slid perilously across the runway as we landed.

Despite our protests officials bundled us onto different buses and drove us to the terminal, or rather terminals! The group had been split and we were minus Olga. To make matters worse it was the domestic airport and it seemed no one spoke English. With every flight delayed the place was overflowing.

Paul started slowly gathering people together, telling them they had to stay quiet and remain as a group. I wanted to go in search of someone to help but he firmly said that I was staying with them. Leading the way, he herded us through the mounting chaos while I shouted, repeatedly, 'Is there anyone who speaks English?' It was mad, reminiscent of something out of a Woody Allen movie.

The crowds parted like the Red Sea and we found ourselves at the far end of the departure hall where Paul told everyone they were not to move an inch. No one disagreed with him, not even the miseries from Birmingham.

'Let's search the offices,' he said to me. And off we went. We knocked on doors, barged into empty rooms and when we did serendipitously chance on someone they didn't speak a word of English. Finally, when things seemed their most desperate, we found someone who could help. Paul explained the situation then asked the man to get an announcement made for Olga. He didn't say a word in response, just picked up the phone, had a very brief conversation in Russian, replaced the handset and said: 'Follow me.'

There, on the other side of the office door, was a distraught Olga. When she saw us she leapt up, screaming and hugging us as she sobbed. She had been within minutes of losing her job.

With the group reunited, Paul simply faded into the background as if nothing had happened. He had been incredible and hadn't even tried to take the credit. Meanwhile, the miseries were thrilled because they had even more reason to be miserable.

After that episode Moscow seemed like an anti-climax. Olga did some additional tours such as the Moscow metro, but now towards the end of our three weeks the group was getting fractious. The miseries happily suggested that a complaint should be made about Olga for losing us in the airport, adding that we might all be in for a bit of compensation. Claire rounded on them and threatened them with Siberia and Thatcher. We all needed something to reunite the group.

'How about the Bolshoi Ballet?' suggested Paul.

'What for? The miseries?' I exclaimed.

'No,' he replied. 'For us all.'

Most people agreed it was a good idea and Olga made enquiries. 'Impossible,' said the hotel.

'How about if we pay in foreign currency?' Paul asked Olga.

Foreign currency held no sway with the Bolshoi. So it was agreed that we should take a chance on it and later that day Paul, Olga and I disappeared to the Bolshoi Theatre. I watched as they haggled, first diplomatically then with increasing assertiveness, for tickets. Miraculously we returned to our group with the precious tickets, at cost price, for the dress rehearsal the next day.

It was an amazing experience. The wonderful Bolshoi Ballet in their home theatre, the superb dancing, a full orchestra playing in the pit; it was magical and the audience broke into spontaneous applause whenever an elderly or retired prima dancer entered the auditorium. We simply glowed, even Olga.

Paul had shown where his skills lay and the 'girls' set him his final task. Our holiday was ending and everyone recognised that Olga had been superb. There was nothing legal that she would not do for her troupe. So, in that British tradition, it was decided that we would have a collection for her. But Claire and Gretl, who had been in service, knew a little about English gratuities and suggested that each couple be forced to pay a 'discretionary' £5. Paul took the envelope round when we were on the coach. I could hear the miseries complaining that it was too much, that she hadn't done that much extra, and besides, a fiver was a fiver! He stood there, hand held out, and repeated 'Five quid', waiting until they spewed it up.

When we presented her with the money Olga was visibly moved, she had no words. She had expected nothing, and certainly not what we gave her. She took out a hanky, wiped her face then let out the biggest laugh imaginable.

We left Russia with new friends, the girls and Olga, and I had a new understanding of Paul. Three years later, in 1988, Olga came to England for good. Though she had visited before, during the permanent move she faced unexpected and bizarre difficulties, so eventually she and her nine-year-old daughter, Anya, came to live with us in Mile End. With our help Olga went on a secretarial course and even though she only spoke few words of English we got Anya into the local primary school. Through sheer hard work, sacrifice and determination they turned their lives around. Olga overcame seemingly insurmountable obstacles to become a very successful commercial operator, and she found the right partner, too. Anya, meanwhile, the non-English-speaking child who had recorded her train journey across Russia in crayon drawings, went on to study law at Oxford.

31

In Russia our lives changed. There was a growing awareness of a major threat to the lives of gay and bisexual men: the HIV virus, which suppressed the immune system, was prevalent in the USA, and was now becoming a real public health issue in the UK. Some spoke of an epidemic, others hoped it would stay in America, but it was already taking hold in Britain and elsewhere. The free gay press raised the alarm, as did a few angry medical practitioners. They could see the figures growing, the rising number of men presenting themselves in the last stages of the illness, and they wanted action.

In New York and on the West Coast activists became hyper-agitated and mounted direct action campaigns against the hostile political and media environment and against an unresponsive medical establishment.

I thought back to the time I had spent in New York just before my thirtieth birthday. It had been a period of unbridled hedonism. In the aptly named Meatpacking District, clubs such as the Eagle, Spike or the Mineshaft (where a door sign stated that anyone wearing cologne or aftershave or was a 'mary' would not be admitted), anonymous sex was constantly available and my curiosity took me there. The bathhouses offered the same sexual liberation, and you could have a shower into the bargain. I found the whole anonymous sex scene a total turn-off. And though I had watched rather than participated, I did have sex while I was in New York. No one knew how far this sexually transmitted disease went back so I knew I could be at risk. In fear, rather than in selfishness, I decided to keep my worry to myself and to wait, watching for symptoms. The night sweats, sudden weight loss, or the purple blotch of the 'gay cancer', Kaposi's sarcoma.

Safe sex with condoms or no sex at all protected you from contracting the HIV virus. Scare stories in the newspapers reported that you could pick it up from sitting next to a gay man or using a cup or glass that they had used. Hysteria took over from fact, and things would get far, far worse before the epidemic would even be properly reported on, let alone understood. Sex now had to be more considered, more careful, and only ever 'safe'. People were dying in constantly increasing numbers. There was no cure if you became HIV positive, and once your immune system failed there was no hope. Death lurked in the places where we had taken refuge and could take refuge no more. Everything had changed. Fear was growing, you could sense it, almost feel it, in the bars and the clubs. And even though the gay papers screamed it from their front pages, some people did not want to address the reality of the threat.

Paul and I had to change too. In Russia our confidence as an open couple had taken root. I was no longer afraid of my jealousy, my anger, or my sense of worthlessness. We settled into each other; we started to find our roles within the relationship and we were in the process of sounding out our compatibility, our incompatibility, and how to accommodate both. For the first time I sensed a shared bond of trust.

Of course we were far from perfect together. We infuriated each other. I'd do the ironing, but not in the way he wanted. He wanted the same coloured clothes pegs when we hung washing out and I couldn't give a shit. I wanted to do a job quickly and get it over with, he wanted to do it properly and take time. He had no qualms about asking for help, whereas I loathed it.

On the other hand, I loved musical theatre and now he couldn't get enough of it; he loved dancing and I did too. I liked a drink and he liked to drink me under the table. If I was shy of new people – it was like always having to perform – he enjoyed nothing better than spotting a new face and turning a stranger into a friend.

And when we breathed out, just let everything go, I knew that we didn't want to be anywhere else other than next to each other.

I found his exhibition of confidence a relief. He was no longer a boy – in fact, I don't think he had ever been a boy in our relationship. Paul was nobody's fool, he loved work and, perhaps as a nod to me, he gave up working at the Lyric Theatre, the place of his first admitted indiscretion. Instead he took a job in another frenetic environment – a men's clothes shop in Hackney, where they were robbed, by appointment, at knifepoint and threatened with death if they so much as thought of calling the police.

He and the other gay man working in the shop also received the most exotic sexual advances imaginable, particularly when someone was trying on something scanty in the changing room. Never one to keep a surprise to himself he would encourage an exhibitor to come home with him, to share. 'A couple that shares together, wears together.' And we wore together well.

We settled into the new safe-sex relationship; it had to be safe sex with other people or it was no sex. The HIV virus did not discriminate: the new rule was not to put ourselves at risk.

Now I was working on Yorkshire television's *The Winning Streak*, it meant time away from home, and that gave the relationship a period in which to develop without either of us trying to prove anything. The series was a good concept with an excellent cast headed by Dinah Sheridan and Leslie Sands, but even I had to admit that some of the writing was not up to the usual standards, and I was not convincing as the hyper-masculine champion rally driver Frank McShane. As a cast of actors, though, we all got on well which meant that our time in Leeds was exhausting socially, with nights typically culminating in us stumbling out of clubs and restaurants in the early hours of the morning. Paul came up a few times and endeared himself with his usual charm and cheekiness, especially to Jane Morant, who played my sultry, pouting girlfriend.

The series was coming towards its final episodes and we started filming a sequence in Bradford. Working at Yorkshire TV was like working with one big family. I felt a real part of it as I knew most of the crew, lighting, wardrobe and stage management from my time on the J. B. Priestley tribute and *Sandbaggers*. Because of this close relationship I discovered in advance that the prime minister, Margaret Thatcher, was going to be visiting Bradford while we were filming in the city centre. She was coming to pay her respects to the victims of the fire at Bradford City football stadium in which fifty-six people had died and 265 people had been injured in May 1985.

Thatcher was not loved in Yorkshire – or anywhere where there were mines and pit villages. The night before her visit we assembled to be told by the producer that, even though the PM was visiting Bradford and there were security concerns, we were still being allowed to film. The cast was uneasy. Some were delighted Thatcher was visiting Bradford, especially Dinah Sheridan – whose son was a Tory MP – but most of us were disgusted that it had taken the deaths of fifty-six people to get her to finally visit Yorkshire. As the meeting with the producer broke up there were murmurings of: 'What shall we do?'

Jane Morant and I shared a worried look. I loathed Mrs Thatcher, who seemed to be on a crusade, backed by the right-wing press including the *Sun* and the *Mail*, to pursue policies that led to high unemployment. There was a callous disregard for anyone who got in her government's way; she particularly despised trade unions and the rights they enforced and defended for their members. Towns and cities were run down, high streets were boarded up, the economy was in freefall and all she kept repeating was that she 'was not for turning'. There had been riots across the country, in Bristol, Brixton, Liverpool, Birmingham and Leeds.

Politically, Mrs Thatcher stood for everything I was against: she was one of the few politicians who fired real anger inside me. She seemed to have no care for the victims she failed in pursuit of her ideology, and she seemed incapable of empathising with British people who suffered at her hand. Those around her felt that 'unemployment was a price worth paying'. Earlier that year I had been so angry that I had come close to resigning my Labour membership over the party's reluctance to back the miners' strike. Coming from a mining area, Paul and I stood firmly together on this subject.

I despised Thatcher's shrill rhetoric, the phony theatricals, her use of scripts honed by playwrights for imagined characters. After the British armed forces' victory in the Falklands War, Mrs Thatcher portrayed herself as vanquisher, the Iron Lady. Meanwhile, unemployment had risen towards a million, the health service was in chaos and single mothers and people on benefits were depicted as 'scroungers', a drain on the country. At GCHQ, the government spy listening centre, trade union membership was banned as if it was a threat to the nation state. The thought of being so close to this awful politician and doing nothing was driving me mad. 'I can't remain silent,' I said to Paul on the phone. He told me to calm down and to talk about it to Jane Morant or Malcolm Drury, the casting director. I went in search of Malcolm but his office was empty and he wasn't in the studio bar, but Jane was; I grabbed a pint and joined her.

'What are we going to do, Cash?' she asked.

I shook my head and stared at my pint of Newcastle Brown.

The next morning we were all taken by minibus to the location in Bradford. We knew what time the prime minister was expected. We got into costume, had our make-up applied in the trailer, then Jane and I got a cup of coffee and an early morning bacon sandwich from the food wagon.

'We have to do something,' she murmured, and I nodded.

A couple of the other cast members asked us jokingly what we were plotting. We just smiled.

Neither Jane nor I were filming at the time of Thatcher's arrival so, clad in our garish shell-suit costumes, we wandered over to Bradford City Hall where the PM was due to appear. A small crowd had gathered, mainly men waiting quietly, but there was also a strong police presence. Then suddenly it happened.

A police outrider came first, then a dark car glided towards the pavement and slowed to a halt, after which followed another car not far behind. Two or three police motorcycle outriders finally came to the rear.

There was a flurry of activity, the back door of the second car opened and an ashen-faced, black-clad Mrs Thatcher stepped from the car. Momentarily she stopped, dropped her head slightly, pulled her handbag close to her and walked away from the car. Adrenalin coursed through my veins, my heart started beating frantically and my nerves locked me into an obsessive focus.

Jane and I quickly looked at each other. And into the eerie silence I started to boo.

'Booooooo. Booooo. Booooo.'

'Shut the fuck up,' said a bobby.

But I persisted. It was pathetic but I didn't know what else to do.

'Maggie, Maggie, Maggie! Out, out, out!' shouted Jane in her poshest voice as I crescendoed my boos onto the end of her shouts.

Unperturbed, not even giving us a hint of a glance, Mrs Thatcher disappeared into City Hall. Jane and I had done our two-person demo, the only ones to speak out from the crowd. Everyone else had met her with sullen contempt, or admiration, but had remained silent.

The policeman, using language more becoming of a docker, asked me what that was 'all about'. I told him that it was disgusting that it had taken all those deaths in the fire to get the prime minister to visit Yorkshire, a place that she had helped to destroy. He told me to stop being a cunt and to fuck off back to London.

Knowing it was not time for an argument, Jane and I walked away, and headed back to the artists' caravan.

By the time we got back word had spread. Dinah Sheridan was furious: 'The woman is the prime minister, for goodness' sake.' Others congratulated us. I felt good. I had wanted to make my voice heard; even though it was a pathetic boo, I had faced up to Thatcher and all she stood for.

At the end of the day's filming Jane and I were separately summoned to the executive producer's office in Leeds. We were told that we had abused the privilege given to us and to Yorkshire TV as filmmakers, and that we had caused serious embarrassment to the television company. I apologised but added that I could not let the chance pass me by because of what she 'was doing to the country'. We argued for a short while, as I tried to get them to see the case sympathetically: but as I left the room it was made abundantly clear that we were never going to see eye to eye on this particular subject.

That night Jane and I got pissed in the bar, mainly on drinks bought for us by staff. We didn't gloat; we knew we had done wrong, that our actions did reflect badly on Yorkshire TV – but in all honesty that possibility hadn't even occurred to us. We had thought about very little except making our dissent known. It may have been selfish and foolish, but strangely I did not regret it, I only wished it could have happened a different way. This incident was never referred to during my time at Yorkshire TV but neither Jane nor I would ever be employed by them again. I understood why.

When I spoke to Paul later on the phone he reassured me that I had done the right thing. He understood my motivation and I believed him.

A final memory of that time in Leeds was at the Queen's Hotel, the beautiful British Transport Hotel perched above the station. It was old-fashioned-style catering, coffee served in silver-plated pots, starched linen sheets and napkins, and breakfasts that approached your table in covered silver trays. When we were filming it was always my treat to stay there and on this occasion Paul joined me. I went to reception and got my lovely Leeds welcome from the young woman while Paul went to retrieve the bags.

'A double?' she asked, smiling broadly.

'A double,' I replied back.

Then she proudly presented the key and two courtesy boxes, one black, one white.

'What is the white one for?'

Every time I had stayed I'd been given a black one: disposable razor, shaving cream, shoelaces, that kind of thing.

'It's for the lady,' she said warmly.

At which precise moment Paul plonked himself beside me.

'I see. Well, this is the "lady",' I replied, pointing to Paul.

She went white with shock, fell into a stupefied silence and swiftly disappeared behind the glass partition to speak to an older man. I saw her mouth the words, 'It's a man.'

Her colleague came to the reception desk with the clear intention of mollifying the situation.

'Sorry Mr Cashman,' he said softly, 'but I'm afraid we've made a mistake and given you a double room.'

'That's what I asked for.'

He caught his breath and looked towards the young woman a short way off.

'But it has a double bed,' he whispered as if by way of explanation.

'Well, we won't be knitting,' I said.

Suddenly Jane Morant arrived and stood beside us.

'All right Cash?' she asked.

The man looked between me, Jane and Paul, totally confused, then he grabbed the white box back and shoved two black boxes towards me.

'Thanks very much,' I said happily. 'And don't worry about her, she's the human bolster,' I shouted over my shoulder as we went to our room, completely unaware that we were breaking the law. In 1985 – and through until the law changed in 1998 – consenting homosexual relations were only legal if conducted in the confines of your own home.

PART TWO

32

By late 1985 the BBC's new soap *EastEnders* had been broadcast for about ten months. It aired twice a week, on Tuesdays and Thursdays, repeated on a Sunday afternoon. At first the tabloids and the reviewers hated it, then suddenly and unexpectedly the show took off. Viewing figures reached into the upper millions and people were hooked. Set in London's East End, it broke the mould of series drama with its documentary-style acting, harsh characters, fast dialogue and storylines of adultery, villains, underage sex, teenage pregnancies and single mothers selling sex. The private lives and indiscretions of cast consistently made the front pages of the tabloid newspapers which added to the on-screen interest. Fact and fiction became interchangeable and led to one nationwide drama. It was also being shown in other countries around the world, including parts of the USA, Australia and Spain.

Paul and I loved *EastEnders* but I never expected to be cast in it. I had worked with the co-creators of the show, producer Julia Smith and writer Tony Holland, on another BBC series and we had a huge row that brought my time on that project to an abrupt end.

So it was with some interest and a lot of trepidation that I went for a meeting in their offices at the BBC at Shepherd's Bush Green, west London.

Success had changed Julia. She was warm, funny and treated me like an equal, while Tony was his usual 'not in the room but watching you' self. Social niceties out of the way, Julia got down to business. They'd been watching my career, she said, and they liked the actor that I had become. There was a part that they were trying to cast, but every time they thought of it they kept returning to me.

'And?' I said.

'We've tried to cast a straight actor,' she said, 'but the part is so right for you.'

My ears pricked up.

'Straight?' I asked.

They both nodded and left a short pause for effect.

'The character is called Colin: your age, the son of a west London builder, a graphic designer who moves into the Square,' said Tony.

'And he is gay,' said Julia.

Silence.

'Now you can see why we were trying to cast a straight actor.'

I took it that she meant the tabloids would be all over whoever took the part on, especially with a media that portrayed the AIDS/HIV crisis as a 'gay plague' and associated homosexuality with effeminacy or paedophilia.

'I see,' was all I could think to say.

They outlined the next two years of storylines, which included that Colin would have an underage, working-class boyfriend called Barry who ran a stall on the market. We talked about the character and about the show for nearly an hour, then Julia asked: 'So, will you do it?'

I seriously did not know how to answer. I had walked into the room without the faintest idea of what would happen. I suppose I thought that they'd ask me to audition for a part, then dismiss me: the settling of scores that sometimes accompanies success. I was flattered, amused, nervous, worried, enraptured, and had no idea how to unpick my emotions. I said something like: 'How do I cope with the tabloids?' Julia replied that they couldn't advise me, but that I should probably speak to Leslie Grantham.

Grantham's past, including his conviction for the murder of a taxi driver, had given him nationwide fame and notoriety. He played Den Watts, the landlord of the Queen Vic pub. I thought of some of the other actors whose lives had been ripped apart and serialised in the tabloids.

'When does it start?'

'Colin's first episode is recorded a week today, so rehearsals start in two days,' said Julia.

I explained that I was going to Paris the next day and wouldn't be available until Monday.

'We'll work around you,' she said and smiled.

'We've thought of everything,' grinned Tony.

'I would love to—'

'Great. Great—'

'But I need to speak to Paul, my partner, and to my mum and dad.'

Julia looked at Tony and said: 'I told you he'd be bloody sensible.'

We agreed that I'd phone her at two later that afternoon.

I left the building on a high and from the nearest phone box I called Paul, who told me without hesitation to do it.

'What about the press?'

'We'll manage that if and when it happens. But we are still going to Paris aren't we?'

He always got his priorities right. I reassured him, then phoned my mum and dad. My mum screamed down the phone with joy, and my dad said it was 'nothing like the bleeding East End'. 'It's up to you,' they said: for them, being gay was not an issue, it was part of who I was.

I could have gone back and told Julia, but I decided to take the Central line home to Mile End and think it through. I ran the prospect through my head and everything screamed 'yes' at me; my CV was impressive: I had been working as an actor for over twenty years, and I had just recorded Ayckbourn's classic comedy, *Season's Greetings*, as the prestigious BBC Two Christmas show. But a show like *EastEnders* would bring financial security, regular employment and stability in an industry notoriously built upon uncertainty. So I sat on the Central line and convinced myself that

I deserved this break. It felt right. What's more, I loved the show and most of the acting.

I rang Julia and she was thrilled.

Later that day my agent came through with the deal from the BBC: a six-month contract with a year's option. If all went to plan and the contract was 'optioned' I would earn approximately £90,000 a year. A considerable sum.

Paul and I danced around the room, went out to get a Chinese takeaway and hit the lager. The next day we drove to Paris with our neighbours, Mike and Marie, fell under the charms of the city and indulged to excess.

The scripts were waiting at home when we got back on Sunday night. There was a message on the answerphone with the time I was needed at the BBC studios in Elstree, Hertfordshire.

The next day I left home and said goodbye to Paul, who was going back on the road with a kids' play, and was about to start rehearsing for the nationwide tour of *The Rocky Horror Show*.

I took the tube to King's Cross, the overground to Elstree and walked the ten minutes to the studio. It felt indescribable. I knew I was embarking on something that would change my life – but at the same time I didn't want it to change me. I had experience of being recognised in public from *Sandbaggers* days, but *EastEnders* was a national obsession. It wasn't that which excited me, however; it was a sense of belonging to something so well-liked and so revered. Each step of the way I had a lovely warm feeling of satisfaction. Life was going to be good – for us both.

I turned down the side street and approached the studios, which I knew well; I'd worked there many times when it was owned by Associated Television. At the front gate I was ignored by a couple of young autograph hunters, and BBC security directed me on the long walk to the reception desk at Neptune House. From there, my heart racing with every step, I took the lift to the rehearsal room, and I waited in the green room.

The green room, which is never green, was empty. Rosters and schedules were pinned to the noticeboard with the famous

EastEnders logo emblazoned on them; there were two phones, in-trays with actors' names on and rows of armless comfy chairs around the three sides of the room. I checked the time, opened my script again, which I had marked up, and silently ran through my lines.

A voice pierced the silence: 'Are you new?'

33

She didn't wait for a response but walked over to one of the phones. It was Gretchen Franklin, who played the pub's ancient cockney cleaning lady, Ethel, famous for her on-screen pug 'Willy'. Gretchen had been in the business for years and had started out as a variety artist with her parents. I stood up and extended my hand, which she ignored.

'Yes, I am new,' I replied.

She spoke into the phone: 'It's me. Gretchen. Could you order my car, dear?' She put the phone down and headed for the door, saying over her shoulder: 'You'll enjoy this job. It's like being shot out of a cannon backwards. You never know where you're going to end up!'

Then she was gone.

There was a flurry of activity in the corridor; I could hear two people chatting and I recognised one of the voices. It was like the first day of school, and I was nervous. A young woman with a clipboard stood in the doorway.

'Michael?'

I nodded.

'Right, we're ready for you.'

As I stood up June Brown appeared in the room. She played the downtrodden and hilariously funny Dot Cotton, Mrs Dorothy Cotton.

'Oh hello, dear,' she said. 'Are you the gay one? I mean, you know dear, Colin. It is Colin, isn't it?'

She drew deeply on the cigarette that was pressed to her lips.

With the reprimand of 'June!' from the assistant, I was led away to rehearse my first scenes in *EastEnders*.

The rehearsal room was stark and resembled a second-hand furniture store. Light streamed in from the windows on one side of the room and different-coloured tapes on the floor marked out the designated houses and rooms of *EastEnders*' Albert Square. The director, Bill, stood in the middle of the room dressed in a suit, an overcoat and a scarf, holding the script in a hardbound folder. His was the old-fashioned approach. He resembled an orchestra conductor.

He looked at the script, then peered at me over the rim of his glasses mouthing 'Welcome'.

I shook hands with Oscar James, who played Tony Carpenter, and then Bill said: 'Let's do it shall we?'

The floor manager swept his hand in front of us and we began the scene in which Colin looked around the flat that he would eventually buy.

The nerves buried themselves as we lifted the words from the page of the script and gave them a life: a hesitation, a caress, a prod. Over and over again for the next half an hour we repeated my scenes, following a suggestion from Bill, a new position to take account of the cameras and the important instruction to keep it real and believable. This was the cardinal rule of working on *EastEnders* – a mantra that was repeated constantly by the actors and the production staff.

The show ran to a very tight schedule and in any one week you could be working on six different episodes. The working week began on a Friday, rehearsing two episodes in Neptune House and simultaneously recording the external sequences for another two episodes in 'the Square'. I would then receive another two episodes to start previewing. My arrival had definitely been noticed because I had upset the routine and the schedules had to be changed for my trip to Paris – something that almost never happened.

Once rehearsals were over on that first morning I made my way back to the green room. June Brown was still there, the air thick with smoke as she puffed away and chatted on the phone. I picked up my coat and started for the door.

'Just a minute, dear,' she shouted at me, then finished the call with an abrupt 'I'll phone you back.'

'Fancy lunch, dear? Mike isn't it? We could go over to the canteen.'

Everyone welcomed me. They were good, kind, down-to-earth people. But as an actor you could never get over suddenly meeting someone that you knew so well on screen, but you actually didn't know at all. Stupid as it seems, it always comes as a surprise when the actor playing the part is nothing like the character in real life. After lunch we did a run-through of each episode in story order and then I was released for the day.

I went home and spoke to Paul on the phone, regaling him with all the details. He reminded me that he had met 'Dot' when she had made a personal appearance at a gay club in Streatham. She had signed a photo to the two of us.

I spent the rest of the evening making sure I was word perfect for the much-feared producer's run-through the next day.

That next morning everything went smoothly. Then, just before two o'clock, we were told to stand by for the producer's run when suddenly a large cream poodle appeared at the far end of the corridor and started running full pelt towards us. It was Roly, the show's famous pub dog.

Adam Woodyatt, who played Ian Beale, jumped to his feet and shouted: 'Julia! – She's coming!' People fled in all different directions, except a few diehards. With that Julia appeared, followed by Tony and two script editors, marching along the corridor, deep in conversation.

Julia saw me and came straight over. 'Everything okay?' she asked, then kissed me on the cheek.

I told her it was all fine.

'Any problems, come and see me. We are all thrilled you're doing it. You are going to be fantastic.' Then she turned and entered the studio, others piled in behind her and the soundproof door slammed firmly shut.

'Fuck me!'

It was Adam.

'She kissed you. She actually KISSED you.'

I told him we had history.

'She kissed you and you haven't got bite marks on your neck!'

Julia was feared. She had made her way up through the BBC over many years and had learned to be tough and uncompromising. I had experienced the tough side of her and she knew my hard side too. We had the measure of each other. It was true that, as a woman at this time, she had had to become hard in order to succeed. She was very protective of her and Tony's 'baby' and she knew that there were people who wanted to get her out and replace her with a man.

That week we recorded my first episodes, just a few scenes, over the two days, but my nerves were shredded by the end of it. After the recording I went to the dressing room that would be mine for the next two and a half years. I'd been told to remain dressed in character and to keep my make-up on. I was then taken on a short walk to the 'lot', Albert Square, to have my official *EastEnders* photos taken.

Part of the show's attraction was its attention to detail; the rooms that characters inhabited reflected their lives and their experiences. Nothing was placed by chance, it had to mean something. Keith Harris led the phenomenal design team, who were always there and were very hands-on. Even after all my years as an actor I wasn't prepared for the shock and the thrill of my first day on the actual Square. I had seen it on screen, but now real and up close it took my breath away: the Queen Vic on the corner, Bridge Street and the market stalls, Ali and Sue's cafe, the launderette, Lou Beale's house opposite and the gardens in the middle of the Square, all of it had been meticulously executed. I stood outside the house in Albert Square where Colin would buy his flat from local builder Tony Carpenter. Seeing the Square without anyone filming on it – that occurred usually on a Friday – gave it a stronger sense of reality. Despite what my argumentative dad had said, it was like someone had lifted the place from the East End and dropped it there.

The photographer and I strolled about the Square and I was struck by how they had modelled the market and Bridge Street on Shepherd's Bush Market just behind Julia and Tony's offices in the BBC, even down to the train line passing over the viaduct. After only about a week I felt at home, and strangely safe, inside the studios. I quickly settled into the routine of rehearsing and recording, filming on the Square on a Friday, and learning the lines quickly. Tony and Julia were sticklers for keeping to what was written. At its best the writing couldn't be beaten; the dialogue tripped off the tongue, the characters and their portrayal were so real, and their situations were either dire or comical. Never anything in between.

The shows were recorded six weeks in advance so I could still travel unrecognised on public transport, which was the quickest way to get across London to Elstree. One morning I set off as usual, made my way to Mile End station, and there I saw a front page headline of the *Sun* that made my heart stop: 'EASTBENDERS', with my photograph alongside it.

The *Sun* had the exclusive from an 'insider' and the story tried to reinforce every single prejudice the media had against gay people at that time. I didn't buy the newspaper (I had refused to ever do that again when Rupert Murdoch took it over). The article described how Colin and his boyfriend Barry would mince into the Queen Vic demanding their gin and tonics, and it would cause uproar. Cast members were said to be 'disgusted'. Inside the paper was a cartoon of two men wearing leather jackets, suspenders and stockings, supping drinks at the bar. At the bottom of the front-page article was a bullet point in bold and the words: 'In no way do we suggest that Michael Cashman is a homosexual, merely that he is portraying one.'

Clearly they had not done their research.

The 'article' made me feel uneasy; it was deeply unpleasant. With the story out, I immediately spoke to Paul and to my family. My mum had seen it on her way home from early morning office cleaning and didn't want to worry me. 'Besides,' she said, 'they don't pay your rent. Worry when they do.'

I got to work, feeling betrayed that someone had leaked the upcoming storyline to the newspapers. 'Get used to it,' said one colleague. 'Congratulations, you made the front page,' said another. The BBC press department said nothing. I was told they did not like to interfere between an artist and the press.

Later that day, however, I finally got a call from the BBC Press Office at Elstree. It was to convey an offer from the *News of the World* for a large amount of money to give them my life story, 'whatever I want that to be'. Without hesitation I said no. Paul and I had agreed that I would not do any interviews because we knew that the tabloids in particular would want to get a negative angle on me the character or both. Julia received a letter from Mary Whitehouse, the self-styled 'moral watchdog' of the National Viewers' and Listeners' Association, expressing her deep concern that a homosexual was being introduced into a 'so-called family show' that was broadcast before the 'watershed' hour of eight o'clock in the evening. Julia had it framed and put on the wall with the rest of Mrs Whitehouse's letters. For Julia and Tony they were confirmation that they were getting it absolutely right; if it upset the establishment then it must be spot on.

When Colin finally appeared it was a bit of a damp squib. He was ordinary, in fact he could blend into a magnolia wall. He carried a Filofax, which was smart and techno; he was posh compared to the rest of the Square, quietly spoken and single. But he wasn't camp. He was just easy. In a few of the early scenes the women made a play for him and he gently fended them off. Three months later when he confessed in a drunken moment to the pub landlady, Angie, that he had 'men problems' the howls went up. Some were delighted that Colin was finally out, as expected; others were less happy. Questions were raised, even in Parliament, as to why with AIDS and HIV 'swirling around' they had put a homosexual into a family show. The tabloids were beside themselves with gleeful moral outrage at the 'yuppie poof'.

34

By now it was becoming difficult to travel unnoticed on public transport. People would stare in disbelief, smile at me, talk to me, giggle inanely, or tell me that they 'never watched the show'. I had lost my public privacy, and while it didn't upset me, it became tiring, like always being on air. But I knew and accepted that it was part of the job.

'You need a car,' said Wendy Richard, who played down-trodden Pauline Fowler, as she drew on her cigarette holder.

'Or a chauffeur,' said Gretchen.

'Nah, get a van,' said Peter Dean, who played Pete Beale.

I had been taken into the inner bosom of the show. Wendy had given me the seal of approval, which meant that on recording days I was allowed to have tea with her, Pete, June and some-times Gretchen, who always complained that the tea tasted like 'gnats' piss'.

'That's because I wash the tea bags first,' Wendy always replied, by way of a put-down.

'Still tastes like piss,' Gretchen would mumble.

June offered me one of her 'old bangers', but I insisted that I would persevere on public transport for as long as I could, as it was the easiest way to get across London.

It was fate, I thought, that the first ever film premiere Paul and I attended together was *Little Shop of Horrors*: it was the play we went to see during our first weekend in London. Obviously I accepted the invitation, along with other members of the cast. On the evening itself Paul and I chickened out and decided to go into the cinema in Leicester Square separately, then take our seats together. Once inside, however, I noticed that our presence together had aroused some attention.

Similarly, when we went to the second anniversary party of the show we travelled in the same car as Wendy and Pam St Clement, who played Pat Butcher, but Paul went in separately with Wendy's husband-to-be. It was ironic, *EastEnders* was giving us financial security, but it was also starting to undermine our relationship. I was a part of the show's success and Paul was not. I could sense the growing tension between us and I knew that we were drifting apart. It didn't matter that the cast members liked him and included him, especially Pam, Wendy and June. He was not allowed to officially be part of my life. He was invisible, but not for long.

It was Sunday, it was early and the phone was ringing.

'Let it ring,' I said. Paul and I had had a late night as I waited for him to get home from one of the regional theatres he was touring.

Finally as it rang for a third time I padded downstairs to answer it. It was Paul's stepfather, Dick, and he wanted to talk to Paul. He wasn't in the mood to exchange pleasantries. I passed the phone to Paul and stood waiting.

Paul pulled a face, repeating again and again that it wasn't true, it wasn't true. I tried to make eye contact with him but he kept looking away, looking down. Eventually I shouted over his phone call: 'What the fuck is it?'

He shook his head, ashen. When he hung up he looked at me and began to sob.

Fifteen minutes later I returned from the shop and we both read the double page spread in the *News of the World*: 'SECRET GAY LOVE OF AIDS SCARE EASTENDER'. The pages featured photographs, and our address. Paul was described as my 'secret love', and the AIDS connection was part of an on-screen storyline, with no truth to it whatsoever. We sat and stared at the pages for what seemed like ages.

I called my family to warn them, but they had already seen it, and were absolutely not interested in the *News of the Screws* anyway. 'Fuck 'em,' said my mum, as she always did. 'Wouldn't wipe me arse on it,' said my dad.

Paul's family were stunned. He had been outed to his family, to their friends and to all friends in the small town of Newark, and in Liverpool where his other relatives lived. The story was snide, full of innuendo and AIDS references, and now wrapped around us and our families, but particularly Paul. The journalist quoted neighbours, who had commented without being named, and they had spoken to Lorraine in our local 'working-class' pub. From their story it appeared that Paul and I were only tolerated so long as we behaved like 'real men', especially in the pub. It was a continuation of all the other awful stories that had accompanied my arrival on *EastEnders* a few months before. But that didn't make it any easier because this time it was about Paul. They had 'outed' him without warning or care.

And deep down that really hurt. I didn't mind what shit they threw at me, it was my job, but Paul was off limits. He was not a justifiable target for their dubious moral code. He spoke to his sisters on the phone and he came out to one. He chose to tell the others a bit later. It was survival time. He, we, just had to get through it.

It was easier for me: I had been out to my family for years. From the very earliest age when I knew I was gay I had got on with it. Going into the theatre gave me a 'gang' to belong to and an environment that helped me come to terms with threats and abuse. Paul also guessed at an early age but he did not have my good fortune or my location. To become himself he had to find distance, a different community and courage. That he was now being outed by a national newspaper was indefensible. But it was what he had to deal with. The irony was that he was already 'out' in London and in our neighbourhood, and this made the story even more unforgivable. How we had never seen this coming I don't know.

I kept telling myself I should have done something. I should have taken control. But deep down I knew it wasn't for me to take control or decide. It was for him.

Lorraine from the pub called by; she had been duped, misled and misquoted. One by one our wonderful neighbours rallied round. It was good that Paul had the *Rocky Horror* tour to go off to as the show would help take his mind off it all. By the afternoon, after one of his Sunday roast dinners, we felt a bit better and cuddled up on the sofa. His bag for the week waited by the door and at around four o'clock I waved him off, but when I closed the front door I felt a huge sadness descend. I settled down to work, to learn my lines for the next day.

After about an hour in the ground-floor study, repeating lines like a demented parrot, I decided to have a break and go downstairs to the basement to make a cup of tea. That's when it happened.

A brick was thrown through the study window.

I rushed upstairs to see the damage, then ran and threw open the door to find the street completely deserted. I slammed the door and went back inside. There was glass everywhere. Suddenly I didn't feel angry, I didn't feel frightened, I felt amazingly calm. All I thought was: how fucking dare they do this to us. How dare they.

The newspaper had even given the location of our home, and they hadn't given a toss about the consequences. As I swept up the glass, effing and blinding, I was so glad Paul had not been here. They could get at me whenever they wanted, but not him. Not him.

After the morning of the *News of the World* article, slowly things started to change. Paul finally came out to his family and they didn't love him any the less – in fact his younger sister, Sharon, thought it was smart to have a gay brother. As we should have expected, his entire family and all his friends were unaffected by the news.

The actions of the *News of the World* had been irresponsible but, despite that, Paul had found the strength to be himself and to occupy his own space, not space loaned to him by pretending to be somebody else. He was like a man who had lost time and lost chances to love. He was not going to waste another second.

Now, however, with our relationship no longer news, the tabloids ignored him in my life. Paul was airbrushed out of photos, left unnamed, or told to 'get out of the picture'. They did not want a happy couple. They wanted scandal. The press sent two young kids to our door to ask for money, while a photographer waited opposite in a car for his opportunity. Our dustbin contents often went missing. One evening I arrived home to be informed by a *Sunday Mirror* journalist that I had just come back from the USA where I had taken an AIDS test. I was, they said, almost certainly dying of AIDS and had decided to break off my relationship. I told her to go and tell Paul this. She said that she already had, but they didn't mean him, they meant another man that I was supposedly having an affair with.

It was all nonsense that nonetheless we had to deal with, deny, refute, then wait to see if they printed. False allegations were given credibility because we were gay. All this time Paul had no official place in my life, except in scandal or shock. His family was incredibly supportive. When he told his mum we were a couple she replied: 'So long as you're happy son,' then she looked at me and said: 'Hey Mike, I always wanted one of my daughters to find themselves a rich man, and me son's gone and done it.'

On *EastEnders* Colin had been joined by his young lover Barry, played by Gary Hailes. Gary also suffered the intrusions of the press and as a young, albeit experienced, heterosexual actor, dealing with the gay label and innuendos must have been harder. One day he turned up at work in dark sunglasses.

'Trying not to be recognised?' I asked sarcastically.

'This is because of you, this is.'

He took them off to reveal a black eye. An elderly woman had spotted him in Tesco and asked if he was 'Barry off *EastEnders*'. When he said he was, she chased him round the supermarket and gave him a thump for giving that 'lovely Colin' such a hard time.

At other times though, the story wasn't so light-hearted. Gary faced homophobic threats and verbal abuse, but he never complained, certainly not to me. We knew we just had to get on with whatever came. It went with fame, or rather the infamy. We didn't expect counselling or support from the BBC and we didn't get it. No one did.

The show was riding a huge wave of popularity. We were the surprise turn on the *Royal Variety Performance* and the Queen Mother adored Ethel's 'little Willy'. Princess Diana even made an unannounced visit to the set and was visibly irritated when I said that Prince Charles's valet, Stephen Barry, was a friend of mine. I didn't know then but the last thing she wanted to hear was anything to do with her husband. The famous were queuing to visit Albert Square and I resolutely refused to meet the Tory MP Edwina Currie, only to bump into her in the car park later. She was charming and came over to shake my hand. Stupidly I was aloof, as I couldn't see the woman, only the politician, a politician who within a few short years would become one of the unexpected champions for gay equality.

Perversely, the more popular the show became, the more the tabloids needed it or us to fail. *EastEnders* was front-page news, it sold their papers. But it meant our lives, personally and professionally, suffered. It was stressful.

Paul and I had our respective work. He was still touring, enjoying all the freedoms, including the carnal ones in the new safe-sex world of AIDS and HIV. I had the bearable boredom of learning lines, weekends off quietly waiting for Paul's return, or a night in a hotel at Elstree with June and the occasional highly paid appearance at a gay club. I was never booked for a straight venue; the heterosexual paying public were not ready for 'Colin' in their discos or clubs.

Paul and I became very close to Wendy, June and Gretchen. When Michelle Collins joined the show she initially had a rough time from some of the other women as competition to be the top dog was fierce. We became friends, but she and Paul formed an especially tight bond. They were similar ages, both loved a good party and they both hated hypocrisy. With Michelle he could be himself. She gave him strength and he never hesitated in speaking his mind, even though he could muster all the tact and diplomacy in the world.

On one occasion, for example, when we were in Joe Allen's, the actors' restaurant in the West End, Wayne Sleep made his way over to our table. He looked at me and asked how I was, as we'd worked together on *The Virgin Soldiers* years earlier. Then after some idle chit-chat he looked at Paul and said: 'I don't like you,' and waited for the reaction.

'What makes you think I would care?' replied Paul, waving Sleep away from the table.

I was impressed. Another time, years before, we were walking home in the early hours of the morning as we passed a hostel from which the residents had spilled out onto the street. Unusually, Paul and I were holding hands, but we let them slip as we passed the throng. A heavily pregnant woman strode out into the road and screamed: 'Fucking queers.'

Paul turned round and from the middle of the road faced her off: 'You wanna try it, then you won't end up with one of them stuck up you.' She shook her fists, screamed like a banshee warrior and, with a stream of abuse, charged towards us, followed by all her mates.

'Come on,' he urged. 'Come on.'

Then we ran, and laughed and laughed – it was mad. It was Paul at his assertive I-know-my-space-in-the-world best.

35

While Paul was touring I rarely went out socially. With the press on my back it wasn't worth the hassle. Then once, I made the exception and I took my cousin Nicky to a premiere. We ended up in the *News of the World* under the headline: 'Real Life Love Notes to a Fan' and our photo had the caption 'Cashman on the town with a "friend"'.

It was another snide piece so off I went to see our astute lawyer Paul Stanley. He always advised me to ignore their reportage, to give them time as one day they would stray over the line. This time they had. It was libellous. Not for the last time we issued proceedings against Murdoch's News International. They printed an apology and made an out-of-court financial settlement. We were thrilled because we had finally smacked News International on the nose for when they had outed Paul and revealed where we lived. It was a doubly delicious victory because I hated Murdoch's empire and the further dumbing down of the press, and Paul Stanley and I loathed what Murdoch had done to the trade unions.

Another time when we issued proceedings against the *Sun*, someone from their legal department rang Paul Stanley to say that the journalists wanted me to know they 'didn't believe what they wrote'. For me that made it worse and we pressed for higher damages. Yet money was never the problem for them: it was our insistence that they include the words 'no truth whatsoever' in their statement. They would offer more money to keep those words out. But we were always insistent, and in every apology they remained.

Then there was the famous kiss.

It was the first gay kiss on a British soap, and it caused outrage when it arrived in 1987. As I left the scene I gave Barry a farewell peck on the forehead.

For Gary Hailes and me it wasn't a big thing. We hardly noticed it in the script and when we recorded it there was no discussion. It simply arose from the reality of these two men and their relationship. It was not imposed. Neither was there any discussion prior to transmission. It was merely another scene. Maybe we were too firmly inside the 'factory mentality' and we couldn't judge how it would be viewed outside. Julia and Tony must have known, but they never said.

In the heady anti-gay, AIDS-plague hysteria it smacked the opposition in the face. The phone lines to the BBC were beseiged; the protest mail piled in; the tabloids misrepresented it as sexual content – and the moral bonfire was ignited. The reaction was nasty. Mary Whitehouse wrote another letter for Julia's wall, the radio jocks spewed their disgust and the BBC did their best to ignore it all.

Later that week another brick came through our window. The bedroom window, just after two o'clock in the morning.

I started travelling by car, a second-hand red Vauxhall Astra, which really confused the public, who thought we were all driving Porsches. I was happy on public transport but Julia had begged me not to continue using it. When I asked why, she just replied that I should make things easier for myself.

I kept a careful eye on my 'fan' letters; yes, there were some unkind ones, nothing really unpleasant though, or so I thought. Unbeknown to me the BBC kept the worst and most threatening ones in case I got upset! Indeed, it wasn't long before my name was added to a 'hit list' of a far-right organisation. The car seemed safer.

Through all the homophobia Julia and the BBC stood firm. They never gave way to tabloid hysteria, the 'AIDS/HIV gay plague' mentality or the bullying politicians. To my knowledge Julia was only once pressured to cut parts of Colin and Barry's episode. As usual it was tabloid misinformation, this time from the *Daily Star*. The front-page banner headline read 'FILTH' and the byline: 'Get this off our TV now'. Alongside was a photograph of me smiling out at an enraged public. It created a nervousness in the upper echelons of the BBC. When I next arrived at the studio the front gate security told me I had been summoned to see Julia.

On my way to her office I passed Leslie Grantham. He called out to me in the huge long corridor that separated us from the office block at Neptune House. 'Oi,' he said. 'I've just been up to see Rosa Klebb [his nickname for Julia] and I've been told I've gotta wait until you've seen her.'

I merely shrugged as we passed but he continued.

'What kind of place is this – where poofs take preference over murderers?' He sauntered off without waiting for a reply.

Only Leslie could get away with saying that.

Once I was in her office, Julia immediately rang the executive on speaker and asked him to repeat the request he had made before my arrival. He refused to have the conversation with me present, so she picked up the receiver and said that the episode would go out unedited, with the Barry and Colin scenes, or she would resign.

As far as I knew they never challenged her again over our storylines. I felt safe working with her and I felt proud of the work we were doing. Everything was going well, but the tabloids never let up on their moral outrage or homo/AIDS-phobia; in fact as more and more people died of AIDS-related illnesses, so the venom increased. Tucked away in our studio in Elstree we just got on with it, day in day out, script after script, and we watched the viewing figures go through the roof, each episode working to normalise the experience of LGBT+ people, and to represent them with humanity and nuance. The show's popularity seemed unstoppable and our viewing figures for the episodes on Christmas Day 1986 pipped the Queen's Christmas Message by a few million. According to newspaper sources 'she was not happy', but Princess Diana – a huge fan of the show – had been 'delighted'. It seemed there wasn't a dark cloud on the horizon, but I was unaware of what was happening in a small committee room in Parliament. Mrs Thatcher and I were about to draw swords again – albeit at a distance – and I was about to test the patience of the BBC.

36

During the eighteen months that I had been on *EastEnders* UK party politics had become harsher and nastier, stirred by the tabloids in particular. Anyone in public life supporting the Labour Party was labelled part of the 'loony left'.

I became involved in the 1987 general election campaign alongside other well-known actors, including Ben Elton, Sue Johnston, Jill Gascoine and Miriam Karlin. A large group gathered at the Free Trade Hall in Islington to support Neil and Glenys Kinnock, with a very young Lenny Henry among us and members of the cast from *EastEnders*. During the campaign I had a request from the Labour press office to go on LBC radio and defend the party's election manifesto. I reread the manifesto the night before and turned up the next day at LBC to see the legendary comedy actor Kenneth Williams sitting in reception. That was when I learnt Kenneth was appearing for the Conservative Party. The SDP were to be defended by Robert Powell, of *Jesus of Nazareth* fame.

We sat waiting for Robert, who was late, while Kenneth, agitated, wailed incessantly: '*Gnawwww*, punctuality is the politeness of kings. Where is he?' It was tiresome, but I too disliked unpunctuality.

Eventually Robert arrived and the three of us sat round a microphone – the poor interviewer trying to get a word in – as we spoke about and defended our parties. It was virtually impossible to debate with Kenneth. He made his point, then proceeded to talk across you with camp comic brilliance, or undermine you with a series of imitations of a castrated cat. At one point he went into an oration about empowering the individual, arguing that Mrs Thatcher was lifting people up, giving them their power.

Pleased with himself and our gobsmacked faces, he then paused and smiled.

I leant into the microphone and quietly reminded him that there were over one million people unemployed who had no economic power. These people had not been 'lifted up'; they had been dispossessed.

'Pardon?' he stuttered, in total disbelief.

So I had the brilliant opportunity to repeat it.

Suddenly it sounded like a fire alarm was going off as a wail started in his throat, rose through his mouth and was emitted from the flaring nostrils with the words: 'Lies. Lies. Wicked Labour lies.'

He replied the same thereafter to every point I made. At the end of the interview he told me he was having terrible trouble with his bowels: 'It's like electricity – *zing*!' and added: 'Like a thousand volts – shooting through 'em. Can you imagine?'

I couldn't. He then swiftly disappeared into his waiting car, casting something behind him about how Mr Powell might be punctual in future. Not all such debates would be as amusing.

In the newspapers, politics and daytime chat shows the obsession with AIDS/HIV was alarming – 'AIDS is the Wrath of God, says vicar' (the *Sun*), 'Britain threatened by gay virus plague' (*Mail on Sunday*) – all ramming home the threat posed by the 'gay plague'. Our pubs and bars were raided by police wearing pink marigold gloves to prevent any infection. The government campaign to deal with the false reportage was singularly noteworthy in attempting to tackle the ignorance being encouraged by the tabloids. Some individuals suspected of being gay or of living with HIV/AIDS were hounded from their homes, their windows smashed and graffiti daubed on their walls. But the gay, bisexual and lesbian community and our straight allies rallied round, giving support, opening hospices, volunteering, holding candlelit vigils. We were a community under siege and we protected one another as best we could.

Along with many others I did gala benefits and fundraising events, and visited hospitals and hospices to try and brighten up the lives of HIV positive patients and those of their carers. The utter loneliness and terror of it all hit me one day when I walked into a hospital room on a visit and lying in the bed was one of my friends. He hadn't had the courage to tell anyone he was HIV positive. I promised him I would not reveal his secret, and sat on his bed feeling totally powerless.

Some weeks later when he died I was one of only a handful who knew. His funeral took place near his parents' home in Sussex. A quiet, ordinary boy who faced an extraordinary death. Some friends were more open about their HIV status, but many others simply disappeared to die with exceptional dignity surrounded by love. I never got used to the homo/AIDS-phobia of the media; I was always shocked by their disregard for the communities, the individuals and the families it was affecting. Ignorance and hatred exact a price, often paid by those least able to.

Paul was young with his life ahead of him, so he tried his very best to rise above it, to get out and enjoy a life that needed living. He had found himself, and he loved his space. Which was just as well because our relationship, now in its fifth year, was going through another difficult phase.

Our working lives kept us apart, and when we were together it became tense because of the pressure on us both. At weekends we would have Sunday together before he left to go on tour again. Sometimes I would drive up to a theatre to collect him on the Saturday night or wait at home for him to arrive in the early hours. It was there that I saw how the show gave him a sense of being, an identity that wasn't linked to me, and a company where he was regarded as second to none. The work was hard, but the audience reaction and the fans made it worthwhile for him. I had my company too, at Elstree, and as usual I lived for my work. It gave me a purpose, especially as our relationship seemed to be in decline.

Christmas was approaching, which meant a break in Paul's tour, and neither of us wanted to spend it with our families – we had grown away from that – so Paul decided on a holiday in Florida, where hopefully we could reconnect. Luckily it worked.

We had a crazy time in the gay bars, clubs and restaurants of Key West, where on the infrequent cold days when the furs came out the smell of mothballs mingled with Chanel. In this paradise the term 'hot tub' took on a whole new meaning, especially after midnight.

One very late night we were cycling back to our apartment when we saw a man dressed as Father Christmas coming towards us on a bike. Paul and I were so drunk that we were literally bouncing off the walls as we pedalled along the pavement. I raised my hand like a demented cop and we stopped Santa. He was young and very attractive. Compliments of the season were exchanged, then I heard myself saying: 'Santa, would you like to come down our chimney?' And, it being Christmas, he didn't refuse.

We left Key West with many new friends – Paul always made them everywhere – and a renewed strength in our relationship. We had rediscovered one another and the enjoyment of just being together and laughing. I had forgotten just how much he enjoyed life, and holidays!

Back in London I leafed through the papers and was amazed to read in *Capital Gay*, a free gay newspaper, about an anti-gay law that had been introduced into a local government bill just prior to the Christmas break. It seemed unbelievable. The intentions of the amendment were clear, the wording spelt it out:

> A local authority shall not promote homosexuality
> or publish material with the intention of promoting
> homosexuality, a local authority shall not promote the
> teaching in any maintained school of the acceptability of
> homosexuality as a pretend family relationship.

The Clause was seen by many as a reaction to the positive campaigning and financial support given to 'gay groups' by primarily left-leaning Labour local authorities, following the media and right-wing political hysteria surrounding HIV/AIDS. It had been introduced during the committee stage of the bill, just as the Labouchere Amendment, which criminalised homosexuality, had been introduced almost a hundred years before.

'Clause 28' had its origins in a private members' bill that passed through the House of Lords and was then picked up by MP Jill Knight (later Dame, then Baroness) but it failed to pass before the 1987 general election. Fellow Conservative MP David Wilshire joined Jill Knight when it was introduced after the election and they received the backing of the government, religious bodies and the tabloids. The intention was clear: to prevent any open discussion of homosexuality, particularly within schools, to restrict information on the subject, and to counter any support or sympathy for the gay, bisexual or lesbian communities. It was an attempt to drive us underground and isolate us from any mainstream support. We were under attack from all sides.

The reasoning for the proposed law was skewed, discriminatory and misleading. It was suggested that action was needed in order to protect young children from homosexuals and homosexual 'lessons'. The press and the bill's supporters referred to two books which became infamous – Danish author Susanne Bösche's *Jenny Lives with Eric and Martin*, about a young girl with gay parents, and *The Milkman's on His Way* by David Rees, a coming-out novel about a young teen's fantasy – which were falsely reported as being given to children in order to proselytise and promote homosexuality. The other protest from the right wing was that gays and lesbians were – shock horror – getting specific services at the 'ratepayers' expense': completely ignoring the fact that we were 'ratepayers' too.

The Clause's viciousness, its stereotyping of gays as a threat to children and families, was of its time: it was aided by the carefully crafted popular myth that equated homosexuality with paedophilia and dubious hyper-sexuality. The introduction of the amendment surprised everyone except the government. For a very brief period the Labour opposition supported it too, when their local government spokesperson stated that they 'would have no problem' with the amendment.

Mrs Thatcher had set the national tone in her Tory party conference speech in October 1987 when she declared: 'Children who need to be taught to respect traditional moral values are being taught that they have an inalienable right to be gay ... all of those children are being cheated of a sound start in life. A sound start.' The delegates applauded and AIDS-related hysteria continued to rise.

It was hard to believe that this amendment was real; it made very little sense and the sentiment behind it was very dangerous: here was a government actively promoting discrimination. A demonstration against the amendment was scheduled to take place in January. I put the paper down and said nothing. I knew deep in my heart that as a gay man, especially playing a gay role on TV, I would never be able to live with myself if I sat back and did nothing. I needed to be on that protest march.

The march was on a Saturday, leaving London's Embankment at midday. I had requested time off so I could attend it, without telling anyone why. But when the schedule came I was still down to rehearse. On the day in question I drove into work and talked to the one person who I knew could sort it out: June Brown. I told her what it was about and that all I needed was a couple of hours to get to London for the start of the march, and then I'd get back. Together we went to see the director and it was agreed, so long as I was back for two o'clock.

'Be careful Mike,' she said, 'and don't get arrested.'

What was incredible was that June and I were at opposite ends of the political spectrum. She was a 'One Nation Tory'; I was 'terrible Mike' who was out on the general election campaign supporting Labour and Neil Kinnock. In the 1987 election, when I told her that I had been out to vote, June replied that she had too in order to cancel me out. Nonetheless we developed a deep friendship. She loved Paul, and instinctively knew that my success was difficult for him. On screen the chemistry of Bible-bashing chain-smoking Dot and gay Colin worked. We were the 'odd couple' of Albert Square. We were also the odd couple of Elstree.

So, thanks to June, and without telling Paul because I saw no need to worry him, I jumped on a train to London. I wasn't prepared for the huge numbers when I reached the Thames Embankment. I tried to blend in, but 'Colin' kept being spotted and people thanked me for being there. The American play-wright Martin Sherman took me to the 'Actors' section' of the march: this was actually the Arts Lobby, a group of people from the industry who met at the Drill Hall theatre, off Tottenham Court Road, and planned media campaigns and opposition to the Clause. Cordelia Ditton, Carole Woddis, Debbo Ballard and Richard Sandells were the powers behind it. The consensus was that I should be at the front, so I was led back through a sea of people, and calls of 'Colin!', and found myself alongside others clutching a banner that had been thrust into my hand.

The crowd was growing; you could sense the urge to get out onto the streets to shout our determination to fight. Standing there, waiting to march, I felt proud and humbled that so many cared. The emotions tumbled one upon the other. The moment was only broken when a journalist thrust his camera at me and said: 'Mr Cashman, would you talk to TV news?'

The demonstration of over 12,000 people set off peacefully but then erupted into a riot and an attempt to storm 10 Downing Street. The march was temporarily halted by the police and, as they grappled with the protesters, I took my cue to jump onto the tube at Westminster back to Elstree and rehearsals, as promised. When my mum and dad watched the news later that day, my dad sighed and said: 'I don't mind him being gay, but does he have to go on the bleeding news about it?'

Overnight I became a media representative for the oppos-ition to Clause 28, along with Ian McKellen. I went with Ian to meetings at the Arts Lobby or the Star Bar in Heaven (the club) – thrown into the frontline of this battle alongside many others, including the lesbians who abseiled into the House of Lords during the debate, and the people who had chained themselves to newscasters live on BBC TV. Ian and I lived in the same part of London and we began night-time plotting on the phone: he had great media savvy, he was kind and, though I hadn't seen him for years, he welcomed me into the world of activism like an old friend. The Clause brought together a powerful spectrum of opposition from the arts, academia, politics, theatre, education and many other industries. The wording of the Clause was so general that it was thought it could be used to censor the arts and culture as well as to negatively affect education.

During the long period of campaigning against Clause 28, the BBC's patience was tested. Julia never said anything about it, one gay actress said I should think about my career, but quite a few others congratulated me. I did notice, however, that the number of episodes featuring Colin seemed to be diminishing. One day when we were filming in the Queen Vic, Mike Reid, the comedian who had joined the show as Frank Butcher, ad-libbed as I walked through the pub door: 'Here he comes, Clause 28!' It survived into the broadcast – a great example of life and soap coming together on screen. When I signed my new BBC contract in 1988 I told them it would be my last. I would be leaving when it came to an end in 1989. A couple of senior executives tried to convince me to stay, but I knew it was time to move on.

Before I left, though, there would be further media and political controversy with another kiss – this time on the lips – in January 1989. The *Sun* led the outraged calls against the 'homosexual love scene between the yuppie poofs' and quoted two Tory politicians who said that 'if the BBC can't stop showing these perverted practices during family viewing time then *EastEnders* should be banned or scrapped altogether'.

With this second kiss I expected the outrage, but I didn't care: I was proud that far from climbing down on the depiction of the love between two people of the same sex we were actually building on it, perhaps even promoting it.

Meanwhile, despite the hostile media environment, opposition to the Clause was growing. Further marches held in London and Manchester attracted over 20,000 protesters. At one I introduced Ian to Trina Cornwall and Wendy Martin who ran the production company Twentieth Century Vixen out of a council flat in

Deptford. They would work with us on several benefits over the coming years. Ian and I also met Jenni Wilson and Lisa Power who led OLGA (Organisation for Lesbian and Gay Action against the Clause) and who would later become pivotal in founding Stonewall.

There were fundraising and awareness-raising events and galas, but for me the high point was 'Before the Act', a benefit organised by Ian, Martin Sherman, Sean Mathias and myself at the Piccadilly Theatre, which sold out within days. It was conceived to demonstrate that if you banned the so-called 'promotion of homosexuality' by local authorities then artistic works by lesbians, gay men or bisexuals could legitimately disappear from theatres, arts centres, concert halls and libraries, let alone schoolrooms. Richard Eyre agreed to be the overall director, with individual directors working on their specific contributions. The show was a series of scenes from plays, sketches, monologues, songs and pieces of music but everything performed had to have been written or composed by a lesbian, gay man, or a bisexual. The list of actors and directors was phenomenal: Dame Peggy Ashcroft, Tom Stoppard, Judi Dench, Harold Pinter, the Pet Shop Boys, Gary Oldman, Patrick Stewart, John Thaw, Sheila Hancock, Stephen Fry, Richard Griffiths, Ian Charleson, Paul Eddington, Timothy West and Michael Gambon, among so many others.

It was one thing to perform the material of the dead, such as Dame Ethel Smyth, Joe Orton, Tchaikovsky, A. E. Housman, Ma Rainey, Noël Coward and Oscar Wilde, but it was quite another to feature the living in our show. Gentle letters (there were no emails then) had to be sent to writers and composers enquiring whether it would be appropriate to include their material given the 'gay theme'.

Martin Sherman had the idea that the entire cast might end the night singing 'There's a Place for Us' from *West Side Story*. Leonard Bernstein replied to Ian's letter that he was proud of the bisexual period of his life and so it was fine by him. The lyricist (and composer) Stephen Sondheim refused to give his consent due to the 'exclusivity of the evening', adding that if we were to make it more 'ecumenical' it would be okay. (I wickedly suggested that we simply hum the tune at the end and let the question be posed as to why we couldn't sing the words.) Martin and I quickly set about trying to find an alternative American musical theatre composer or lyricist who was 'out' and whose material we could use – dead or alive. However, apart from the British Sandy Wilson, who was already on board, there was no one. Musical theatre may have been chock-a-block with gay men, but few were 'out', which, as Martin commented, told you a lot about Broadway, especially with the AIDS epidemic hitting the industry.

A raft of 'known-to-be-gay' performers were suddenly 'unavailable' or heading 'out of town' for the weekend – at one point, Martin believed there might be one bus collecting them all. But to be fair it was not a good time to come out. If you did you faced severe discrimination and the synonymy with HIV.

Others were kind and considerate in their letters but still said 'no', such as Sir John Gielgud and Sir Alec Guinness – who went so far as to condemn the Clause and enclosed a cheque in his letter to Ian. I arrived one day as Ian was opening the letters. He opened the refusal from Sondheim and, saddened, passed it to me. As I was reading it Ian let out a cheer and punched the air. Beaming, he handed me Alan Bennett's reply. Alan thanked Ian for his letter and indicated that he knew what Ian was 'alluding' to. He had faced the same question in Cologne some weeks before, 'and my reply is now as it was then: I have had a bit of both in my life, but not quite enough of either. I would love to be included.'

A cheer indeed.

Bennett would outdo himself by appearing on the night to introduce Dame Joan Plowright in one of his 'Talking Heads'. He told the packed theatre that he had received a letter from Ian McKellen about his sexual 'proclivities' and he had come to the conclusion that he 'was rather like a man who had dragged himself across the Sahara and when you get to the other side they say would you like "Perrier" or "Malvern"?'

A specially written sketch by Tony Holland for *EastEnders* and *Brookside* cast members was another great hit, but nothing could beat the final line-up of artists, poets and writers. The government had picked a fight and we had signalled that we were up for it. The evening raised over £15,000, which went to anti-Clause 28 organisations, but the significance of what the artistic community had done had far-reaching consequences that would ultimately lead to the founding of the LGBT+ rights group Stonewall.

37

During the campaign against the Clause, Ian and I became close. He had the ability, the passion and the address book to engage so many people in the fight. We talked tactics late into the night. We took to the airwaves together, or separately. I capitalised on my fame from *EastEnders*, while Ian used his not inconsiderable influence as the greatest Shakespearean actor of his generation – and he had a CBE from the Queen. We were a perfect double act: Shakespeare and Soap, and without competing egos. The media was keen to have us. The famous American chat show host Phil Donahue broadcast three shows from London and he invited us to appear for a Clause 28 special.

Early on in the campaign Ian took part in a lively BBC radio discussion with the editor of the *Sunday Telegraph*, Peregrine Worsthorne. Worsthorne had vigorously defended Clause 28 and in a signed editorial had suggested that homosexuals had brought intolerance on themselves as they had become 'a bold and brazen, proselytising cult'. The discussion was highly charged and Ian cut the ground from underneath Worsthorne when he said: 'I think it's [Section 28] offensive to anyone who is, like myself, homosexual...'

Ian had 'come out' on national radio; it was a brave and stupendous move, but he thought he had better tell his stepmother Gladys and sister Jean before it was broadcast. When he finally managed to get the words out to tell Gladys, her response was that she already knew, and they moved on to other matters. Now he was out it meant that Ian's campaigning, like my own, was deeply personal as well as political. Armistead Maupin, the writer of *Tales of the City*, had encouraged Ian to 'come out' and remained a rock for him. Others warned him it would destroy his career.

As I now knew Ian well, I was able to ask him something that had stuck in my mind for many years: why he had snubbed me when we worked at the RSC, albeit in different productions. I reminded him that I had tried to reintroduce myself following a dinner party but he had virtually ignored me. 'What did I do?' I asked.

He was incredulous. 'What did you do? You know what you did.'

Then he explained. The night of the dinner I had flirted out-rageously with his boyfriend and it had been reciprocated. They then went home, had the most awful row and later split up. I was mortified, I hardly remembered the incident and told Ian that. Then it began to dawn on me.

'Wait a minute,' I said.

'You admit it, then?' he smiled.

'Ian! Oh Ian. I was after you!'

He laughed.

I told him that it was him I fancied and I thought that the best way to get to him was to flatter and charm the boyfriend. Lovely though the boyfriend was. He waved the subject away and we got stuck in to campaigning.

But despite the brilliance of the opposition against the Clause it passed into law, though with an important amendment that Ian and others had argued for. The amended phrase had just one new word: 'A local authority shall not *intentionally* promote homo-sexuality.' It had been blunted but it was still a defeat as on 24 May 1988 Clause 28 became law as Section 2A of the Local Government Act. We had lost and it was devastating; it seemed incredible that despite having won the argument we had lost the battle.

There was no time for self-pity. Besides I had a new idea. The public momentum and support we had worked up during the cam-paign was still there. The anger had not gone away and we had to build on it. So, one Sunday morning I left Paul in bed – he had arrived in the early hours from one of the *Rocky* dates – and drove the five minutes down to Ian's home on the banks of the Thames. The house had served as informal campaign headquarters over the previous months. Here his two phones were commandeered, our Filofaxes raided for volunteers and donations and his wine cellar drunk dry.

We sat out on his terrace as the Thames coursed by and I told him that we had to form an organisation to make sure another Section 28 never happened again. I went over how the campaign had been so successful, so well organised and media savvy. I tried to push more buttons, reminding him that I had good contacts in the Labour leadership, and that the Tories were still keen to seduce him, including the local government minister Michael Howard. We knew all the right people and the timing felt good. He listened politely but no conclusions were formed and we left it there. I went home to one of Paul's afternoon dinners.

The following Sunday it was Ian's turn to ring me, so I drove down to see Douglas Slater, our mole in the government Whips' Office of the House of Lords. I sat and listened as Douglas outlined an idea similar to the one I'd put to Ian the week before. Ian asked me what I thought. This was the day the most successful European lesbian and gay lobbying organisation, Stonewall, was conceived.

We had an idea but now we needed others involved and that wasn't going to be easy. It was necessary to capture the moment and work quickly, so we threw ourselves at it like maniacs. Ian was better at managing his time, and I rode on the back of excitement and enthusiasm. I hurled everything I had at it to the detriment of my relationship with Paul, squeezing him out of my life once again. I said a sad goodbye to *EastEnders* – though not to Colin, who would always remain with me – and drove out of the studio for the last time. The show had changed my life in so many different ways, and despite it all there was nothing that I regretted. I knew it was time to move on if I had any future life left as an actor so obviously associated with one programme, one character and now one issue. Appearing in a soap was considered to be artistic suicide, but I didn't care. I had loved the show before I went into it and loved it even more as I was leaving. I had experienced unimaginable opportunities, the curt exchanges on set with Princess Diana when I had mentioned my friend Stephen Barry, her husband's valet, a late-night dinner invitation from a royal prince, standing up to the Thatcher government, championing HIV activists and people living with AIDS, and meeting some of the sexiest men in London.

Now it was all about to change as I went on a national tour with post-war film sweetheart Marius Goring. Marius had been a leading actor in films such as *The Red Shoes*, and an even bigger television star in the sixties, and now had the biggest blue-rinse following in the country. At certain matinees women could be heard swooning as he came on stage. We were doing a classic Agatha Christie, and by slightly altering the end of the play – the management got the trustees of the estate drunk on the opening night so no one noticed – we had the audience jumping out of their seats.

Marius and I were good on stage but we were not a good political mix. He was a right-wing, libertarian Tory and had supported Clause 28 when the actors' trade union, Equity, had debated it. At the press conferences around the country I talked about the awful Tory government and how Labour could make a difference while he waxed lyrical about the play, the acting and our marvellous cast. In the end we became deeply fond of each other because of our differences, not despite them.

So there I was: away from home, away from Paul, and on the one free day a week when we should be together I was chasing my latest obsession: I would commit to Stonewall meetings that went on all day, or evening. In the end he asked me whether it was worth him coming home at all. We were in a destructive cycle; I resented the pressure he put on me, and he resented my ignoring him. It couldn't last.

Eventually he brought in a lover. What made it worse was that I understood and just accepted it, secretly hoping that they would forget about me.

After many months of cajoling and charming key people we were finally in a position to go public about Stonewall's ambitions. It had been an exhausting year of personality clashes and verbal fights across boardroom tables. A year of chairing and attending interminable meetings and sub-meetings, of minutes, action notes and attacks from some LGBT+ activists and gay media. However, in May 1989, a year after Section 28 became law, we publicly launched Stonewall at Limehouse, with me as the founding chair. We also set up the Iris Trust, an associated charity, and Ian became its chair, with Pam St Clement on the board. The thinking behind this was twofold: 'closets' would not give to a known gay organisation but they could give to Iris, and charities could not work for political change. But Stonewall could.

Paul's two and a half years with the *Rocky Horror Show* finally came to an end. He was now at home and I was either on tour or absent at meetings. His first lover had long gone but soon another moved in, the incredibly handsome and hitherto 'straight' Essex lad, Hudson.

Poor Hudson was not prepared for life with Cottingham, let alone me. He wasn't out to anyone and now he was living with the other half of one of the most famous gays in the TV village. He almost wore a veil to go off to work in the City. But Paul gradually teased Hudson out, dropping him off at his City offices and blowing him a kiss goodbye, and essentially gave him the strength to be himself, to feel his own worth. Not worth within a hidden relationship. Paul had learnt the difficult way and he wanted it to be easier for others. It worked for the three of us. Hudson did ask how I could let Paul go 'off with someone else' if I loved him. It was difficult for him to understand that if you really loved someone, rather than wanting to possess them, then you had to have the courage to let that person go and not tighten your grip. Yet while Paul could manage his love life, his career was unravelling.

Soon after *Rocky*, he went on a tour of Stephen Sondheim's *Sweeney Todd*. But the production was doomed and closed after one week in Blackpool when the set collapsed and the management with it. In the same week that he lost his job his agent went bust. I tried to help him through this difficult time but it was June Brown who really did it. She convinced him to work more on *EastEnders*, as a background artist and as a regular, with featured parts. Now that I was no longer on the show he had his own distinct identity, and they loved his honesty, his lack of bullshit and his loyalty in the face of challenge.

While I toured I still had to work on Stonewall, which was an idea with a purpose and a board, but which had no substantial funds for the creation of an organisation with staff and offices. We knew that independent funding would be crucial to Stonewall's success. Section 28 had put the curse on any lesbian and gay organisation receiving public funding, but our intention had always been to challenge Thatcherism by doing it with private funding. If all they understood was money and power, then so be it.

When I left *EastEnders* I bought the rights to *Bent* by Martin Sherman, the harrowing and uplifting play of two gay men in a Nazi work camp and the love that sustains and liberates them. It had been my intention to take the play on tour, but with anti-LGBT+ sentiment still high, certainly outside London, I was advised to put the plans on hold. Investors would be impossible to get.

So one night when Paul, Ian and Sean Mathias and I were talking about raising private funding for Stonewall, Paul said: 'Why don't you and Ian do *Bent*?'

Ian's response was that he was far too old, and it had been ten years since he had done the original production with Tom Bell. I thought it was a genius idea but said nothing.

'Amazing,' said Sean, 'but how do we sell it to Martin?'

'But I'm too old,' protested Ian.

Sean fixed Ian with both eyes: 'Course you're too old. And so is he,' he said, tossing his head in my direction. 'But after that campaign against Clause Fucking 28, you two are a director's dream team. So you're doing it.'

Ian remained silent. And there was still Martin to convince.

We decided to take Martin to dinner at Joe Allen's. The plan was that we were all meeting there to think up a benefit for Stonewall, and at the right time Paul would pitch up as if it was a brand new idea. Though I had the touring rights to *Bent* I did not hold West End rights, nor the option on them, and Martin was protective – quite rightly – of his gem. We knew we had to play it carefully.

The conversation flowed between us but the three of us were obsessed with getting to our common goal. The dinner was nearly over, when Paul innocently asked on cue: 'If you want to raise money, why don't you and Ian do *Bent*?'

Martin looked up from his vanilla ice cream with hot fudge sauce.

'*Bent*?'

There was a short pause.

Paul nodded. We looked at him and then across at Martin, who shrugged, pulled another spoonful of dessert towards his mouth and replied: 'Fabulous idea.'

And that was it. Now we just had to get a theatre, and other actors.

38

We rehearsed in London while I was touring – at one time commuting daily between Liverpool and London – and we opened for one night only at the Adelphi Theatre in London on Sunday 25 June 1989. It was a star-studded cast, led by Ian, Ralph Fiennes, Richard E. Grant, Nathaniel Parker, Alex Jennings, Ian Charleson and me. The play was produced by Trina and Wendy of Twentieth Century Vixen, who badgered, borrowed and stole to get the show on from their Deptford council flat. We pressured our agents, accountants and various others to buy space in the programme to boost our fundraising. I also offered to ask Cameron Mackintosh for help.

Cameron was the West End's most successful producer; *Les Mis*, *Cats* and *Phantom of the Opera* were among his prestigious offerings. I had known him professionally for some years and had worked on some of the many benefits that he had produced and supported for the AIDS/HIV charities. My then agent, Barry Burnett, who knew everyone who was anyone in the showbiz world, arranged a meeting. In the plush offices I told Cameron about our production of *Bent* and Stonewall's aims. After about five minutes he intervened and asked about our production costs.

'Ten thousand,' I replied.

'Right. I will give you five.'

'Thousand?' I asked hesitantly.

He nodded and smiled, and I told him that I had prepared to pitch a lot harder. He shook his head and said I didn't need to. I left ten minutes later promising to keep him updated.

On the Sunday of the performance we were still rehearsing the last scene of the play on stage when the theatre manager, at his wits' end, demanded that he be allowed to open the theatre to the waiting public. But Sean would have none of it and sent him packing. With the audience spilling onto the road outside and blocking the traffic of the West End – apparently the first time this had happened since a Judy Garland concert in the 1960s – Sean had to relent.

Backstage in our dressing rooms the excitement and the nerves mounted as we heard the audience taking their seats. Just after 7.30pm the house lights dimmed and the curtain went up. We stepped into that dark arena and as the performance proceeded you could sense the emotion building and building. It was one of those rare, magical moments in theatre when the actors and the audience become one.

As the lights went out on the final scene a silence descended over the auditorium that I had never experienced before. It seemed to go on for ages. Then a shout went up, and a standing ovation erupted that went on for over ten minutes, which allowed Martin Sherman, at Sean's insistence, to make his way from a box in the circle and get onto the stage. After which another ovation followed.

It could not have gone any better: we raised all the money we needed to hire our executive director and made a staggering profit of £30,000 in just the one night. As promised I wrote to Cameron Mackintosh, and said how grateful we were that he had donated half our production costs, adding that no one had matched his generosity. By return of post he replied: 'Now your production costs are covered' – and enclosed another cheque for £5,000.

Paul's instinct about *Bent* had been spot on and Sean's judgement superb. The combination of Ian and me, the star casting, the message of the play, its reminders of where intolerance can lead, and the inspiration of Sean to flood the stage at one time with over 100 work-camp inmates, gave the production an eloquence and a grounding that shook the audience to the core.

That night we got well and truly drunk on complimentary champagne that 'the Vixen' had wrenched from a villain they knew in south London, and Sean and I talked about taking the show on tour. I had demonstrated that there was more to me than 'Colin', as fond as I was of him, and it would be wise to capitalise on it quickly.

On Tuesday morning Ian rang me at home. Richard Eyre had just phoned him and asked whether we would be interested in doing *Bent* at the National Theatre.

'You serious?'

Ian giggled and said he was indeed serious.

'The National?' I squeaked.

Paul looked across the room at me. I nodded to him and he came over and listened in on the call: Lord (Laurence) Olivier had been scheduled to perform in a play and his death that summer meant a slot had to be filled. It would be filled by us, and the Olivier family could not be happier.

So, weeks after the Berlin Wall came down, *Bent* opened at the Lyttelton Theatre on 19 January 1990. The location was incredible: just a few hundred yards along the River Thames from Parliament where Mrs Thatcher and her government had spent so much time and energy trying to prohibit the 'promotion of homosexuality'. And here we were doing it!

We had a successful but not uneventful few months at the National. On opening night, I was summoned to the stage door to find Miss Edna Davies, the ballet mistress from Scarborough, in the clutches of two security men. She had been found front of house scattering 'blessed witches salt' and muttering incantations to ward off evil critics. I convinced them that she wasn't mad and she was released into my charge. The salt obviously worked because the reviews were good. On another occasion it was the 'understudy business'; I had volunteered to cover Greta the drag queen. It was just a gesture to prove that we really were a collegiate company and it was feasible to play both parts in the same night. The gesture caught me out when I arrived at the theatre to be told I was going on! I played Greta for about five performances and I loved it, but I never offered to understudy again. The real fun was working with Ian and getting to know him as an actor as well as a friend.

When we eventually moved to the West End the excitement followed; for the first time in my life I saw my name in lights *above* the title. However, despite the reviews and the audiences loving it, the depressed economic situation – given expression in riots across the country against the much-hated poll tax – soon put paid to our run and after four months the neon lights were switched off and we closed.

When I wasn't working, Stonewall occupied my time. Now we had our first member of staff, executive director Tim Barnett, I had a workload to respond to. Tim wanted a hands-on chair who would attend meetings with him, introduce him to parliamentarians and effectively represent the organisation. Thankfully I had the time and the motivation to do so. At the beginning we operated on a financial shoestring and our office for a few months was a bedroom in Rectory Street, Islington. But eventually Tim Barnett's pleas for a professional set-up were heard and we relented. A couple of us opened our cheque books and we took the plunge and leased Stonewall's first tiny office, in Greycoat Place, Westminster. It felt like a real milestone. We were all so proud.

The political fallout from the poll tax riots was the end of Mrs Thatcher's reign. She had been in office too long and there were not enough people close to her who felt able to stand up to her. The Tories were galvanised by the prospect of electoral defeat and after a 'stalking horse' started the leadership challenge, Michael Heseltine declared himself a candidate. John Major, Thatcher's quiet chancellor of the exchequer, was suddenly missing with toothache. Finally, he declared that he was standing for the leadership and, in a battle she eventually knew she was going to lose, Thatcher stepped aside and left Downing Street in tears.

A strange twist of fate played out in the dying embers of Mrs Thatcher's tenure: Ian's name was put forward for a knighthood. He was on an international tour as Richard III and watching Thatcher fighting for her political life on television. His hotel phone rang, and he was surprised to learn that it was the prime minister's office at Downing Street. They explained that they had not received a reply to the letter regarding the knighthood, and now needed an answer. At first Ian thought it was a hoax, but it soon became clear that this was not the case. Then he saw some irony that as Mrs Thatcher was departing government her office was chasing him about the honour. Maybe she had thought it was time to promote homosexuality too.

The knighthood was eventually announced but it was not universally welcomed: there was trenchant opposition from filmmaker and artist Derek Jarman (he wrongly considered it acquiescence to Thatcher's anti-gay stance) among others. When Ian took that phone call from Downing Street he immediately consulted three friends, including me. My reaction to the news was enthusiastic and ecstatic. I told him to accept it, that he could use it for the 'cause' and I added that he bloody well deserved it for his talent alone. But the newspapers, led by the *Guardian*, perpetuated the criticism of the knighthood. They loved pitching one gay man against a better and more deserving queer. It was deeply unpleasant, hurtful and very personal.

Because the issue needed balance, Martin Sherman and others organised a letter to be published in the *Guardian*. It opened with the phrase: 'As gay and lesbian artists ...' and went on to lend our support wholeheartedly to Ian and his decision to accept the honour. I was given the job of getting a few names on board; one of them was Cameron Mackintosh.

We were working within a tight timeframe and I was struggling to get an answer either way from the Mackintosh office. Ten minutes before our deadline I was getting desperate so I rang for the third time that day. Cameron's PA asked me to wait a minute, then came back and confirmed that Cameron would add his name. I was overjoyed; it was a real coup.

The next day, 9 January 1991, the letter was published and the *Guardian* ran a front-page story that Cameron Mackintosh had 'come out' as gay in support of Ian.

My phone rang very early. Cameron hadn't properly read the letter and was surprised – as was his family – by the outing. I had inadvertently revealed his private life and I felt terrible, but there was no bad feeling: he was stoical and gracious. When he was subsequently knighted in 1996 I wrote to congratulate him. He thanked me for my letter and said that it was nice that no one had had to come out this time!

With John Major now in power a few key jobs had shifted in Whitehall and there was now a handful of LGBT+ allies in various departments: politicians, civil servants and the staff of hugely influential lobbyist, Ian Greer. During a visit to the National Theatre, Ian cheekily asked the new prime minister if he might 'pop along to Downing Street to have a word about some "social issues"'. Major agreed and that September, Ian made his way to Number 10. It was the first time a sitting prime minister had publicly met an out gay activist and the meeting would have a profoundly positive effect.

Ian reported back to us that in his meeting with John Major he had raised concerns affecting the gay community: police harassment, the discriminatory criminal law and abusive press language; and then presented our draft 'Homosexual Equality Bill'. Major was relaxed and open and he indicated that civil servants would indeed work with Stonewall. As Ian left he suddenly got the attention of the media, who were awaiting the arrival of the French prime minister, Edith Cresson. Madame Cresson had caught the interest of the British press because she had said that 25 per cent of Englishmen were homosexual. Given that a famous, openly gay man was seen leaving Downing Street the media wanted to know what was going on. It was unknown whether Ian's presence confirmed Prime Minister Cresson's opinion, but our agenda, and Stonewall, made the evening news and the newspapers the following day.

The meeting was effective and showed that Stonewall, referred to by the press as a 'pressure group', would work with a Conservative government. It helped too that Ian looked part of the establishment and knew how to talk to the media. Civil servants quickly engaged with Tim Barnett and Stonewall, and though our Homosexuality Bill came to nothing John Major delivered on his promise swiftly by ending the ban on homosexuals serving in the intelligence services and the Foreign Office. It was Stonewall's first success and it mattered that it came from the highest level of government.

Months later another connection with John Major would set the precedent for equality: the media-savvy Edwina Currie.

39

Within a few months of becoming PM John Major had decided he'd had enough of the Eurosceptic right-wing 'bastards' who were rebelling over the European Union and the Treaty of Maastricht, and called a general election. It was fiercely contested and I hit the ground running for Neil Kinnock and the Labour Party. But now I had to strike a delicate balance. I could represent my own views but had to be careful to distinguish between them and the non-party-political position of Stonewall.

There were a couple of key Tories in Stonewall, Matthew Parris among them, but Tory confidence in the group was low, and people felt suspicious. Labour felt like a stronger ideological match as we had a similar equality agenda. As far as I was concerned achieving equality meant having a Labour government. Nothing else made sense as Neil Kinnock and Roy Hattersley, then deputy leader of the party, were now both committed to delivering equality. It was true that there were Neanderthals in Labour, but there seemed fewer than in the Tories, and some of the trade unions could be relied on for their support. In the years since the 1987 election Paul and I had worked closely with the Labour leadership team, building connections within the arts community, in particular. Paul spent his free time working with 'Arts for Labour' at party HQ, increasing support from famous actors that he knew or met, drawing on his contacts in the soaps and beyond. Working along-side Ken Follett we had produced a star-studded gala benefit in the West End to raise money and the profile of the party and Neil Kinnock.

In the immediate run-up to the 1992 election Paul worked full time with Ken in the 'celebrity unit', supplying famous names and faces to the campaign teams across the country. Meanwhile I was out on the road whenever I had the opportunity with Glenys Kinnock in Suffolk and Norfolk, or stumping the streets with candidates and activists. But the Tories and the tabloids threw everything at us, and busted us with the shadow chancellor John Smith's budget, dubbed 'Labour's tax Bombshell'. Nevertheless, it remained a time of hope and, after three terms of Tory rule, it seemed like it was our last chance for a Labour government.

Politically Paul and I were joined at the hip; he genuinely liked people and expected the best of them. He had no side either – he was the same person whoever he came into contact with and his authenticity was refreshing. Working passionately together was fun, and it was good for the relationship. At the celebrity unit he regaled colleagues with stories of sexual conquests. Ever curious as a writer, Ken Follett asked if Paul would mind guesstimating how many people he had slept with?

'Slept? Slept!' He paused and then replied: 'Not slept with many. But I've had sex with about a thousand.'

Ken was stunned into silence, mouthed the word 'thousand' and shook his head. The celebrated wordsmith was lost for words.

In the final days of the election Labour was ahead in the polls and Neil and Glenys asked us to join them at the eve of poll rally, on 8 April, at Neil's constituency in South Wales.

The sports hall was packed out. Sue Tully from *EastEnders* was there, and celebrated Labour peer Barbara Castle, and I spoke to the assembled crowd. Barbara had them cheering to the rafters as she denounced the Tories and talked of the brilliance of Neil as our future prime minister. Afterwards, at a small dinner, Neil confessed the polls were not as good as we had been led to believe, but despite what the Liberals were saying in public they were prepared to enter into a coalition with us. We went to bed the worse for drink, with bruised egos, but still hopeful that a change of government was imminent.

The public decided otherwise and John Major was returned as prime minister with an overall working majority. In the early hours of the morning Neil announced that he would step down as leader of the Labour Party once a new candidate had been chosen. Overnight our hopes were pulverised and we descended into weeks of depression. Before we said farewell I passed Neil a garish tie of mine that he'd admired. 'Now you're free,' I said, 'you can wear outrageous things like this.' He graciously accepted it but had the good sense to return it by post a few days later.

With the general election campaign out of the way and a Labour government no longer in sight it was clear that Stonewall had to really work up a strategy with the Conservative Party.

When John Smith took over from Neil Kinnock the celebrities were put on the back burner. We were given the distinct impression that the new leader wasn't keen on the 'Cheyne Walk set' – a reference to where our meetings were held at Ken and Barbara Follett's house. But during the election a stroke of luck happened. I was a guest on a live late-night television discussion hosted by the celebrated political journalist Vincent Hanna. Alongside me were moral crusader Mary Whitehouse, who had written all those letters to *EastEnders* about Colin's moral depravity, and the ex-chief rabbi, Lord Jakobovits. When I arrived and learnt that Jakobovits was fast losing his voice and that Mrs Whitehouse had such a bad attack of piles that she had to sit on an inflated rubber ring, it was the one time I thought that God might exist. Eventually his voice disappeared, as did the air in Mary's rubber ring, so they went home early and I was left alone.

At the end of the show I gave a last direct question to the remaining politicians: would you support an equal age of consent, I asked? Edwina Currie replied that she would. When we came off the air I told Edwina that she had made a promise on live TV and that I would hold her to it. She looked taken aback, smiled at me and said: 'Michael, I will not only vote for an equal age of consent, I will campaign for it. You have my word. Okay?'

She smacked of total and utter decency, and it was a promise that she would fulfil two years later, supported by Neil Kinnock.

With our post-election strategy agreed by the board it was important to keep Stonewall's profile prominent, as well as taking every opportunity to fundraise. Armistead Maupin came to London and put on a night for us at the Theatre Royal, Haymarket, which raised over £15,000. The Joseph Rowntree Trust kindly supported us with a one-off grant, but new sources of money were scarce. Then 'Eddie' came along.

One night in Joe Allen's a middle-aged man approached me out of the blue, thanked me for what I was doing, then thrust a cheque into my hand for £500. The payee's name was absent. I protested that I couldn't accept it but he walked away saying, 'it's to help the boys'. Thinking it might be a sting by a tabloid I asked the head waiter to endorse it to Crusaid, an HIV charity.

Paul and I saw Eddie again at Joe Allen's and we got to know him well. He was about fifty-five years old and had been round the block; he not only knew 'where the bodies were buried', he had probably put some of them there. A thoroughly decent man, he loved to create an air of mystery. He was also absolutely sincere, threw money around like confetti and would dispatch a lot of it to Stonewall. He had been a Labour councillor, and was now in 'business'.

Eddie and Paul got on well as fellow Liverpudlians, and he became a good friend to us despite his habit of appearing then disappearing just as quickly. There would be a call out of the blue to join him for dinner somewhere, or to inform us that he needed his driver to drop off a 'package'. Invariably it would be about £3,000 in £50 notes, which would be quickly dispatched to Stonewall. When we asked questions he merely replied he liked doing what he was able to do. Many years later, in a television programme, he 'blew the whistle' on a slush fund which he operated on behalf of a multinational company to grease the wheels of lucrative deals in the Middle East; unbeknown to the company he vasolined the wheels of equality too.

However, I had other fundraising ideas in my head, and that's when Paul and I decided to head for David Hockney and California.

40

As we had been out of work a couple of months Paul planned another of his holidays: life was becoming easier between us – we were getting on well again, and he kept me young! Paul decided on six weeks' travelling across America and all I had to do was turn up on time. As usual we started in New York, grabbed our dose of Broadway and musical theatre, then watched from the bars the depressed state of the gay community and the long shadows of AIDS and HIV, but also the growing activism of groups such as ACT UP and others that demanded action. Everywhere in Greenwich Village and the surrounding areas was graffiti and posters reminding us that 'SILENCE = DEATH'. People were dying in increasing numbers and there was a deep outpouring of anger. In the bars that were still open, people tried to lure themselves into distraction or denial, but it wasn't working for us. The spontaneity of sexual encounters had ended, now everything had to be calculated or negotiated. The safest sex was no sex at all, or simply fantasies in your head.

As predicted the holiday brought us slap bang together. Being in each other's company 24/7 worked and Paul loved having me all to himself; the affair with the live-in lover had faded away, but we were all still friends.

In LA we booked into our hotel, which turned out to be a whorehouse. The receptionist read the rules out clearly, emphasising that any guests we had over would have to leave their ID with him until they left. I protested at this intrusion but he arched an eyebrow and lisped: 'Mary, I've had people disappear in this place.' So we checked out and found a new hotel, the Ramada

Inn, in the gay district of West Hollywood. After we were settled in, I nervously called David Hockney's number.

A soft, warm Yorkshire voice answered with: 'Hallo?'

'David, this is Michael Cashman—' I had my script all ready but he interrupted.

'Hello love. I've been expecting your call. Why don't you come up for tea?'

We were buzzed through the front door of the house off Mulholland Drive. With its multicoloured rooms and gardens it was like stepping into one of the artist's paintings, except the famous pool was sadly absent of men diving into it. It was a feast for the eyes and senses.

We saw the dachshunds, Boogie and Stanley, before we saw David. Then we met John Fitzherbert, his gorgeous new cook who had just arrived from London and who would subsequently become David's long-term partner. David was welcoming, charming and funny, and conducted a running commentary on the worst excesses – 'well, all the excesses' – of the Thatcher government. A cigarette never far from his lips, within minutes we were whisked off to his vast studio. He was excited about his new electronic camera and, using it with the fax, photocopier and coloured pens, hey presto! He presented us with a multi-technique-produced painting and photograph, which he signed 'with love, David'.

Over tea I did the talking, but David wasn't interested in me. He couldn't take his eyes off Paul. I told him of our ambitions for Stonewall and finally got his undivided attention when I said: 'And I wondered if you would give us a painting.' Given that his works sold for millions it was a bold move.

With a wry smile he asked: 'Only one?'

'Only one,' I replied.

He then very quickly changed the subject back to the Tories and why they hated sex: 'Because they can't get any, so they don't want anyone else to have any. Simple, love. Simple,' he chuckled away.

John, his cook, had joined us and he could tell I wanted to get back to the subject of Stonewall, so he started talking about

EastEnders and the importance of Colin, and 'the kiss'. I believe that if John hadn't intervened David would have seen me as yet another chancer trying to get his support, kudos and cash. The 'tea' ended at two in the morning and, ignoring David's suggestion that we stay, I selfishly and stupidly drove us down Laurel Canyon to West Hollywood, under the influence of marijuana. At one point when another twist in the road seemed too much I pulled over and confessed that I was 'stoned'. We had two options; get out and walk and be killed, or drive on and get arrested. Paul started singing songs from Broadway shows and, singing along, I gained a degree of presence, enough at least to get us safely back.

We met up with David a few times that trip, in the Hills and the house at Malibu, and he made his promise to give us a painting. He took a shine to Paul and Paul felt similarly in response. They were both from the north, and they both had the same dry sense of humour. Their friendship really developed, and I tagged along merrily. While I went on drives with David in the Malibu Hills, carefully choreographed to Wagner's music, Paul would stay behind at the beachside house cooking roast dinners and home-made Yorkshire puddings for our return. David used to say while pouring the gravy: 'Look at that! You can see next door through that!'

Moving on to the next leg of the trip, we said goodbye to David and headed to San Francisco. As we drove into the city an 8.7 earthquake struck. The car shook and lurched. 'The tyres have gone,' I shouted, then I looked in the rear-view mirror to see that the police car behind us had disappeared in a cloud of dust. There was devastation; parts of the city were burning, the Bay Bridge and stretches of highways had collapsed and people were terrified. Initially we had no idea what had happened but at the next petrol station it was obvious. The place was wrecked. We reached the safety of Armistead Maupin's apartment in the Mission District using a tourist map, a great deal of luck and riding bumper to bumper with a police car. Armistead was away travelling so waiting for us at the apartment was the beautiful

AIDS activist Steve Beery and a joint pinned on the bedroom door with a message from 'Mrs Anna Madrigal', Armistead's wacky character from *Tales of the City*. We slept in our clothes and the tremors continued, including our own with the stunning Steve. On the radio they talked of a tidal wave, and further shocks to come; uncertainty reigned.

It was not the best time to experience San Francisco, but here too the rising death toll from AIDS-related illnesses had impacted deeply. The communities were angry and active and determined to get the health, social care and intervention necessary. The famous gay Castro Street felt more like a war zone than the infamous fleshpot it had once been. Steve kept us well entertained and after a few days we moved on to complete the last leg of our holiday.

After six blissful weeks, once we were back home I set about convincing Stonewall that we should construct an art exhibition and sale around the Hockney. We would call it 'Art For Equality'. It was a risk, but we hired the ICA Gallery in the Mall and, thanks to the support of the brilliant British painter and sculptor Maggi Hambling, we managed to get other prestigious artists to donate. Maggi was never keen on the title of the exhibition and insisted on calling it 'It's For Queers, Dear!' Her cajoling and gentle harassment, not two words that generally go together with Maggi, made the show an artistic success. Artists wanted to be involved and the hype created through the quality media made it a commercial success too. We raised about £150,000 – a considerable sum.

Ian had managed to get the Pet Shop Boys to support us again, and we had the backing of the wonderful Paul O'Grady (and alter ego Lily Savage), as well as the ever-faithful drag scream (Her Imperial Highness) Regina Thong, aka Reg Bundy. They worked together in the variety show we did at the London Palladium entitled *The Equality Show*. But we knew we needed to reach wider to other artists and supporters. I had been trying, in vain, to get in contact with Elton John and his manager, the royalty of pop, John Reid. Unfortunately, I was getting nowhere. Meanwhile BBC television asked me to script and present a thirty-five-minute documentary on a subject of my choosing: I chose discrimination against lesbians and gay men, and its origins. With a reference to my time on *EastEnders* I called it *A Kiss Is Just a Kiss*.

Paul and Michelle Collins had gone to LA for a couple of weeks, where they called in on David, shopped like maniacs and partied like there was no tomorrow. I turned up at Gatwick to collect them. I hated airports at the best of times, but especially when waiting for someone. I kept my head down and loitered on the edge of the arrivals hall. I felt a gentle tapping on my shoulder and heard a soft 'Hello'. My heart sank. I was grumpy and not in the mood to discuss the entrails of *EastEnders*. Slapping a tired grin on my face I turned and came face to face with Billy Connolly.

'Hello!' he lilted, and my face lit up. 'I am a huge fan of yours,' he told me.

'I am a huge fan of yours!' I replied, and I hugged him. He was as warm and easy as he was on television and I took to him immediately.

'C'mon,' he said, 'let's throw caution to the wind and get a cup of coffee. I'm paying,' and we trotted off to the bar opposite. Billy was there to meet his wife, Pamela Stephenson, who was on the same flight as Paul and Michelle.

'Loved your documentary,' he continued. It had aired on BBC Two; with its focus on discrimination it had been hard on the media and politicians.

We had a hilarious ten minutes together before Pamela appeared and he jumped up.

'Right, I'm off,' he said.

'Billy, you're with John Reid, aren't you?'

He nodded.

'Why is it he never returns my calls?'

'It's nothing personal, he doesn't return my calls either,' he replied.

We swapped numbers, he gave me a hug and off they went. I continued to wait for Paul and Michelle. After an age they appeared and Paul was shaking. 'What's wrong?' I said.

'I've been arrested. By customs.'

In LA they'd been given a couple of video tapes by professional porn-makers and Paul had forgotten to dump them before boarding the flight to London. Paul told customs and took full responsibility for them. In the end nothing came of it but the videos were confiscated and during the process they decided to go through Michelle's LA purchases, and she ended up paying hundreds of pounds in duty.

I bundled Paul into the car and beamed. It was wonderful to have the naughty, carefree wastrel home. That night our little reverie was interrupted by a phone call. 'I hear you've been slagging me off to one of my artistes,' announced the caller in a soft Glaswegian accent.

It was John Reid. Billy had come through – and quickly. We had a lovely chat; he too had seen the documentary and he wanted to know how he could help. It was such a relief to finally get offers coming through.

'We need money,' I said. 'And your influence.'

A few days later Ian and I drove to Reid's palatial house in Buckinghamshire for dinner. Paul Gambaccini, who I knew from the Labour Party, was there too.

'We are just waiting for one more,' said John as the butler topped up our drinks.

The door opened and the unannounced guest walked in. It was Elton John. I thought I had died and gone to gay heaven; Elton was the Emperor of Entertainment and was hugely admired for his talent and his AIDS activism. Ian and I exchanged glances, we all shook hands and I glowed like a ripe pumpkin.

'Dinner?' beamed John when he saw my reaction.

As we walked into the dining room John took me aside and muttered: 'He's sat on your left and he's got no one next to him. So work him.'

Elton was the easiest person in the world to chat to. He loved a bit of gossip, humour and a lot of camp, and I gave it to him. Then I dropped into the conversation that my mum cleaned Sarm studios, where he recorded.

He shouted to John at the far end of the table: 'John, Kitty's mum is a cleaner at Sarm.'

'Kitty?'

'That's your nickname. Kitty. Cos you're a cash man.'

'And your nickname?' I said to Elton.

'Tell him, Beryl [Beryl Reid the actress],' he said to John Reid.

'Sharon. Because he is one. A Sharon.'

Then we ditched the camp and got back to talking about the documentary. He wanted to know all about Stonewall.

'What do you need?' he asked.

'To be honest? Money. To hire more staff and to keep the organisation working.'

'Okay. I'll give you £50,000.'

I nearly choked. I couldn't even imagine £50,000, let alone raise it in one conversation.

Elton then waved his hand to get John's attention: 'Kitty's told me about Stonewall, and I'm giving £50,000.'

'Okay. Okay,' said John. 'I'll match it.'

Now Ian was turning white as a sheet, and Gambaccini chuckled.

That night we sang all the way back to London. We had raised £100,000 in a single night. It was the equivalent of probably a year's work on three or four theatre benefits. And more followed. I asked Billy Connolly if he would do a benefit and he gave us one of his charity gigs at the Dominion Theatre, Tottenham Court Road, where they organised everything. All I had to do was go on stage and introduce him, then Stonewall collected the cheque.

Elton topped the bill when Stonewall migrated from the London Palladium to the Royal Albert Hall for its annual *Equality Show* in 1994, attended by the new leader of the Labour Party, Tony Blair. A deeply moving moment for me and for many others was to see the rainbow flag flying above the Royal Albert Hall, a place that was such an emblem of the English establishment. Symbols like this were few and far between, and they meant so much. We belonged; it didn't matter that the flag would just be there for one night, it felt like we finally belonged.

As the annual *Equality Show* grew, with Ian producing every one, so the stars' fame rubbed off on Stonewall. Ian relentlessly worked all his connections to make sure each year was unique: Sting, Antonio Banderas, Melanie Griffith, the Pet Shop Boys, Peter Kay, George Michael, Stephen Fry, Jason Donovan and the cast of the *Rocky Horror Show*, Joanna Lumley and Jennifer Saunders all featured at one time or another. The celebrity seal of approval helped to build and improve our public profile and our image. Looking back I always thought maybe, if Paul and Pamela Stephenson hadn't been on the same plane and he hadn't been 'arrested', it might have all turned out differently.

When Tim Barnett left Stonewall to go to New Zealand, we entered a very difficult phase with a new executive director who only lasted a couple of months. It was clear that radical action had to be taken and I was tasked by the board with the dismissal of the director. The other two members of staff threatened to resign if I dared to replace their boss. I knew it was survival time and I faced them down. Decisively the board adopted a shortened recruitment process and offered the job to 'left-wing' lawyer Angela Mason, but the appointment was not universally welcomed; some considered her too radical. Most vocal of all was the Tory Campaign for Homosexual Equality (TORCHE) with whom we had quietly worked over a number of years.

I decided to meet the board and its chairman, the historian Dr David Starkey, in his rooms at the London School of Economics. The assembled men of TORCHE said that if we appointed Angela then they and the government would sever all connections. I listened quietly as Dr Starkey told me that it would not be long before the tabloids would be pursuing Stonewall and its new chief executive. The board looked at me and waited for my response in a long satisfied silence.

Slowly I explained that I understood their concerns, that it was my deepest wish for us and the government to work together, but I had it on good authority that the tabloids were not interested in Angela Mason but were much more interested in the private lives of members of Stonewall, like me, and members of TORCHE. I smiled; I was well aware that there had been recent salacious visits to gay Berlin. It was my turn to sit in satisfied silence.

Conversation resumed and common sense won out as it was agreed that if Angela was given security clearance by the Palace of Westminster then goodwill and good relations would prevail.

And they did. I had got through by the seat of my pants.

Angela threw herself into the work and charmed, coaxed and argued her way around every Whitehall department. Her brilliant intellect and persuasive arguments, her ability to work with people, rather than rub them up the wrong way, and her generosity in giving credit to others, was one of the major reasons why equality was achieved relatively quickly, and why she was eventually poached by the government to head up their Equalities Office. Stonewall, with its huge celebrity support, political credibility, media savvy and status, had the wind behind it.

It was ironic that although Paul had been key to Stonewall's success, he disliked the organisation primarily because of what it was doing to us as a couple. Even I started to recognise that our relationship was again on the brink. He didn't even ask me what I was doing at weekends any more, simply organising his life without or around me. I had found my voice; everything had come together, the on-screen, the off-screen, the politics, the identity I had worked hard to forge. Suddenly I was confident like I had never been before. But I was beginning to see that I was also becoming a problem.

As chair I had done my work well, helping to steer the organisation through some difficult times, but now I was becoming resistant to change. While I was obsessed with the cause I was also beginning to resent the time I was giving to it. Angela Mason was so inclusive but I could see she needed someone more flexible and open to new ways of working. I noticed that during my time on tour my deputy, Elaine Willis, had shaped the organisation in a much more collegiate way and, being an open person, was less defensive than me.

After thinking about this for some time, one Sunday afternoon I drove to our offices, now in Farringdon, for our monthly board meeting. I had a plan in my head, one that I had discussed with no one. At the start of the meeting I announced that I had an additional item under 'any other business'.

Angela Mason gave me a quizzical look.

I had made my mind up to tender my resignation. When it got to the business item I told them the news. I would be stepping down in three months. Angela was taken aback and afterwards expressed her anger that I had not told her before the meeting. She was right. But I knew that if I told anyone I would have allowed myself to be talked out of it, or into delaying it.

That night when I got home I told Paul; initially he was shocked but not surprised that I hadn't raised it beforehand. Another partner would have been furious that such a key decision had been taken without prior discussion, but not him. He knew me, and more importantly he trusted me to do the right thing for us both.

It wasn't going to be easy. A distance had grown between us, especially as Paul's showbiz career seemed to have ground to a halt. But he never let the grass grow under his feet. He decided to train as a counsellor; he was a good listener, a great problem solver and his new view on life dramatically altered our relationship. Now my games and guilt transference no longer worked. He was able to identify them. Seeing how brilliantly he had flourished, I decided to undergo therapy.

It was one of the most important decisions of my life. I began to realise the tricks I played on myself, the scenarios I would invent, the low self-esteem that led to self-sabotage, and I also got the first fleeting acknowledgement of my addictive personality. Paul's change of profession and the subsequent changes in our relationship were fundamental to the two of us staying together. No longer would we argue and lurch from personal crisis to denial or diversion; we now committed to exploring our way through. It proved what he had been saying for all these years, that honesty was central to a relationship and imperative to our growth as a couple and as individuals. There were no reasons to lie, not to one another, and there was every reason to trust. It was both liberating and terrifying.

Other changes were coming, too, in which Paul's people skills would come to the fore. During his time working with Ken Follett in the different elections for Labour, Paul was acknowledged as an effective 'celebrity catcher', using his contacts and his charm. With Tony Blair as the leader he was persuaded to join the Labour Party as a senior staff member six months prior to the 1997 general election.

Top: Dining out no expense spared in Key West, Florida

Bottom left: On holidays in 1985 with Paul Cottingham, the model of cool

Bottom right: Well behaved (in public) in the Soviet Union, 1985

Above: At Elton's home in Old Windsor

Left: 1997, our first trip to 10 Downing Street – and the smiles show it

Below: Elton's 50th – being led astray by the Mistress Savage and Brendan Murphy!

Above: Blissfully boasting of our civil partnership outside Vinopolis, 2006

Left: The ceremony that nearly didn't happen; Ian and Michelle as our witnesses

Below: Two become one

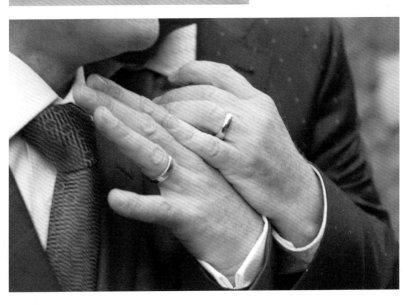

Above: Relaxing at Hillsborough Castle, Northern Ireland (we had the decency to take our shoes off)

Below: My last speech to a Labour Party conference as chair of the NEC

Above left: Jo Brand, Ed Miliband and a fit of the giggles at our home in London

Above right: Gay Pride March with the then prime minister's wife Sarah Brown!

Below: Section 28 gone, but still defiant

Collecting my CBE at Buckingham Palace – and Paul's 'new look'

Above: Our outing at Buckingham Palace

Below: The day of my introduction into the House of Lords as Lord Cashman of Limehouse

Never happier

On the morning of 2 May we both had such amazing hangovers that we overslept and missed our date at Downing Street to see Tony and Cherie Blair walk through the gates. We had stayed late at the Southbank Centre to welcome in Tony and the first Labour government in eighteen years. The dawn had started to rise over a new, optimistic London and we didn't want the night to end. What had seemed an impossible dream had become reality, but things *were* going to get even better.

England won the Ashes and then for the first and last time in a generation we won the Eurovision Song Contest – Paul's other great passion, alongside Nottingham Forest! Britain, it seemed, had found a golden age and with it a young and energetic prime minister. The country felt fresh, bright and adventurous.

Paul was on the inside, working at Millbank as a high-value fundraiser, and his celebrity contact book was a vital part of the toolkit for the dinners, campaigns and other money-raisers. He worked closely with key members of Tony Blair's team: Alastair Campbell, Anji Hunter (Tony's political secretary) and Labour's first female general secretary, Margaret McDonagh.

Paul was hugely sociable, a good team member and he wasn't precious. But he hated the nine-to-five culture of the office. If he was late in the mornings no one took account that he had been out working and socialising with his contacts the night before. Being at your desk mattered. But not to him. He hated the concept of time-serving and let it be known. He was out about his sexuality and in a male-dominated political world that wasn't always easy either. He noticed that some other men wouldn't stand at the urinal with him but instead locked themselves away in the cubicle. When he started work he had the tag of 'Michael Cashman's other half', but not for long. Difficult though the work was he had found his niche, especially with the counselling tools, and he soon proved that he was nobody's 'other half'.

At Labour HQ he was the only openly gay man. He spotted a few others, but they kept their heads down. Then one day Mary Doherty, one of the longest serving members of staff, called out across the desks to him in her Irish brogue: 'Paul, there's a new fella starting,' she said. 'And I think he's one of yours.' Then quietly she added: 'Look after him.'

And Paul did. By the time he left two years later to join the pro-EU group Britain in Europe, he and John Watts were no longer the 'gay Lone Rangers'. By simply being himself: honest, charming and cheeky – forever cheeky – he set the example that others would follow.

Work was going well for me too. I still couldn't get a television role, but the acting that I was doing in the theatre was reshaping my career and redefining what employers thought about me. In fact, I was working so much that I was missing out on the best treats. Elton John rang and invited us to dinner. His dinners were fabulous, always interesting, always funny and packed with stars, but this time I couldn't go because I was starring in two plays by Joe Orton at the Birmingham Rep, so Paul took Ian instead.

On the night of the dinner Paul went to Mayfair to collect Ian from a party. He rang the intercom, entered the building and was let into the flat by none other than Joan Collins. Joan was elegantly attired and coiffured, purred a welcome and told him that he must stay and enjoy the party, 'darling'. Never a man to refuse a bit of glamour and celebrity flirting he stayed for about half an hour before he and Ian set off to the dinner. Elton was waiting outside to greet them and told Paul it was going to be a fun night. 'You'll know everyone, they're all soap stars,' he said and swept them in.

Sat on the floor in full flow was Princess Diana, Sylvester Stallone, Richard Gere, George Michael, a couple of other Hollywood celebs and Dawn French. As the evening progressed something in the air changed. Testosterone and tension filled the room; suddenly Stallone and Gere squared up to one another, leading to Stallone storming out. Apparently, there had been competition between them for Diana's attention. Dawn plopped herself on the floor and told Paul to sit beside her: 'It's my turn to hold court now,' she shouted.

After dinner most people slipped away. In a corner a Hollywood star quietly pleaded with Paul to stay the night with him. When he told me who he had refused I was gobsmacked: 'Are you mad? Why? Why?'

'I told him it wasn't my house, and I had to take Ian back to London. Besides, I didn't know what Elton would say.'

I couldn't believe he had turned down this gorgeous hunk and told him he should have stayed. Ever the honest one he confessed: 'It was because I was driving and I hadn't had a drink. Otherwise I would have shoved Ian in a taxi.'

The next day I read about the night, the party and the bust-up in the papers, but not the covert invitation.

After Birmingham Rep I had the joy of being in other prestigious productions such as *Noises Off* by Michael Frayn and *Kvetch* by Steven Berkoff. I appeared alongside Sheila Hancock in *Gypsy*, Warren Mitchell in *King Lear*, and gave an acclaimed and daring interpretation of Antonio in *The Merchant of Venice*; after seeing my performance Ian said that it was the first time he had wanted to do the play. Then there was a lead role in the premiere of Fay Weldon's *The Four Alice Bakers*, followed by *The Rocky Horror Show*, with Jason Donovan. Yet politics was becoming more important to me. I had been elected to the council of the actors' union, Equity, with Miriam Karlin, and took on the job of turning round the union's finances and negotiating a pension scheme for members, which beforehand had been deemed impossible. We had our fights here too with both the left and the right.

I was still doing work on equality campaigns for Stonewall as well as for the Labour Party, and I loved it. Then politics shoved forward and in 1998 I was elected by the Labour membership to represent them on the National Executive Committee. The NEC is the powerful governing body of the party; it oversees the policy-making process, sets strategic objectives and guides the overall direction of the party. Crucially, now we were in government, Tony Blair needed unity between the government and the NEC. The Labour Party could not be split down the middle as it had been before.

Paul had played a pivotal role in my election; Downing Street had rung him to sound him out about my running for the NEC, and he advised me to do it. In the same year we both decided that I should have another go at becoming one of Labour's candidates for the European Parliament. I wasn't sure whether I should do it again. I had tried in 1993 and had come a strong second for the internal party nomination as the candidate. It had been a bruising battle and I was attacked from both sides. I was dismissed by the right for being a part of the liberal elite and cast aside by the left for being a successful actor. Worst of all, despite my roots, I was told I was not working class. At that point I didn't need much dissuasion: I believed that other people went into politics, not me. I hadn't completed my education; I hadn't gone to university. I'd grown up in a council flat, I didn't fit. Equally, back then I wasn't sure that the voice I had found could sustain and develop itself. In a nutshell, I didn't have the confidence.

Paul decided it needed to be different this time and he had a word with the general secretary of the Labour Party, Margaret McDonagh, who took me to one side and told me to do it. I was still tentative. She just said: 'You're mad. You'll be brilliant.' Paul shared the sentiment, adding that whatever I decided I would have his backing. That was it. I took the plunge.

The party selection process was again tough and controversial, as it was used by the party to clear out some of the sitting MEPs. The lengthy process of meetings, hustings and internal nominations got under way, and I found myself enjoying it. The secret was to think on your feet, to listen as you spoke and to engage. It was like acting without a script; but if it went wrong you were on your own. Camaraderie might have been in the concept but it was not always in the practice.

After the all-members ballot the successful candidates were then interviewed again by the National Executive and regional bodies of the party. Depending on how we performed we were ranked on lists and then placed in a region. Prior to the final interviews Paul tipped me off that I was about to be shafted by Downing Street. He passed me the phone and said: 'Ring them'. I had been the overall members' choice in London, but now they were planning to place me at number four on the list, which meant that I might not get elected.

'Absolutely not,' I said to the startled political adviser in Downing Street. 'You place me in an electable position or you take me off the list.' She reasoned that I was popular and that putting me in a precarious place meant members would work harder to get me elected.

'I see. So I stood for the NEC because you wanted me to, and now you're going to fuck me.' It wasn't a question. She promised to call me back after she had spoken with the wider team. I put the phone down and I was shaking with anger.

Paul said: 'Fuck 'em. I'm proud of you.'

Later that afternoon Downing Street agreed that if I performed well enough in the interview the next day I would be placed at number two, in the West Midlands.

When the lists were announced there was uproar. Some sitting MEPs had been effectively dumped while newcomers had been 'parachuted' to safety. London members accused me of disloyalty by going to the Midlands, while parts of the West Midlands said they hadn't voted for me as their candidate and they didn't bloody want me. Even the Tory leader William Hague chipped in at Prime Minister's Questions and said the only reason I had been selected was because I'd appeared in the *Rocky Horror Show* in Birmingham.

'Talk to Mo,' said Paul.

The MP Mo Mowlam, who had been brought up in Coventry, came to the rescue and invited me on an official visit to the city.

Mo was the first woman to hold the position of secretary of state for Northern Ireland. She was widely loved and had famously experienced one of Ian Paisley's rants and, after a short but studied silence, had merely replied: 'Oh, fuck off,' and thrown her wig on the table. Mo could do no wrong in the Labour Party's eyes; she loved people, she was open and she had seemingly successfully fought a brain tumour, so her endorsement gradually brought all but the staunchest opponents on board.

Paul and I had struck up our friendship with Mo in 1989 and one weekend, prior to the 1997 election, we travelled up to Newcar, her parliamentary constituency in the north-east, to spend a weekend with her and her new man, Jon Norton. The booze flowed and Mo and Paul were inseparable, while Jon and I behaved like a couple of houseboys, tending to their every whim. Paul and I stayed on for a few days and Mo left instructions for us to place the house keys on the kitchen table, and to 'wedge the mop against the back patio door because the lock isn't working'. The security services were going to love her, I thought!

The internal opposition among Labour's candidates in our region continued and got so bad that staff had to bring in a counsellor to try and moderate. The approaching election campaign heightened the simmering resentment. As ever the party wanted to spend money, but not their own. So we had to put together a fundraiser, or rather, Paul did. It was a celebrity launch and auction at Birmingham Airport. One of the star items was a theatrical costume that Elton had performed in, along with a signed Hockney poster, but the Cottingham coup was getting Graham Norton to come and host it.

The excitement was palpable as Graham stepped forward to deliver the immortal words: 'I am so pleased to be here in Birmingham Airport' – pausing for effect – 'and I never imagined, insane or in my worst nightmare, that I'd utter those words.' He wooed us, insulted us and, conducting the auction, got a fortune out of us. It was the best start to any regional election campaign I could have hoped for, but the opposition to my candidacy was not giving up easily. Their goal was to remove me from the list so that someone below me could become electable – and they were prepared to go low with their tactics.

At the end of a long day's campaigning I was summoned to regional office as the officials wanted a chat. When I entered the room suddenly it began to empty. In no time at all, only three senior officials were left; one of them closed the door very firmly and they all turned to face me. 'This isn't easy,' said one. 'But we know you've made a porn film,' continued another. 'We've had a tip-off.' I made a jokey remark that was met with studied silence. That was when I knew they were serious. It was incomprehensible; I knew these people, we were in the same party, and I was being questioned as though I was a criminal. The allegations then came thick and fast. It was clear they believed the source of their information and if I couldn't convince them otherwise they were going to drop me like a brick.

Around and around in circles we went, until, after about thirty minutes, they told me the title of the 'porn film'. At first it meant nothing to me; then it slowly dawned. I had appeared in an AIDS/ HIV-awareness video years before, for which Ian had done the voice-over. This was their pornography. After some wrangling I was allowed to call the film's producer. He assured me that they had not 'doctored' the video in any way during post-production, and said that it had a British Board of Film Censors certificate. This was all communicated to the three men in the room with me. Then the video was ordered to be sent down to Millbank to be viewed by a senior staffer.

That night I went back to my rented flat in Birmingham. I wanted to be anywhere other than in this election campaign. It felt dirty and so did I. I was on the verge of throwing in the towel but Paul was angrier than me, and told me to stay and fight. I felt wronged and bullied. The party officials were understandably terrified of media manipulation. I ticked the tabloids' list for a front-page scandal: gay, politics, *EastEnders*, AIDS/HIV and now porn. Such a story would have run for days with banner headlines.

The party received the video and I was sent out campaigning as if nothing had happened. The other candidates knew about the allegation but everyone pretended that they couldn't smell the shit on their shoes. Despite my daily and then hourly requests for information I received none. I was told the official hadn't seen the video yet, but I was done waiting, so I demanded that they either clear me or sack me, anything but this interminable limbo. I had gone from celebrity poster boy to porno poofter. I understood, indeed I had to understand, that the party was going to protect itself, and like everyone else I was dispensable. But it wasn't pleasant.

Paul protested to people at Millbank and the official told him she had cleared the video the day after the allegation had been made. Maybe someone at my end had wanted to prolong my misery or had just forgotten. I licked my wounded ego, got on with the campaign and I was elected to the European Parliament in June 1999, with Paul by my side. That I had been elected as the UK's first openly gay Member of the European Parliament was something Paul and I were proud of, even more so given that we had fought fair and maintained our integrity against some bastards who had sunk to the depths.

42

Tony Blair's government was in its second year and Stonewall was building on the trust it had established by emphatically working across party political divides, working with ministers and civil servants on equality legislation as well as with non-governmental organisations and the media. But the opposition to LGBT+ equality was still strong in Parliament, as witnessed during the earlier attempts at reform.

When Edwina Currie and Neil Kinnock put down an equal age of consent amendment to legislation in 1994 they were defeated in the Commons and the Lords, but a compromise was agreed and the age lowered from twenty-one to eighteen. However, inequality was once again enshrined in law and the debate had emboldened homophobic and religious zealots; the stereotypes were rampantly reinforced without any nod to reality. My friendship with Mo Mowlam paid dividends on the thorny issue of the ban on lesbians and gay men serving in the armed services, which was working its way up the political agenda. It was a ban that was vigorously defended and ruthlessly employed to end the careers of service men and women. It had the additional effect of destroying their outside career chances.

A brave group of ex-service personnel, led by Robert Ely and Elaine Chambers, co-founded Rank Outsiders and worked with Stonewall to try to end the ban. Because a change to the law seemed remote it was decided to pursue equality through the courts, and a long-awaited judgment from the European Court of Human Rights was imminent. Angela Mason tipped me off that there was some serious objection in government to lifting the ban should the case be won; there had been a discussion in

Cabinet and she asked if I could get some inside information so that Stonewall could focus its strategy. Mo confirmed that there was no clear agreement in Cabinet. She had spoken in favour of lifting the ban, but had been faced with opposition. Chris Smith, the first openly gay member of Parliament, and now secretary of state for culture, media and sport, had also spoken in favour, but Tony hadn't yet made up his mind.

I reported back to Angela and we agreed that we would talk when we had more news. It was a week before the Labour Party conference in Blackpool, which would prove fortuitous.

The Friday before the conference began I received a call on my newly acquired mobile from Lance Price, Alastair Campbell's deputy at Number 10, telling me that the Strasbourg judgment on 'gays in the military' was expected and that the government's position was merely to note the judgment and continue with the ban until the Armed Services Act came up for renewal. None of this was news to me but I knew it was a political cop-out; I hadn't fought inequality to now have my political party enforce it. Lance asked if I would accept the government's position (though he remembers it somewhat differently in his version of events) and my reply was quite simple: 'Absolutely not.' I told him I knew of at least two Cabinet ministers who were of the same opinion and that there was no way I would support this flabby approach. He asked me if I was happy for that message to be reported back and my answer was firm: 'Absolutely.' I reported the conversation to Angela and promised her that I would raise it with the prime minister at the first opportunity, certainly before the expected judgment.

The following Sunday we gathered in Blackpool and I waited nervously for Tony's arrival. Tony and I had developed a good working relationship from his time in opposition and particularly around the age of consent debate. It helped that both he and Cherie liked and admired Paul too. I saw it as my role to give him opinions that he might not otherwise hear, especially on equality issues.

As he walked into the room I went straight up to him and said: 'Prime Minister, can I have thirty seconds of your time?' He smiled and replied: 'Michael, if you're calling me prime minister it's going to be at least ten minutes. Where're you sitting? I'll come over.'

'No,' I said. 'We can do it here,' gesturing to a vacant corner.

I gave him a very quick run-down of what had happened, what the government's reaction to the judgment was going to be and added: 'It's wrong. You have just been defending the international rule of law in East Timor and here we are ignoring it when it comes from Strasbourg and it affects us. Accept the judgment and then enter into consultation with the military. If you want to you can stretch that consultation to the other side of the election, but accept the judgment.'

I waited for his response. He thought for a few seconds then said: 'You're right. Leave it with me.'

Once the lunch was over and conference business had been discussed, I realised that my nerves were in shreds. Why was it that at crucial moments like these I always doubted myself? I nagged myself and regurgitated every single second of my short exchange with Tony, looking for evidence of where I might have got it wrong.

Later that afternoon Lance Price rang me to say that I had 'changed government policy' and I was to be in the media briefing room the following morning just before eight. It was a great success for equality and Angela was thrilled, but I had not endeared myself to some key people around Tony, nor in the Ministry of Defence. The government announcement on Monday morning barely raised an eyebrow. We had done the right thing and it made sense, but I honestly believe that if I hadn't alerted Tony he wouldn't have found out about it until he opened his red boxes that night, when it would have been too late.

I took up my NEC conference duties and tried to hide the profound sense of pride that I felt; we had achieved an astounding victory and it went right to the heart of the establishment, the armed forces.

In the early days of the long campaign to end the military ban I had come face to face with how the hatred of LGBT+ people could have devastating consequences on people's lives. In 1991 the City of London Police had arrived unexpectedly at our home with a matter that apparently could not be discussed on the phone. They had carried out an investigation into an attempted murder and the man they'd charged had confessed that he wanted to attack me. They'd found in his possession newspaper cuttings referring to my attempts to end the ban on gays in the military. It was likely that this evidence would be heard at the Old Bailey and that if the accused, Alex Rees, was found guilty the police would have to stay in regular contact for my future safety.

This was surreal. I didn't even know the man. My initial reaction was disbelief: it was an old and accepted defence tactic to establish that an abhorrence of a homosexual advance brought out uncontrollable emotional reactions resulting in a physical attack. It even had a name: the 'Portsmouth defence', or 'guardsman's defence', presumably because it had been used by service personnel previously. These two towering detectives assured me that I was 'at risk' and should be more aware. They left with the promise that they would keep me informed and they stayed true to their word. Alex Rees was later found guilty of attempted murder and sentenced to sixteen years in prison. The judge expressed grave concerns should he ever be released.

Many years later I received a letter from Alex Rees in Maidstone Prison. He wanted to explain things to me, and what had happened to him, so he invited me to visit him in prison. I never had the courage to accept his invitation, but we engaged in correspondence that went on for years. He had suffered terrible abuse, he explained, both at home and in the army; he had resorted to drugs, self-harm and self-abuse. But through prison he had found himself and a vocation in writing. His letters were deep, funny and moving. During his later years he developed terminal cancer and I helped to get him home for his final weeks. I knew he wanted closure so I took courage and phoned him. Alex sounded fragile, but at last he was with his mother and his sister, and soon after he died peacefully at home. I don't know if he ever made peace with the man he had attacked; I hope he did, but I felt deeply privileged that we had reached out above everything else to find one another.

So when the judgment came through from the European Court of Human Rights in Strasbourg I knew it meant that the culture of bullying and hatred in the military that had destroyed so many lives could be challenged and finally brought to an end.

43

Mo Mowlam loved to throw a party! Trying to keep the feuding political parties of Northern Ireland together was difficult to say the least, so during weekends when she was at the secretary of state's official country residence, Hillsborough Castle, Paul and I were often invited.

Our first visit to Hillsborough was with Anji Hunter, Tony Blair's trusted advisor, and her family, Jackie Ashley and her partner Andrew Marr, and the actor Richard Wilson. We arrived on the Friday ahead of the rest of the party. David, the butler, said 'the secretary of state has told us to make you comfortable. You are to choose your bedroom and she should be here by supper.' He then whisked us around the palatial building, set in beautiful landscaped grounds, and showed us the options for accommodation.

First we inspected the Queen's bedroom, with its grand double bed, then Prince Philip's bedroom, which adjoined the sovereign's, both of which had separate bathrooms. Finally we were shown a couple of smaller royal bedrooms. It seemed the lower down the royal pecking order you went the smaller the bed and the less luxurious the bathroom. 'And have you chosen a bedroom?' asked David.

'Well, the Queen's bedroom...'

There was just the faintest shake of his head. 'Prince Philip's has lovely twin beds,' he said.

'He put you where?' asked Mo when she arrived.

'Philip's.'

'Fuck me. If ever there were two men who should be in the Queen's bedroom, it's you two. Okay. Next time.'

Friday evening was a raucous affair with just Mo, Jon, Paul and me. David the butler hovered in case his services were required. Mo laughed, saying: 'He thinks you're gonna pinch something, he's keeping a careful eye on the silver.' David, who we became close to over the next few months, reassured the secretary of state that we seemed perfectly trustworthy gentlemen, but did regale us with a story of how he had once needed to remove a number of silver ashtrays and spoons from the pockets of a Commonwealth high commissioner. When the others arrived on Saturday it was a bit more sedate, although Jon's teenage kids (H and Freddie) did their best to liven things up. We played 'Country House weekends', croquet on the lawns and boating on the lake. But there was a hardcore who stayed up late, Anji among us.

Sunday lunch was served in the grand dining room, after which we started our departures for the airport. As Paul and I were leaving one of the staff members, in her late forties, discreetly asked me if she could have my autograph, saying: 'I love *EastEnders*.' I happily obliged and then without any prompting she said: 'It's so wonderful, Mr Cashman. She's brought laughter back to this house.'

Mo had brought hope, too. It was a critical time in Northern Ireland and she had been central to negotiating the Good Friday Agreement, which sought to reconcile the historic sectarianism. That she had worked quietly and tirelessly when she was opposition spokesperson paid dividends: she knew who to talk with, she knew how to listen and she had a brilliant sense of humour. Crucially she was a radical break from the patrician attitude to Northern Ireland politics – and she loved people. She physically demonstrated this when she broke with tradition and opened up the castle and grounds of Hillsborough to the people of Northern Ireland. And she enlisted Paul to assist BBC Northern Ireland in the organisation of a celebration of the 'ordinary people' of Northern Ireland. Working with the producers, Paul helped to assemble a group of celebrities and flew them over for the show to be recorded before a live audience at the magnificent Grand

Opera House in Belfast. A host of TV personalities in the show included Patrick Kielty, Eamonn Holmes and 'Lily Savage', and Michelle Collins and television actor Paul Moriarty, who were billed to sing a duet. Unfortunately, when Paul Moriarty arrived he told the production team and full orchestra that he couldn't sing a note. A solution was quickly found; he would introduce Michelle and Paul Cottingham, who would do the duet! Another famous English actress hated the orchestration of her song, refused to sing it and took the next flight back to London. I did my party piece, 'Bring Him Home' from *Les Mis*, which musically overlapped with a young boy who sang 'Where is Love?' from *Oliver!*. The artists named and celebrated people in the audience who had 'made a difference' to their communities, and the show felt like a success.

At the reception afterwards in the adjoining Europa Hotel, Mo was mobbed by people from both sides of the sectarian divide. The outpouring of love was unbelievable to witness. After forty minutes she still hadn't reached the front door of the ballroom. She dispatched Paul to get her a Bushmills whisky and slowly made her way towards it. When she left some time later she said: 'Cottingham, get some stars to come back, some fun people. I need to party.' And he was as good as his word.

With the party at the castle in full swing I convinced Mo to stay up a little longer on the promise that I would wake her in the morning. A little longer turned into a lot and the next morning I woke abruptly to the alarm and a memory of Lily Savage/O'Grady, carrying me to my room. Quickly I pulled on a shirt over my pants and stumbled to the secretary of state's bedroom to wake her. As I came out a minute later, unsuitably undressed, I came face to face with an armed RUC man patrolling the corridors. 'Good morning,' I said.

'Good morning, sir,' came a stern reply.

A week later Mo said she had heard the gossip that she was 'now sleeping with gay men'.

Mo left for work while I sensibly went back to Paul for what I hoped would be a quiet morning in bed. But before I could drift off there was a loud banging at the door. 'Mr Cashman! Mr Cashman! There's someone sleeping in the Queen's bed!'

I remembered. 'Savage!'

Mo loved it all. There was nothing shocking or unacceptable when it came to letting your hair down and living. We took her to see the *Rocky Horror Show* at the Belfast Grand and she invited the entire cast, including Jason Donovan and Nicholas Parsons, back to the castle for the night. The party of all parties ensued. We sang, danced and drank until daylight. As Mo recorded in her biography, the sight of the stretch limo leaving with arms and legs draped out of all the windows was unforgettable. The comments her visitors recorded in Hillsborough's official guestbook – which included entries from Diana, Charles, the Queen and others – were so lurid that Mo ordered for the book to quietly 'disappear'. She later told me that some of her Special Branch officers thought that in going to see *Rocky* – she had taken them with her – she had scraped the very bottom of the barrel.

At the root of Mo's relationships were loyalty and love. Even after Peter Mandelson replaced her in Northern Ireland in late 1999, people never forgot her because she showed such formidable courage, not the least when she entered the notorious Maze prison to talk to the loyalist paramilitaries to encourage them to engage in the peace process. For her there weren't any 'no-go areas'; she was determined to have the peace settled and secured. The Ulster Unionists (UUP), led by David Trimble, and the DUP, led by Ian Paisley, found her difficult to deal with. She hated male obstinacy and to her they personified it. When asked by Hillary Clinton how she coped with it in that particular political environment, she merely replied that she always factored time into the agenda for 'willy waving'.

In 1998 Tony Blair had asked Mo to leave Northern Ireland but she refused. She knew where she was needed; despite huge advances and her role in brokering the Good Friday Agreement, she knew her work wasn't done there. We were at Hillsborough the weekend the call came through from the prime minister.

She returned shaky and ashen from the experience, which had come out of the blue. We all told her to stay firm. 'He daren't sack you,' I said. She called Tony back and said she wanted to stay and finish the job of creating lasting peace in Northern Ireland. But she had enemies, and not only in other political parties; her popularity ratings, which at one time were higher than the prime minister's, also bizarrely threatened her position. A few months later Tony told her he was replacing her with Peter Mandelson, and she was shunted off to the Cabinet Office where she wallowed with nothing really to do.

She was angry, confused and hurt. After years of impeccable service and devotion to the cause of peace in Northern Ireland – built up from those unseen years of work in opposition – they had, in her words, 'fucked her over'. When I said that it was unfair she merely replied: 'It's nothing to do with "fair". The party always will.' It was a political fact of life for her, but she felt betrayed.

Mo and Jon moved to Hackney and the glamour-seekers started to slowly fade away. Dawn French was always there for her, however: she never forgot the weekend in Hillsborough when she and Lenny Henry were going through a rough patch. The tabloids traced them to the pub along the road from the castle. Mo took control and had her bulletproof car backed up to the pub's exit so that Lenny and Dawn could slip away, unnoticed and not photographed.

One of the last things Mo asked us to do was witness her living will: her brain tumour was no longer the issue, she said, but she was adamant that if she was ever in a coma she should not be resuscitated. The final time we saw Mo we travelled down to a small cottage she and Jon had bought in Kent with their diminishing capital. When Mo came to the door they both looked and smelt like a couple of chimney sweeps – the flue from the fire was blocked and neither of them had noticed. Between us we sorted the chimney, got the fire working properly and then had a wonderful, boozy early dinner.

The next day a gathering of friends from London was expected for lunch. Not all of them turned up and her old Parlimentary

Private Secretary didn't show up either. She tried not to show it but she was upset and got very pissed over lunch. 'Fuck 'em! Fuck 'em!' she suddenly shouted. Then she stood up from the table and went to bed. After lunch we helped with the dishes then took the taxi to the station.

Barely a couple of months later it was reported that Mo had fallen and sustained brain damage, whereas the truth was the brain tumour had never gone away. During all those years she lived with it, worked despite it, and barely told a soul. In accordance with her living will, she was not resuscitated and died in a hospice on 19 August 2005. Even in death her love for the people of Northern Ireland was reaffirmed when, as she requested, some of her ashes were scattered in the gardens of Hillsborough. But someone like Mo can never really die. Decency always lives on in the work people do, and in the courage with which they lived their lives.

44

After the May elections to the European Parliament I travelled to Brussels to start my new life. I put the difficult election campaign behind me and reminded myself that I had been given the privilege to serve, even though the turnout was the lowest in the EU at a miserable 22 per cent.

For us new arrivals there was an air of excitement as we rushed to induction courses, and had our photos taken. The seasoned 'old guard' looked on pretending they were bored while those who hadn't been re-elected wore their pain for all to see as a reminder of what befalls most politicians – rejection. Once I had found somewhere to live and got through the entirely new experience of interviewing and hiring staff for the Brussels and West Midlands office in West Bromwich, I was ready for a holiday.

Paul and I spent our summer in Turkey, during which time I started reviving my knowledge of French and learning how the EU institutions functioned; it was obvious to everyone that I was chomping at the bit to get to work. The summer break over, I arrived at the parliament building and from my office on the thirteenth floor I began the preparatory work for my committees. Each MEP was expected to take two committees but as Labour's numbers had dramatically decreased in the election – we had switched to proportional representation, which hadn't helped – I was asked to take on three. I shrugged my shoulders and got on with it; I would learn on the job, it's what actors had to do. My lead committee was 'Citizen's Freedoms and Home Affairs (LIBE)'. On every committee each political group had its own coordinator. Ours was an affable German called Martin Schulz, and we got on immediately.

'Ah, New Labour! Welcome "Comrade",' he laughed. He thought it would be an insult but I loved it. Thereafter I was Comrade Cashman and he was always Comrade Schulz, which often raised a quizzical eyebrow from others.

Two weeks into committee work Schulz tapped me on the shoulder and asked if I would like the legislation on 'Public Access to Documents' – a European Freedom of Information Law. It sounded like a huge task, and I wasn't yet confident in my abilities, so initially I said no. But another voice in my head said 'Do it. Do it.' This voice had been steadily growing louder since the Stonewall days and it was extremely persuasive. I told Schulz I had changed my mind: I would do it. Working with the LIBE Committee and the Constitutional Affairs Committee over the next twelve months the Public Access dossier became one of the most important pieces of legislation in years. The German, French, Spanish, Greek and Luxembourg governments did their best to get my approach rejected by the EU Council (the government ministers). We were successful in preventing the rejection of this EU-wide freedom of information law because the UK government formed a blocking minority in conjunction with Sweden, Finland, Denmark, Ireland and the Netherlands.

The job was arduous and we were up against a tight treaty deadline, but working alongside brilliant advisers on effective amendments across the different committees we achieved a substantial majority in the parliament. After tense and difficult negotiations with the Council, which was working on behalf of the governments of the EU countries, we reached agreement and it became EU-wide law in May 2001. I had flown by the seat of my pants, trusting officials in the parliament, having the courage to work with other political groups and seek compromises, and as a result we now had a major piece of law that gave access to all documents held, received or produced by the three EU institutions. It was truly groundbreaking. I had amazed myself; I never believed that I could do work like this. I found new confidence and the liberating ability to listen, to take advice and to learn. The feeling was one of utter relief.

Paul and I were invited for a formal dinner at the plush residence of the UK ambassador to the EU, Sir Nigel Sheinwald, and his wife, Lady (Julia) Sheinwald. The titles quickly disappeared and it was only when we sat down to dinner that I realised, to my shock, that the event was in my honour because of the new legislation. Nigel said that I had achieved 'the impossible'; the fact that the French and the Germans had tried to dilute it, and failed, evidently added to the success. People truly thought I was worth something. As for Paul, he assured me that he had always thought I was.

45

I was beginning to find my rhythm and balance the demands of serving the West Midlands and the European Parliament. Paul quickly adjusted to my being away three nights every week; it was like the old touring days, minus the scandalous landladies. We settled into a haphazard routine but Paul was drinking too much, and becoming worried about it.

I was wrapped up in work on committees, including writing and amending law on non-discrimination programmes, visa agreements and the Schengen Border Code, as well as overseeing the entry into the EU of countries like Bulgaria and Romania. Despite an earlier hesitation not to just fall into what was 'niched out' for me, I took a decision and quickly became active on LGBT+ matters both within the Socialist Group, to which Labour was attached, and in the wider parliament. We relaunched the cross-party group on LGBT+ issues, which would prove vital in ensuring that concerns were properly addressed – even when some would rather ignore them. It would become the most successful cross-party group in the European Parliament.

On the Foreign Affairs Committee, I joined a group of MEPs on a mission to Bulgaria to assess progress. At our pre-meetings with commission officials in the capital Sofia, it became clear to me that equality issues were not being prioritised and as such I argued for more commitment to them in the final communiqué, effectively our recommendations for the future. Neither the Bulgarians, nor our right-of-centre MEPs, would give way. After discussion with my Socialist Group colleagues, the Liberals and the Greens, we threatened to block the communiqué unless the problems surrounding LGBT+ communities, disability rights, women's rights and children in institutions were addressed. I was told by the British Conservative MEP leading the delegation that what I was doing was 'unprecedented' and that I should withdraw immediately. I refused and we stood our ground. It didn't endear me to the opposition, but it worked. We included our demands in the final report, pushed the issues to the top of the political agenda and, because countries joining the EU had to address such inequalities, eventually Bulgaria changed its laws.

Satisfying as the work was, it was lonely; Paul and I were back to the days of a relationship conducted primarily by phone. Brussels was bearable but in Strasbourg, where we went for the monthly plenary sessions, conversation time was almost impossible. The routine was twelve hours a day, followed by a meal, mostly eaten alone, the hotel, then back to work in the morning, often hung-over.

Occasionally Paul would come out to Strasbourg or Brussels, but for the most part he stayed in London. Sometimes in Brussels I might have supper with Glenys (now an MEP) and Neil Kinnock, who was vice-president of the Commission, and our MEP friends Arlene McCarthy and Linda McAvan. More commonly, though, I'd go to my flat to sink a bottle of red wine in order to sleep. I also started abusing my body with binge smoking, getting through twenty cigarettes in a few hours. In the morning I would feel dirty and guilty and regret it, vowing to end the stupidity. Until I got back to my room in the evening when I would start all over again. I knew deep down that I had a problem, that I was trying to self-medicate, but I did nothing about it and just tried to ignore the warning signs. When I went home to London the binge smoking would stop; I had no yearning for it; but once I was alone in a hotel, or away from home, it felt like an inevitability.

The difference between Paul and me was that he was prepared to talk about his excesses, while I preferred to bury them. Loneliness and discomfort seemed natural to me. Eventually he cottoned on about the smoking. As a smoker you fail to notice the smell. I was angry. He had caught me out, again, and I didn't like it. Could I hide nothing from him? 'You need help,' he said gently. But I brushed it off aggressively. I knew he was right, and still I could do nothing.

Being a British MEP meant the UK media considered you fair game in all seasons. I did not go in search of headlines or media hype, and hoped my work record would speak for itself. I was naive. The press attacked me and then tried to set Paul up in a sting. A few months after I joined the European Parliament, Paul started working for me on an administrative basis. Years later the *Daily Telegraph* regurgitated an old press story, which was picked up by the *Daily Mail* and others, but with the new allegation that I was paying him £8,000 a month, and using language that was tinged with homophobia ('Pays Gay Lover ...'). Buried in the reportage was the fact that the money was paid to Paul so he could pay my staff – his job was administering the payroll as an MEP could not directly receive the payments. Paul was paid £8,000 a month because that was my total staff bill.

The day after the *Telegraph* piece, ITV contacted me to say they wanted to run with the story. I informed them that I would be issuing a short rebuttal. Number 10 Downing Street, where Gordon Brown was now in office, was discussing the issue in a conference call of his senior advisers and I could say nothing until they had taken a decision. I asked the leader of our European Parliamentary Labour Group if I could be in on that call but was refused. My future would be decided without my input. Meanwhile I went to see the secretary general of the European Parliament and asked him to investigate the leak of information as well as the allegations. He told me they had already initiated an investigation and were satisfied that all the rules had been abided by and that payments were properly used, though the source of the leak had yet to be established. As far as they were concerned there was no story.

Nonetheless the allegations continued to be reported by the media: ITV news called again and said they needed the rebuttal before twelve, an hour away, in order to decide whether to run a story that would undoubtedly end my career. I called to get an update: the conference call had not taken place yet. Paul was in Brussels and with him and Renaud Savignat, my senior staff member, I prepared a three-line rebuttal. At 11.45 a.m. UK time, having heard nothing from either our leader at EU level or Downing Street, we sent the rebuttal to all media outlets and informed Downing Street. ITV called me for a couple of clarifications and then concluded that there was no story.

Downing Street had dithered, not for the first time. We thought about legal action against the newspapers but were told it wasn't actionable, and we considered a complaint to the Press Complaints Commission a waste of time. So we let it rest, where it would float in the ether for ever. I wish we hadn't.

The attempted sting against Paul some years earlier was pure entrapment. I had recently joined the Parliament and he had set up his own company as an events organiser; he was contacted with a lucrative 'money no object' proposal. The directors wined and dined him at a posh London hotel, the lunch continuing long into the afternoon. But something didn't add up. This 'young, aggressive company' would do anything and pay any sum to expand their work and their contacts into the institutions of the EU. Paul and I talked it over and agreed it seemed too good to be true, but also too big a contract for Paul to handle. So he declined their generous financial offer to use the services of his company to supply contacts and access to MEPs and commissioners. They were angry, but he stayed firm. Overnight the website of the company disappeared.

In the West Midlands I showed the party members that I was ready to work to earn their trust and respect, and they in turn overcame their initial reluctance towards me. That I was close to the Labour leadership helped, especially with the unions. I ran my office from the heart of the West Midlands headquarters, in West Bromwich, and usually, after returning home to London from Brussels or Strasbourg on a Thursday evening, I would spend the next day or two in the Midlands at party meetings, visiting businesses and doing my constituency work. In vain I tried to get people to see that European politics worked, but I found that most of my constituents were turned off by politics, and I got used to being insulted and abused. There was the added confusion that people sometimes recognised me from *EastEnders*. After the initial glow, though, they usually reverted to type.

At the end of a normal week I was driving back to London from a constituency dinner when my phone rang. It was Paul. My mum was in a coma.

It came without warning. She hadn't been ill. She'd had trouble with her 'nerves', but nothing serious medically. Indeed, we used to joke that she was as strong as an ox.

Life had never been easy for Mum – her early years had been particularly tough. In her large family she was such a rebel that her father applied to the courts and had her placed in an open prison. Even that couldn't confine Mary Clayton, and she escaped in a baker's van and returned home, whereupon her father had her rearrested. During the Second World War she had served with the Women's Land Army, working the fields with farm hands and Italian POWs. After she married she worked round the clock and brought us four boys up on a pittance. She was always in debt to the 'tally men' and balanced the competing demands of different loan sharks like a seasoned city financier. Even when we were teenagers it didn't get any easier for her, especially with the added expense of my stage school. I came home from school one day to find her on the floor with the rental television on its side as she attacked it with a knife to prise the coins out of the meter. When the man came to empty it he complained that there was 'hardly anything in it'. She'd flick the ash of her fag, adjust her stockings (she always had good legs), and say: 'I know mate. We never watch it. There's never anything on.'

At other times she risked life itself trying to rewire the electricity supply so it bypassed the meter. Uncle Charlie found a way of taking the gas meter off and reconnecting it so that the readings went backwards. My dad just tutted and wished it wasn't happening. All of these habits Mum found difficult to leave behind. Her attitude was always 'waste not, want not'. Often she worked three or four jobs at the same time, and later in life when she went on holiday she expected her sons to cover her work. We would think nothing of getting on a bus at 4.30 in the morning, Paul and I having left a nightclub a couple of hours earlier, in order to cover one of her cleaning jobs. Life to her was a grind in which you had to fight to grab your chances, and only friendship and graft got you through it.

I parked up at the Royal London Hospital in Whitechapel and dashed into the Accident and Emergency Unit, where the first person I saw was my dad. 'She's as right as rain,' he said.

'What?'

He nodded me into an adjoining room where Mum was sitting upright on a trolley, with an oxygen mask over her face, holding court with the nurses, my brother Johnny looking on. 'Here he is,' she muffled, 'the actor. *EastEnders*.'

'You okay?'

She hadn't been. At home she'd collapsed, turned blue and had to be resuscitated by the emergency services. She was kept in hospital for a couple of days, but tests showed no clear indication as to what had caused the attack, so Mum was sent home.

Within a couple of months, she had another two attacks. Yet still they never came close to the source of the problem. Once, at the Royal London, on a recurrence, I was in the ward when the consultant did his round. I was firm in my 'posh boy' voice that she should not be discharged until they got to the bottom of the problem. I can see her now, sat on the bed like a small girl, her hands smoothing out the bedclothes, never asking the questions, just looking from one to another as we spoke. The consultant said they were panic attacks, which caused her to hyperventilate and black out. It was then the cardiac arrest occurred. Blinding us with science he continued that she had been a heavy smoker for many years and it had affected her lungs. 'Mrs Cashman?' he asked.

'Yes dear?'

'Is there anything that you are worried about?'

She shook her head and smiled.

'Anything you're unhappy about?'

Her head dropped slightly and she looked down at the hand-kerchief in her hands. After a few moments she glanced up, her bottom lip started to quiver, then she said: 'I'm not very happy. At home.'

My heart sank like a stone.

Two days later she was discharged. Within a week or two she was back in hospital, and three weeks later she died when we agreed to switch off the life support machine at St Thomas's Hospital. Only later did they realise that the problem had been an arrhythmic heart, which could have been dealt with by a pacemaker.

As she had carried us into life, so her four sons carried her to her grave. When we lowered her into the earth on that cold, damp September morning I felt the umbilical cord snap. And I howled.

Through it all Paul was my rock. Always there with me at the hospital, supporting my dad and my brothers. At these times he was at the centre of our family and, with my sister-in-law Ellen, he helped hold it together. They knew how difficult the Cashmans found expressions of love, grief or any other emotion, with the exception perhaps of anger. He was especially strong for my dad. Only later, reading Paul's notes, would I realise the pain and the loneliness that he was quietly going through, and how, in his words, he was losing one of the few people who understood: my mum.

46

My dad died alone, in a hospital bed in Alicante, on 27 December 2004. It was two years and three months after the death of his wife, our mum.

How they ever stayed together was beyond us. I can only put it down to the fact that they loved one another and simply struggled to show it. Certainly they never expressed it in front of us. When they did talk it was always about problems, or coping with life, or family. Perhaps they just kept their other life for when they were alone at night, or their times together in Spain.

He was a man of few words, arguably a shy man, except when he had the courage of the drink, and then he would be the life and soul of the party – or the biggest pest imaginable if he had a fight to pursue on someone else's behalf.

Dad was born in 1923 in Stepney, east London. His upbringing was tough: his mum was a big woman – not fat, but what other women called 'big boned' – and she was deaf. His dad, John, had fought in the Great War and came back minus a testicle, a leg and a future. His parents rustled up a living as much as they could, surviving the Great Depression of the 1920s and 1930s. As soon as my dad was old enough he was sent to work, and by the age of twelve his schooling was abandoned. As the eldest of five he was expected to provide the income that his disabled father could not. The docks were a hard place to live, work and exist, so he added another string to his bow and became a boxer. Athletic and disciplined, he eventually became a London amateur boxing champion and he had the cups and medals to prove his proficiency. One of his earliest jobs was lighting fires and running errands for the Jewish community on their Sabbath, and every ha'penny went home.

His mother ruled the roost over them all. In her opinion no one was too big to take a good beating. Once she was arrested for assaulting a tradesman who was harassing a neighbour. Upon hearing the facts the magistrate awarded her a small amount of money and dismissed all charges. Later in her life, at the age of seventy, she knocked a young man unconscious for swearing at her. This was the stock my father was from: the brawn of his mother, the brains of his dad.

At the age of eighteen my dad was called up to fight in the Second World War. He served in the desert campaign in North Africa, during which he continued boxing and gained a good reputation, before being injured by gunfire and captured by the Italians. With the Italian armistice, my dad was sent to a Nazi slave-labour camp in Poland to dig iron ore. His parents had no idea at this time whether he was alive or not. They had received a telegram stating that he was missing in action, presumed dead. But they were given hope when Charlie Clayton, the man who would be his future father-in-law, heard his name mentioned during a German propaganda broadcast by Lord Haw-Haw. Charlie was soaking in a tin bath when he heard the news on the radio that a 'German boxer had beaten the army boxing champion John Cashman'. He dashed out of his flat and ran downstairs to tell the Cashmans, and the neighbourhood erupted into a celebration. It was some rare good news in the bombed-out East End.

When Dad arrived home he was given a hero's welcome, but his celebrity status soon wore off and he sought escapism from his experiences as a prisoner of war, 'ducking and diving' in the docks. Some time around 1948 he became emotionally aware of one of Charlie and Nell Clayton's daughters, Mary. The two families had lived in the same block of flats beside the Rotherhithe Tunnel, and the siblings from each grew up together and mixed as friends. Our mum always maintained that she had lifted my father to the heights and that when she met him he was 'licking the drips off the coffee stall under Stepney East station'. Whatever the truth, their courtship presented challenges. He would ask her to go to the 'pictures, up the Troxy' with him. If she said yes, he would arrange to meet her inside, bunking his way in through one of the exits while she paid for her own ticket.

Dad believed in having a 'good time', but that it wasn't something to be shared with women. That was the way of many of his generation. You married a lover, who then became your wife, who became your mother.

The proposal too, by all accounts, was unromantic. My brother Johnny had been born 'out of wedlock', and my dad disputed that he was his. Mum's father, Charlie, thought the courts should decide and took out a paternity order at the magistrates' court in Stepney. Three days before the case was to be heard Johnny Cashman marched up the alley at Ratcliffe Orchard, where the Claytons now lived, and thumped on the door. He was met by Nell Clayton, my mum standing behind her with their baby.

'What do you want, Johnny Cashman?' sniffed Nell.

'Your Mary.'

'What do you want, John?' said my mum.

'I'll tell you what I want. You, me, tomorrow morning, Limehouse Registry Office.'

'What?'

'I'm fucking marrying yer.'

And with supreme confidence, he turned on his heels and left.

The next day they were married and immediately afterwards he disappeared on a bus to the magistrates' court to quash the paternity order. Nine months later I was born, virtually a carbon copy of my older brother, after which no one said another word.

The difficulty of Dad's life, the insecurity of work in the docks, his drinking to escape, the pressures of marriage and kids, it all piled up. In reality he was a single man who never really adjusted to married life. But despite the awful rows and fights with my mother, when he was fun, he was really fun. He would lie on the floor when we were young and pretend to be dead to the world as our mum encouraged us to 'beat him up', feign surprise when booby traps were set for him, or put one of us on his shoulders and carry us through the streets as a 'flying angel'. He brought home stolen fruit and toys from the docks, and he was so proud when Stevie came home with sporting medals. He knew how to work hard but then he wanted to play hard. In the sixties, when the London Docks were in decline, he had got out, and, after becoming a park keeper, blossomed. Maybe it was because of his time as a prisoner of war, about which he never spoke, but he seemed freer and more alive when he was head park keeper at King George's Stadium. He was around the people he liked best – sportspeople – and he had an identity: he was 'Johnny Cashman', the man who ran things, and he could slip off unnoticed for a pint too.

Dad's sense of camaraderie never left him and he later became a shop steward and rarely shied away from fighting injustice. At home, however, he was a different person. Sadly, I believe he felt unloved; my mum's flirtations, or affairs, must have driven him mad with jealousy. But he had a roving eye too, and occasionally he followed it. Perhaps that is why the violence sometimes flared: they both felt trapped.

Because of that violence his sons withdrew, emotionally and physically, from him – all of us except Steve, who as a sportsman and fantastic amateur football player exemplified all that my dad had been as a young man, and still wanted to be. Although I always stood between my dad and mum when there was a fight, I was the only one he did not hit physically. I was his emotional match and we both knew it. I had his stubbornness, his madness, his flash of temper. Steve, Johnny and Danny adapted differently. They had little choice. I effectively left home at the age of twelve and, even when I did return, I existed in another place, in another universe. I had my escape. They had none.

Despite my being gay, or probably because of it, Dad and I saw in each other many similarities: a determination not to be trodden down, a common politics – which we rarely discussed – and an obligation to speak up against a wrong. Yet I wouldn't acknowledge these similarities for many years. My closeness to my mother blinded me and it was Paul who opened my eyes due to the relationship he had with my dad. Paul disagreed with me; he told me that I couldn't see the good, and I refuted absolutely his assertions that my dad and I were so alike.

Two experiences brought me up sharp. When Paul became a trained counsellor in psychotherapy at the age of forty-one, I started what would become years of therapy and analysis. In one session we started dealing with my feelings as a young boy: I remembered that I would let down my dad's tyres on his bike to stop him going back to work at lunchtime. It hit me like a brick that I loved my father and that the reason I had spent my time hating him – pushing him away from me, taking Mum's side whenever I could – was because I had no idea whether he loved me back. That was why I had punished him. Because I wanted him to love me. I told no one this except Paul.

After I left *EastEnders* and made the documentary *A Kiss Is Just a Kiss* for BBC Two, my mum and dad phoned me the night of the broadcast. It was their usual call to tell me they were proud of me. So I was surprised when Dad rang again the next morning. He had just come from his pub where the landlord had put a free pint on the bar for him because of my programme – 'And he's tight. He wouldn't give you the drips off his nose in winter. So I just wanted to tell you that I'm proud of you, son.'

I thanked him.

He started to speak again but his voice fell away: 'And I want to tell you … I want to tell you …'

He couldn't finish the sentence.

'What?'

'That I love you.' He took a deep breath: 'I love you, son.'

I held back my emotions, just, and muttered: 'I love you too.'

Nothing more was said in that beautiful silence.

Then he said he was heading back for the pint 'before the fella changed his mind'.

That was the day I became my father's son. The day I know he realised that if he had been gay and had the same experiences and opportunities, he would have done exactly the same as I did.

It was the day I realised that he was capable of love and being loved. The conversation was never referred to again.

As he grew older my father mellowed but his love of politics grew stronger. When I was elected to the National Executive Committee of the Labour Party it was for him the greatest achievement of my lifetime. His words on the phone were clear and precise, his tone completely felt and rounded: 'I never ever believed a son of mine would get elected to the National Executive Committee of the Labour Party. Never.' It was wonderful too to see him and Paul bond over their same sense of humour, their love of a pint, and their shared interests in sport and politics. Paul brought me closer to him than I could ever have imagined because I saw the side to the man that his friends enjoyed, and that my mum once probably enjoyed too.

When Mum died he was lost. They had been married for over fifty years and, though I never knew it at the time, it left a huge hole in his life. Going to bed alone and having to face the morning, and the days ahead, without her. He had the company of his mates from the docks and the parks, and the community of the East End, including his pub, but it wasn't enough. He never complained, though; only once as he was making us a cup of tea did his voice tremble and he said how much he missed her. I hugged him, but instead of that big strong man inside my mind, I held a frail old man of bones.

When our mum was on life support for three weeks and had shown no signs of unsupported life, my brothers and I were told we should take the decision to turn off the machines. But Dad refused and quietly railed against the doctors, challenging them as to whether they thought they were gods. Alone with us in the room reserved for relatives he wept silently, his back turned so we couldn't see him as he left the decision to his sons.

He was on a Christmas holiday in Spain with my youngest brother, Danny, when he was taken ill with pneumonia. Danny did his best ferrying between the hospital and my parents' little house in Torrevieja, but emphysema took hold and he declined very quickly. Our dad, who could never resist a pretty face, was last seen by Danny flirting with the Spanish nurses. He died that night in his sleep, and Johnny and Stevie brought his body home to the East End, where he belonged.

The whole community turned out for his funeral and as the cortege passed his pub, people stood outside and raised their glasses 'to Johnny Cashman', a tribute rarely seen in the London of today. We buried him with my mum, in their plot near Ilford, alongside other family members. Their own little place in the country – the City of London Cemetery. As we'd done for Mum, his four sons carried him to his grave, knowing that as a family we four would never carry together again. An ending had begun.

47

After only seven years in government, Labour had managed to reverse some of the most significant excesses of Thatcherism. The changes introduced, specifically on the equalities agenda and LGBT+ rights, were groundbreaking. But opposition never melted away and it was particularly prevalent in the Lords, especially after the Blair government removed 90 per cent of hereditary peers.

Every step of the way we were opposed by the Conservative Party at Westminster, and by religious fundamentalists. The government showed that it was determined to achieve equality; the House of Lords rejected an equal age of consent for a second time and Tony Blair employed the rarely used Parliament Act to override them (it would be used again to ban hunting with dogs). Section 28 was quickly repealed by the newly created Scottish Parliament, but for the rest of the UK it would be three more years, and two attempts, to finally get it off the statute books in 2003. Justifiably there was some anger in the LGBT+ community because it had taken so long to get rid of the much-hated Section 28 and people questioned Labour's commitment. There was a mistaken belief that maybe there had not been enough push at ministerial level and that the government should not use valuable parliamentary time pursuing unpopular measures that would be blocked. With this in mind, I kept up the pressure when I saw Tony Blair on the NEC or during my occasional visits to Downing Street.

I never got over the thrill of going to 10 Downing Street. The first time Paul and I were invited, just after the 1997 election, I stopped halfway up Downing Street to bend down. Paul asked me what I was doing and I told him I was doing up my shoelaces. 'But you're wearing slip-ons,' he said. I smiled and then owned up to the fact that I never thought I'd get up Downing Street without being arrested halfway – and I just wanted to savour the moment. At that first reception, after the party had spent eighteen years in opposition, I will never forget Tony's speech about the sacrifices and work that had finally got us there, which ended: 'But never forget, it will all end in tears. It always does.'

Being on the NEC gave me frequent access to the prime minister and to Cabinet ministers, and the chance to ask difficult questions in a semi-private situation. When I was elected to the NEC to represent the Parliamentary Labour Party it was no mean feat; that I had beaten a seasoned Labour parliamentarian and ex-chair of the Parliamentary Labour Party was also notable. There were highs and lows on the NEC. The highs were various: finding an exceptional candidate to stand in a by-election, interacting with constructive members over policy and chairing the annual conference. The lows were many, especially the bitter left–right fighting, and important discussions leaked to an opposing media.

Even though I was a committed moderniser of the party – building on the work done by Neil Kinnock, who had faced down the militants – I did not always agree with Blair. It was only Dennis Skinner and I who opposed Ken Livingstone's acceptance back into membership: Livingstone had stood against Labour and that was an automatic five-year suspension. On Iraq I opposed Tony for months, both on the NEC and in the media, until Clare Short tried to sabotage him and the prospects of another UN resolution. But the meetings that I had at 10 Downing Street were often about future policy – as they would be with Gordon Brown – or getting around difficult ministerial colleagues, whips or reluctant civil servants.

I was due to see Tony just before the Westminster parliamentary summer recess of 2003. I sat in the tiny waiting room off the main entrance and was then escorted to the Cabinet Room to see the PM. Except he wasn't there. The flustered assistant left me in the room and disappeared to find him. Suddenly Tony popped his head round the door from outside and asked me to join him on the garden terrace.

It was a lovely, warm summer's afternoon and we sat there soaking up the sun and exchanging small talk. As we got to the crux of why I was there, Sally Morgan, his political secretary, appeared. 'I've been looking for the two of you,' she said.

'Thought I'd get some sun,' Tony replied.

Sally and I had a good relationship by now, and after the 'gays in the military' intervention I think she trusted my judgement. She certainly trusted Paul's.

Knowing their time was limited I cut to the chase, as advised by Angela Mason, and explained that we needed to get the LGBT+ community back on board, citing the delay in repealing Section 28. I thought I had a way of doing it: 'I know there have been inter-departmental discussions around civil partnerships for same-sex couples, primarily led by Barbara Roche.' Tony nodded. Sally sat forward in the garden chair. 'So, I wanted to ask you to bring it forward in the Queen's Speech.'

The traffic in Whitehall droned in the background.

Tony looked to Sally and said: 'We can do that, can't we?'

She thought for a couple of seconds, then nodded. Tony looked to me, smiled and said: 'Okay, there you are.'

I was stunned. I added that I was prepared to work a lot harder, the same phrase I had used when pitching to Cameron Mackintosh to help us set up Stonewall fifteen years before. Like Cameron Mackintosh he replied: 'No need,' then said: 'Anything else?'

I raised the other equalities issue that Angela had requested and he agreed to look at it and get back to me. Then we talked about Paul and the work he was doing with high-profile supporters, even though he was no longer officially working for the Labour Party.

I left Downing Street on a high and immediately phoned Paul and Angela to give them the news. True to the prime minister's word, in the next Queen's Speech on 26 November 2003, same-sex civil partnerships were announced by the sovereign to the assembled Houses of Parliament.

48

There was no pleasing some people. The longer we were in government, people, including our own supporters, became more obsessed with what we had got wrong rather than acknowledging what we were getting right. There were ministerial resignations and the in-fighting between Gordon Brown's and Blair's teams was becoming bitter and public.

It wouldn't be long before a small group of lower rank parliamentary private secretaries, known as bag carriers, would gather for a curry in the West Midlands to plot against the prime minister. Tom Watson, Chris Bryant and Siôn Simon were among them, which was sad as I liked them all, but I loathed disloyalty and told them that directly. In my usual subtle way, I referred to their resignations as the Uprising of the Lilliputians, and texted Tom and Siôn to say that I believed that what they were doing 'would inflict long-term damage on the Party'. I wasn't against Gordon, it was just that I believed it was wrong, unseemly and irresponsible to behave like this. Tom took it on the chin, disagreed with me, and we got on with our friendship. Siôn and I didn't speak for years.

But I was right.

We also had high-profile supporters publicly criticising the government and Tony, and this needed to be managed. Paul was called in to help and I was asked to assist, along with the actor, Sir Patrick Stewart. Paul arranged for small groups of directors, writers, musicians and actors to meet the PM so that they could air their views, and to hear from Tony about the difficulties of government.

Getting the balance right between the almost inconsolable and the slightly disaffected was key, but most of the meetings, certainly the ones I attended with Patrick, were fairly well mannered and balanced. One was held in Tony and Cherie's flat in Downing Street and included Liz Dawn, best known for playing Vera Duckworth in *Coronation Street*, and a loyal stalwart, and an angry Sheila Hancock. Tony opened the session, then asked people to give him some feedback. Sheila didn't hold back and let rip. Liz Dawn sat there open-mouthed in amazement, before jumping in to staunchly defend Tony and the government. Shortly after, the meeting concluded. But Sheila never came back to the Party, while Liz remained and campaigned like a Trojan.

There was rarely any rancour, and never from Tony. The meetings were for people to feel included and listened to, and also for them to understand something of the difficult choices faced by those in power. As Tony said on one occasion: 'In opposition we have all the answers, knowing that when we go to bed someone else has to make the decision.'

One of the places from which I did not regularly receive invites was Buckingham Palace, and my first visit was nearly my last. When we were asked to the small reception at BP it was the first time that same-sex couples had been officially invited. Of course they had been before, but never as recognised couples. As the Queen Mother's chef had said to me many years earlier: 'If it wasn't for gay men, dear, it would be self-service at Clarence House' – and to my certain knowledge for a while it had been true of Buckingham Palace.

Selected Members of Parliament and our partners gathered and waited in the Picture Gallery to be presented to the Queen. The doors at the far end of the room were thrown open dramatically and light from the adjoining reception room streamed in. Instinctively everyone turned to approach the room and the waiting royal couple. It was pure theatre. I presented our invitation to the announcing official and, when he saw the names, he shook his head slightly in disbelief. The Queen gave him an enquiring look and with raised eyebrows he boomed: 'Mr Michael Cashman, Member of the European *Parliaaament* AND MR Paul Cottingham!'

In the photo taken at the event the Queen is clearly enjoying meeting Paul, probably because he was among the youngest of the small gathering. As Prince Philip shook Paul's hand he asked: 'You one of them, too?' Quick as a flash Paul replied: 'Yes, I suppose I am. I'm his partner.' And off we went to mix and mingle.

But you never get the last word with Philip. The wine flowed, we were having a great time – especially when I had a stand-up row with Philip over Europe. He barked at me about how terrible Europe was and, after a bit of to-ing and fro-ing, he attempted to leave our debate. Undeterred, I clasped the royal arm and promised to put a pamphlet in the post so that the next time he piped up he'd know what he was talking about.

A little later the Queen approached our group. Her courtiers tried to steer her away from our direction, but I stretched out my hand and she warmed to the initiative. The MP Paul Farrelly told her Philip and I had had 'an interesting exchange of views'. 'Oh really. On what?' she asked.

'Europe,' I replied.

She winced, then added: 'I can imagine that that was most fascinating.'

As we left, Paul, who never missed an opportunity to have his say, nobbled Boris Johnson, then MP for Henley, regarding a vote on equality measures, which was imminent. Boris gnarled the English language into something unintelligible and walked off saying that he didn't really believe in much, so not to give it a second thought. Two other Tories, whose sexualities were dubious, passed by. Paul knew one from their Westminster gym and with the same gusto he pounced on them. I mentioned to Paul that I had no idea he was gay, to which Paul replied: 'Neither did I until he put his hand on my dick in the jacuzzi.' Cottingham diplomacy!

To our surprise, some years later we were invited back to Buckingham Palace. With a drink in hand and her gloves off, the Queen approached and mumbled: 'How are you both?'

I replied that we were good and added that a lot had happened in the time since we last saw her.

The royal reply was a trifle tart: 'Well, obviously' – which had just a hint of 'what an idiotic thing to say' in its tone.

'No, Ma'am, what he means is we have had our civil partnership,' quipped Paul.

After a little quizzical pause, she came closer and said: 'Oh! Has it made a difference?'

The conversation deepened and widened as we described the many other couples who, after years together, had now publicly declared their commitment and been afforded legal protections. She was genuinely interested. 'Then it's obviously a good thing,' she replied, and a little later on she left. Philip was nowhere to be seen, so the night ended quietly.

49

Living with someone who is a professional organiser spoils you for life. So when Paul and I agreed that after nearly twenty-two years together we should have our civil partnership, it was also agreed that Paul would organise it. He researched into places, catering, entertainment and transport, and he drew up the guest list, selected the music, the readings, everything. His choices were perfect and I simply had to agree.

The first thing he discovered was that we needed to get permission from the registrar of the borough we lived in. Off we went for our appointment to the old offices on Bow Road, where we sat on the bench under the stairs beside a young man and woman. Looking at this lovely couple I suddenly realised neither of us had proposed to the other. I turned to Paul and asked: 'Paul, will you marry me?'

'Don't be daft,' he said, grinning from ear to ear. The young couple looked up, startled.

'No,' I said. 'But we haven't proposed.'

'You always pip me to the post, don't you?'

He held his finger up to his lips for silence, then said: 'Michael Cashman, will you be my civil partner?'

'Yes,' I said and we settled into smug silence while the young girl next to us smiled and blushed.

On 11 March 2006 we turned up at our venue, the impressive Vinopolis, a huge Victorian cathedral of a warehouse in Southwark, and our guests assembled.

Inside, now secure with the late arrival of our registrars, the ceremony started and I took part in something that I believed would never happen in my lifetime. It was incredibly personal and emotional. In front of our families and friends proudly and publicly we declared our commitment and our love to one another. My only sadness was that my mum and dad had not lived to see it and experience it. They would have been so proud, and boy would they have partied – my dad might even have appeared as an old lady.

We celebrated till late. Chancellor Gordon Brown, who was waiting to go back to finalise his budget, took his leave early but Sarah stayed on. Cherie joined us from Chequers, leaving Tony with their youngest son, Leo. June Brown kept up with the best, Sue Johnston danced literally until she dropped, but it didn't go unnoticed that, even on this day, the Brown camp sat on one side of the room and the Blair camp stood on the other. My Aunt Margie tried to pick an argument with Barbara Windsor, and left with a flea in her ear; Paul O'Grady and Ken Parry, meanwhile, became inseparable.

It was a perfect night, and the next day the press were unusually kind to us. The *Mail on Sunday* even declared it a beautiful day when 'Westminster meets *EastEnders*', before taking a sideswipe at Cherie for being 'hungry' when she arrived. They failed to report that she visited every table (apart from the Browns') and made sure that anyone who wanted a photograph had one taken with her.

It had all gone spectacularly well, and Paul had done it with minimal help from me. A few days later we jetted off to Budapest for a short celebration which ended in the most almighty row and me threatening to throw my wedding ring into the Danube. The stress of getting spliced had obviously taken its toll. As we had been together for over twenty-two years we decided we couldn't go on a honeymoon as such, so instead in November we went on a 'funny moon' to South Africa, and the big game reserve of Shamwari, where we met Virginia McKenna, Martin Shaw and Amanda Holden, who were there to celebrate the return of a lion from captivity. The breathtaking beauty of days and nights among the big game in the bush rounded off our celebrations superbly. He had planned it all. I had just done my bit and turned up, and not argued. Well, nearly not argued.

It was the perfect end to a perfect year, and despite what they called it, we were married.

50

After I was re-elected to the European Parliament I told Paul that I would not seek re-election in 2009, as ten years back and forth to Brussels and Strasbourg would be enough. I wasn't tired of politics but I did worry about getting tired of the job. The media sniping was exhausting and I was sick of the public's reaction to politicians.

So, shortly after our civil partnership in 2006, I went to see the Labour Party regional director of the West Midlands. It was decision time. Over a curry lunch in West Bromwich I told him that I did not intend to stand again, but by the time we'd finished the meal I had changed my mind. He was determined that I should not give way to the other Labour MEP, and as I had a very difficult relationship with her, he pressed all the right buttons.

That night I told Paul and his reaction was generous: so long as I wanted to do it it was okay with him. Deep down I did want to do it. Politically I had found my stride; I had proven my worth as a debater and legislator, and I had successfully led the challenge against the Italian EU commissioner designate, Rocco Buttiglione.

Buttiglione, who had a worrying record on equalities and women's rights, was Silvio Berlusconi's candidate for the human rights portfolio! It beggared belief, but Berlusconi and the other European governments stuck to their position; there would be no backing down. Working with colleagues we achieved cross-party commitment that if this candidate was not removed then the European Parliament would reject the entire European Commission. It was daring and it was unprecedented; everyone, including some of our colleagues, thought we would surrender.

The media were entranced as the two institutions stared each other down.

I became a spokesperson for the Buttiglione affair – before I deferred, inexplicably, to the leader of the European Parliamentary Labour Party. On the crucial issue of rejecting the Commission I had crossed swords with Peter Mandelson (also a commissioner designate) who was adamant that we should accept the Commission without adjustment. Leaders of the political groups had lost control of the votes, a majority of the Parliament backed the line I and others proposed, and after weeks of negotiation and postponed votes the composition of the Commission was changed. I refused to take the credit; it was the job that gave me the opportunity to do the right thing.

When a proposed EU-wide equality law was going to be watered down by the European Commission I led the fight to stop it. Martin Schulz, my earliest friend in the Parliament, who was now president of the Socialist Group, asked me to negotiate with the president of the European Commission, José Manuel Barroso, on behalf of the entire Socialist Group, and I delivered. Quite rightly the law was proposed undiluted.

I was leading on many human rights issues in the European Parliament, amending and improving the transparency law, and fighting for the rights of property owners in Spain who were having their homes demolished and ownership ripped away from them. On another dossier Schulz joked that: 'Only Cashman would work for those who will never have the vote.' This was with reference to the repatriation of mortal remains – people who had died outside their countries and needed to be brought home. The changes I sought were not agreed and it was ironic that years later, through a death in the family, we too would encounter the numbing bureaucracy faced by so many others. The battles were endless and I wonderfully lost myself within them.

But after work in Brussels there was, as ever, nothing other than the same routine: meal alone in a restaurant, a drink alone in a bar, home alone, tired, fantasising, unnoticed yet happily surviving. But surviving for what? In absence of an answer, I worked on.

At home my relationship with Paul had settled into easy mode. Live-in lovers had long gone and I made more of an effort to do what he loved: socialising. So instead of vegetating on the sofa, as I preferred to do, we would go out. Nearly every weekend was spent chasing a play, or off for a meal. It was good. In fact, to my utter surprise, it felt very good. On the weekends I had to work we managed it and compensated elsewhere. I had finally learnt to let go, to embrace Paul's spontaneity and to stop worrying about the future.

His wonderful holidays sustained us too: the brilliance of our time in Mayan central Mexico and the Yucatán Peninsula, the evening when we chased the setting sun and arrived at a beach-side hacienda to find we were the only guests. Waking early and walking along deserted beaches for mile upon mile and then lying in the hammock at night listening to the ocean. Paul and I being the only 'gringos' in a remote Mexican cantina: we paid the bill to the dancing waitress and then in a crazy gesture she demanded I partner her; so I grabbed her hand, swirled her round the tables and we left to the sound of a Mexican cheer! In the rainforests of Honduras we were happy as larks, soaked to the skin; in Amarillo, Texas we had to lock ourselves in a hotel room to escape the drunken locals (the only reason we visited the city was because Paul loved the song).

There were trips to Paris, the museums, restaurants and gay bars with their dark rooms: even there they had a knack of making you feel like your French just wasn't up to it! The outrageous naughtiness of Amsterdam, and that one crazy winter night when we passed a man who was standing on the pavement dripping from head to toe with water. As we walked by I said to Paul: 'It's freezing. He'll freeze to death,' so we turned back. He was Irish and had been thrown into the canal by his friends. He had no idea where his hotel was, so I decided that we would book him a room in our hotel. 'You're coming with us,' I told him.

'I love you gays,' he replied and kept repeating it.

At the hotel they refused to give him a room, so we took him to ours. We were planning to give him some dry clothes, get him into the shower to warm him up and then take him to the police station.

'I love you gays.'

'So you keep saying.'

I shoved him into the bathroom and laid out spare clothes. Ten minutes later he reappeared, still loving us 'gays'. I told him to get dressed. He was blond, with a well-defined, muscular body and was about twenty-five. Paul was sitting on the bed and the guy unexpectedly leant forward and kissed him full on the lips. The towel dropped, a clinch ensued, I was pulled into it and a night of incredible passion followed. When we woke in the same bed in the morning he jumped up and shouted 'Jesus!' I asked if he knew where his hotel was, to which the reply was 'of course, near Amsterdam station'. It was just around the corner. He thanked us for 'saving his life' and made for the door, saying that he was flying out that morning and that he had to meet up with the other 'gays'.

'You're with a bunch of gays then?' I said.

'No. No. Not gays. *Guys*.'

We sat there, speechless.

'We're firemen. On a stag weekend.' Then he left, never to be seen or heard from again. Strangely enough the episode reminded us of the parable of the Good Samaritan, and we never passed by thereafter.

Then we rediscovered Turkey and the mesmerising Aegean/Mediterranean Datça peninsula. There we fell in love with two beautiful, derelict stone cottages on 1,000 square metres of land. Within four days we'd bought them and, not speaking a word of Turkish, Paul began the renovation process. The Turkish builder delivered on budget and on time. We painstakingly nourished, designed and loved the garden into a Bougainvillean paradise with olive, orange, almond, lemon and pomegranate trees.

Now that Paul and I had life balanced out, dealing with some of my own political comrades – though at times awful – felt more manageable. However, when Paul stood with me at the election count in June 2010 and I was returned as the only Labour MEP for the West Midlands (we had started with three in 1999) it was decided I would definitely not stand again. This time I left nothing to chance and publicly announced my pending retirement very early into my third term. When I was re-elected onto the NEC I informed my colleagues that it would be my last election to that body too.

Paul was thrilled. I had given him my word and this time I had stuck to it without any prompting. There was no going back and we had it all planned. I worked out our finances, as I always did, and we would be okay. There were the holidays to be taken, continents yet to be visited, and our love of America to be indulged. So much to do, so much to look forward to.

During my final parliamentary mandate I took over as president of the European Parliament's Delegation for Relations with South Africa, which had its challenges and its charms. Among the breathtaking charms were the country and its people, and I made sure that when I led the delegation there, at our own expense, Paul came with me. Of course my MEP colleagues loved him, especially the right-wingers. He knew how to listen, flirt and cut the politics.

The challenges were many. The African National Congress (ANC) in government was difficult to deal with and never allowed us to forget our colonialist past, especially when we raised human rights issues in Africa, including LGBT+ issues. We narrowly avoided an international diplomatic incident when the South African foreign minister passed a letter to me from President Sarkozy implicating France in the invasion of the Ivory Coast. I refused to allow our MEPs to publicly use the letter and within minutes Renaud, my French head of staff, revealed it was a fake. This was later confirmed by the French embassy – and thankfully we managed to stop it getting into the public domain.

Then there were endless debates about what they would allow onto the agenda. There could be nothing critical of the ANC regime or policies. Sometimes we would go to the wire as the

ANC fought against important items on the agenda, and minutes from the start of the meeting I would have to threaten cancellation in order to achieve a compromise. But when we socialised as colleagues the South African parliamentarians were joyous, and they liked Paul, too. They had to because he never took a back seat. If I was there, he felt that he had as much right as any other spouse to be there too, and a party was a party.

On a parliamentary trip to Papua New Guinea, where homosexuality is illegal, we gave them a lot to talk about. A call came through from the prime minister's office requesting the presence of Mrs Cashman at the spousal events. Eamon, our head of protocol, giggled and delightedly told them that 'Mrs Cashman' was actually Mr Paul Cottingham. The Papuan prime minister's PA, Barbara, was fascinated and insisted he attend. I told Paul not to go and said it would be boring among all those soldiers that were required to escort us everywhere. That did it, he was off!

At first he was the 'gay' curiosity item, but he then charmed them all, including the captain of the battleship. The spouses ended their three days with a party and Paul serenaded them and the prime minister's PA with Barry Manilow's 'Mandy'. At the end of our work in South Africa we decided to stay on for a few more days and finished off by returning to the Shamwari game reserve on the Eastern Cape. I waved the delegation off, said farewell to our EU South African ambassador and Paul and I settled down for a late breakfast.

'I think it's getting bigger,' Paul said, pointing to the small bump on the left side of the bridge of his nose. He asked me to take a look at it. It looked perfectly normal. Just a bump. The GP had diagnosed it six weeks before as an ingrowing spot and gave him some ointment. But there were no signs of it diminishing. I reassured him and told him to see a dermatologist when we got back to the UK.

PART THREE

We flew back to London and Paul made an appointment with a consultant dermatologist at the old Jewish Hospital in Stepney Green. There they took a biopsy, put in a couple of stitches and told Paul to return in a week. In the meantime there was Paul's fundraiser at the Café de Paris, and we were both excited about it.

The event was another success. The politicians and glitterati turned out, Ed Miliband made a wonderful speech, referring to Paul and me as the 'Posh and Becks of the Labour Party' and Paul O'Grady did the introductions and a hilarious stand-up spot. Long after the night was officially over a group of us stood drinking by the bar and congratulated Paul on the substantial amount of money that had been raised. The morning beckoned, but as always we had 'another one for the road'.

Hung-over, the next day we weaved our way through Stepney to the hospital and I waited in the ground floor cafe while he went to get the result. I got a coffee, nestled into a chair and tried to avoid mentally counting the bottles we had drunk the night before. There was a newspaper in my hands that I was just staring at as the vision of a builder's breakfast entered my head: the perfect cure for a hangover.

Lost in a reverie, I didn't notice Paul until he was suddenly standing in front of me.

'That was quick,' I said.

In his hand he twiddled what looked like a post-it note.

I stood up and he turned towards the main exit.

'Everything okay?' I asked.

'Let's go outside,' he replied and led the way.

On the pavement outside he stopped, turned to me and said: 'It's cancer. I've got cancer.'

He passed me the post-it note the consultant dermatologist had given him.

'I asked her to write it down,' he said.

I read the words 'subcutaneous B-cell lymphoma'. It was a foreign language, and one I never wanted to learn.

A state of shock overwhelmed me; I had expected us to breeze through this appointment, then get on with the rest of the day. Now it was going to be dramatically different. I heard myself saying it would be okay, that we would get it sorted, but I didn't know – was I trying to convince him or myself?

The dermatologist would email a referral letter recommending a specialist before the end of the day and then we had to make an appointment quickly. It was serious. In less than ten minutes Paul had been told he had a rare form of cancer and was then bounced onto the streets with nothing more than a fucking post-it note.

I was silent and angry, and I wanted to get angrier, but Paul just wanted to go home. We retraced our steps and barely said a word. I didn't know what to say. The word cancer was screaming in my head, filling every space. We entered our building, walked into the lift in silence and I saw Paul's terrified, uncomprehending face in the mirror. And we hugged and hugged.

In the flat he sat down at the computer and began to cancel some appointments that he didn't feel 'up to'. I stood behind him. I was frightened for us both. I could only imagine what was going on in his head, and I wanted to get inside there and take all his fears away. But I knew I couldn't. I placed my hands lightly on his shoulders, and moments later together on the bed we quietly cried, holding one another tight. Eventually, though, we got up and decided to do something.

'I'm going to get this sorted,' he said, and I breathed out a sigh of relief that I had never experienced before; the organiser was taking control. I followed his lead; I needed to cancel my weekend meetings, I couldn't face them.

My UK office was deserted and the phone clicked into answer-phone. I started to leave a message that we had been to the hospital and that Paul had been diagnosed with – I couldn't say the word. I forced it into my mouth, I shaped the 'C' and instead I burst into tears. Through those tears the anger formed itself into 'cancer. Paul has got cancer.'

It was a Friday; the day was slipping away and there was still no email from the consultant. I cursed her, not under my breath. Paul asked me to be quiet and told me it didn't help me getting angry.

I took to the internet. I thought, if this woman who calls herself a doctor couldn't bring herself to do the specialist referral then I would do it. All the time I ached to hear that 'ping' in his inbox, the sound that someone cared, that they were in command and they knew how to sort it. But it didn't happen.

How we got through that weekend I don't know, but by Monday we had found the specialist for his type of lymphoma online. We spoke to his GP and he made an appointment for the next evening, Tuesday. Finally things were moving forward, there would be no more paralysis.

That Monday night, when we got in from an escapist dinner, the dermatologist's referral letter and her recommendation of a physician were sitting in his inbox, three days later than promised. We ignored the recommendation. And we never heard another word.

52

Stephen Morris was part of a multi-disciplinary team based at St Thomas's Hospital in Lambeth, where he worked alongside countless other specialists. I had printed off the referral letter with the diagnosis and had it clutched in my hand as I sat in the office as an observer on a life I wanted to protect.

Stephen was about forty-two, warm, gentle and sexy, as doctors sometimes are. He had a soft, quiet way of talking and a naughty smile that slowly crept across his face. He explained that there were two groups of lymphoma, and although Paul's cancer was rare, it was treatable. We breathed an outward sigh of relief, and mentally punched the air. Nevertheless, he said, it was important to move quickly.

Stephen would arrange for a battery of tests and scans, and then finally a painful bone marrow biopsy, for which he apologised in advance, to ensure there were no other cancerous sites. He was insistent that his team needed to physically see the biopsy slides that had been taken previously so that their own pathologist could confirm the diagnosis that Paul had been given. We left, and Paul was bright, cheerful. 'Sounds positive,' he said. And it was. Very positive.

There was a tremendous feeling that we had locked onto someone who knew what we didn't and that we would not have to fight this alone. Without Paul and me sharing a word we knew we could trust Stephen, who had the air of a consummate professional, and we were relieved that we no longer had to lead the charge. The emotional labour and the reassurances could be shared.

It was time for a drink! I put work on hold: what had existed before me could exist without me. Paul was my only priority, and to their credit, my colleagues rallied round, while my staff were wonderful. Over the next two weeks we saw Stephen several times. All the scans and tests confirmed that there was no other diagnosis, and no additional cancerous sites. It was good news.

'But,' said Stephen, 'we still need to see your slides, and we're having trouble getting them from King's College Hospital. I've called personally and they've promised to send them over this week.'

However, he did not want to wait. Time was of the essence and the quicker they treated the cancer the greater the chances of success. They had no idea of knowing how long it had been growing, so it was better to start the treatment sooner rather than later.

That's when we started our journeys to Earl's Court for radiotherapy. Three weeks of daily intensive radiotherapy to the face was scheduled, followed by six weeks of chemotherapy. Stephen warned it was not going to be pleasant, or easy. We laughed when Paul had his 'phantom of the opera' lead mask made to ensure that the radiotherapy only destroyed certain cells. He met Lena, his lovely radiologist, and all was set to begin the following Monday.

Yet still the pathology slides from King's were nowhere to be seen. Stephen decided that, given the other tests had shown nothing 'sinister', we should proceed. That word 'we' was so important throughout these early stages. It made Paul and me feel included, that we were not on our own in what we were going through. And, of course, we were not. The support and the expertise around us was mind-blowing. We had moved from the utter desolation of the original diagnosis to a sense of relief, enveloping care and experts who were in control. It all felt manageable. It felt, dare I say, easier than we had imagined.

Paul's attitude too was so unexpected. Before this diagnosis every pain was a heart attack, every ache a brain tumour. But now, due to the reality of what he had to deal with, he became a warrior. 'I'm going to live through this cancer,' he said. And live we did.

The darkness that had taken over our lives, and made me want to rewind every single minute back to a time before the diagnosis, gave way to hope. I started to plan the holidays. Me! Weekend breaks to see our friends in Holland who we'd met at our home in Turkey. I looked out for 'once-in-a-lifetime' experiences, because I now knew for certain that was all we had: one lifetime. I realised too that all my carefully worked out plans and financial strategising meant nothing. Cancer came into our lives first as a threat, then as a teacher. Now, we were ready for it to go. The days of putting up with shit, and shit people, and doing things we didn't want to do were well and truly over.

For the first week of radiotherapy we planned a few nice things – nothing too extravagant – like having dinner together, seeing fun people, catching theatre; an awayday to Brighton for fish and chips and a seaside stroll, or the Botanical Gardens at Kew. Brussels ticked along without me, primarily due to my brilliant team Renaud Savignat and Bruno Selun. When I popped back for a day I was overwhelmed by MEP colleagues of all parties and nationalities who were concerned and kind. The Labour leader, Dame Glenis Willmott, forbade me from even thinking about going back to work, and Martin Schulz threatened to ban me from the Parliament!

On the Sunday evening Stephen rang to see if Paul was okay. He would see us at the hospital just before the treatment started and would catch up with us again on the Wednesday or Thursday. A bag of medication would be waiting for Paul to deal with the nasty burns and side-effects of the radiotherapy.

To watch Paul in the hospital you would have thought he didn't have a care in the world. He was smiling and happy, and his attitude was infectious. The sessions took no longer than about thirty minutes, after which we would go for a long walk back into central London, before deciding on our treat. After three days the burning started at the back of his throat, but he was armed with sprays, and pain relief. We were getting into a routine and he suggested that I could stay at home if I wanted or meet him after his sessions. I told him to fuck off and that he couldn't get rid of me as easily as that. I didn't tell him that deep, deep down, I felt that I had lost so much time with him over the years that losing any more was unthinkable.

When Thursday morning came around Paul and I arrived at the hospital in high spirits to see Stephen, but immediately we could tell something was wrong. His radiologist Lena was visibly upset and she looked away when we approached.

Inside the office Stephen asked us to sit down. He opened the file in front of him, shook his head, then frowned.

'Something wrong?' asked Paul with a big grin.

'Paul.'

There was a long pause.

'Yesterday we finally got your original biopsy slides from King's. I am afraid there has been a misdiagnosis.'

He turned his body completely towards Paul. I felt like I was no longer in the room. Again I sensed that in these situations the observer needs to remain silent and passive.

'We are not dealing with subcutaneous B-cell lymphoma. You have a very rare form of cancer that we only see about one case in every three million.'

He paused to see if Paul was taking it in.

'It is called angiosarcoma and I am afraid we will have to halt your treatment. This kind of cancer doesn't respond to radiology, or chemotherapy. We can only cut it out.'

Out of the corner of my eye I looked at Paul.

'I want you to go to St Thomas's where I have arranged with Professor Whittaker to do an urgent biopsy.'

My head was spinning; frustration and anger began to rise; I felt there would never be anything straightforward. I held back my emotions and quietly asked why they were doing another biopsy. I didn't want to intrude, but I needed to know. I wanted Paul to know.

'We need to match these slides, to confirm...'

Stephen suddenly broke off mid-sentence and in a flash of anger he said that it was almost impossible to mistake these two cancers as they are so different. Then a ray of hope.

'We need to confirm that what our pathologist saw last night is *your* biopsy. You'd have to be drunk to diagnose angiosarcoma as subcutaneous B-cell lymphoma. Drunk or insane.' He then said that he and Professor Whittaker would meet us later. Paul asked some questions about treatment, and about how the cancer would be cut out. Then we thanked him and left.

Outside Lena was waiting. She apologised to Paul and they went off to a room together. I watched through the glass door. She talked animatedly, using a tissue occasionally to wipe away her tears. He touched her arm and for a second the tables turned as he reassured her. I could see it in his face: that soft understanding smile, his hand on her forearm, the kiss he placed on her cheek as he left.

We had two hours before we needed to be at St Thomas's, on the banks of the Thames. Outside the world was revolving normally, it was only ours that seemed off its axis.

As we walked towards Knightsbridge, Paul said that Lena was devastated by the misdiagnosis and was so worried about the treatment that she had filed a report. Strangely, it didn't seem to matter. We had entered a void where time was on hold and all that mattered was the appointment with Professor Whittaker. At some point we grabbed that ray of hope: Stephen's quiet aside that 'it might not be his biopsy slide'.

We walked, side by side, passing places that we had passed so many times, but never seeing them like today. Everything was different: the colours no longer there, the sounds muted, the people merged into a background of grey. The only place I wanted to be was in my head, and inside his. Inside Paul's head listening to his fears and his questions and soothing them. Yet I was faced with the mind-numbing reality that I couldn't take anything away, I could only walk this path alongside him.

From Hyde Park Corner we walked towards the Mall and Buckingham Palace. Behind us came the sound of horses' hooves and the magnificent Household Cavalry went by on their way to change their guard at Whitehall Palace. We stood in a quiet vigil, watched them pass, saying nothing.

I found myself catching sideways glimpses of his face and remembering Stephen's words, that they would 'cut the cancer out'. Cut across his beautiful face. Again and again I tried to imagine what he was thinking, what he was going through. But he showed nothing. St James's Park was packed with tourists and Londoners soaking up the April sun. Silently we edged our way through them and over Westminster Bridge.

The Thursday afternoon before Easter, St Thomas's was deserted. We walked down the long dark hallways and followed the signs to the west end of the old building, St John's skin clinic. Breaking the silence, I told Paul that Somerset Maugham studied here as a young medical student. He didn't respond. A receptionist explained that Dr Morris and Professor Whittaker were on their way, and we waited on a wooden bench. Never a couple for overt shows of affection, I subtly squeezed his arm. He squeezed mine back.

'You okay, babs?'

'Not really,' he replied.

Professor Whittaker apologised for the appalling and inexplicable misdiagnosis, then rolled up his sleeves. He explained that if the cancer was caught early it was manageable and Stephen added that it was usually found on the scalp and in old ladies. I asked Paul if there was something he should be telling me.

We laughed. The medics seemed confused.

While Paul disappeared with Professor Whittaker and a nurse, I looked out of the window at the meaningless desert that London had become. Alone for the first time since we'd heard about the misdiagnosis, I stared at the sky and realised my anger had subsided and time had frozen. I knew that I had to shake myself out of this stupor: I had to fight like I had never fought before. Then suddenly he was back in the room as if nothing had happened and with two bright blue stitches on the left side of his nose.

'Matches his eyes,' I said, trying to smile.

We wouldn't receive the biopsy results for another ten days, due to Easter, so the next day we flew to Turkey, determined to live as normal a life as possible. And to a certain extent we did. We tended our beautiful garden, walked the quiet beaches and hilltops and visited the harbour at night. A couple of bars and restaurants were open, and the fishing boats nudged one another gently on the night winds.

Although at times I could escape the cancer at the forefront of my mind, I knew it was there and I knew his head was filled with it too. Unbeknown to him I had asked our GP to let me know by email if any news came in before we got back. Nothing arrived and I breathed easily each time I left the internet cafe.

53

St Thomas's was buzzing and the skin clinic packed. Paul and I waited on the same wooden bench until Stephen emerged, extricating himself from a group of clinicians.

He said that he hoped Paul had had a lovely holiday, and that he would find a room for us. He spoke quietly; they had received the results of the biopsy and the pathology confirmed the rare cancer. He paused, then added that he wanted Paul to see the surgeon, Jenny, as soon as possible. My heart sank as we listened to news we had hoped to avoid.

'It is vital that we get it out as soon as possible, so that the team can start six weeks of radiology in order to kill off any microscopic cells that might migrate to the lungs and replicate.'

Secondaries.

If Jenny was able to successfully cut the cancer out then there was a good chance. He smiled reassuringly, as doctors often do, and Paul smiled back.

'Mr Cottingham? Paul?' Jenny Geh beckoned him in.

Paul asked if it was okay if I went in too. Once inside I explained that I was his civil partner. Jenny was warm and efficient, about forty years old. She asked if she could take a look and explained that until she was actually able to open up the face we wouldn't know how much she would need to remove. But she would try to keep well away from the eye.

Inside I winced, but all the while Paul just listened.

With a sketch pad Jenny showed him how she would cut into him and where she would take a flap from his forehead as a blood supply to the skin that would eventually be grafted onto his face. There were two operations scheduled within ten days. The first to cut the cancer out, along with a safety margin of healthy cells, and then get the lab reports before doing the plastic surgery. She opened her diary to find a date. Paul said that he had a problem: Eurovision.

Jenny closed her diary and was suddenly very interested. Paul explained that he visited the host country every year for the grand final and it was the highlight of his year. I told him he was mad and must cancel the trip. Jenny didn't even acknowledge me.

'When is it?' she asked.

It was only a week away.

'I want you to go,' she said. 'It is better that you have a good time and come back in the right mood for this op.'

A date was agreed and she ushered us out, wishing him a good time at Eurovision.

'I like her,' he said. I nodded.

Spontaneously, we decided to go to the mad Italian restaurant around the corner where they had a singing Elvis. Unbeknown to us, though, it was Elvis's night off so the entertainment was karaoke and Paul performed Barry Manilow's 'Mandy' to wild applause. We chatted to a lovely couple, drank far too much bad red wine and limoncello, and eventually staggered into a taxi home. He said how thrilled he was with Jenny and Stephen, his 'team'. Drifting off to sleep later in our bed I released him from our cuddle and turned over, my foot curled around his ankle to make sure he was there, as I always did.

'Pleased you're going, babs?'

He nodded.

As usual I did the packing for him. Paul loved Eurovision but I always stayed home. It was his world, his friends, his space. On the night of the final I always watched from the comfort of our home in London, while he was there inside the hall. The text messages connected us. This year it was in Germany.

There is a year-long run-up to the final, with each country choosing its entry before the fans descend from around the world on the host nation. It is one of the largest gay male gatherings on the planet. There is a series of parties, then dress rehearsals – where the show gossip bursts out onto the streets – followed by two semi-finals and ultimately the live grand final, which is broadcast around the world.

Paul always went with his mates, John Watts and Mitch, and he had other friends that he only ever saw at Eurovision. There were always the local men to be enjoyed too – and the occasional Russian oligarch. This side of his life fascinated me – I lived with it, waking every morning to ESC (Eurovision Song Contest) Radio – but I didn't totally understand it. So, we agreed he'd keep this world for himself. I only ever knew it as his guest, with him as my guide.

Each year when the event was over he would return home and together we would watch the semi-finals and the final on DVDs, curled up on the sofa, singing along, as I gave a running criticism and he threatened to kill me.

'All done,' and I zipped up his bag.

Instinctively I reached out for him and he was in my arms. He whispered into my ear that he was frightened that this might be his last time.

We held one another for ages.

In the morning he left for Düsseldorf with a spring in his step, his other world waiting, unquestioning, unconcerned. I stood alone in our bedroom, trying to push unwanted thoughts away.

54

I found myself packing Paul's bags again on his return, but this time for the hospital. It was only for one night. Jenny would operate and all being well he could go home the following afternoon.

We were both quiet. His room was on the third floor, overlooking the Thames and the City of London. Upriver, to the left, you could see St Paul's Cathedral. It was a good omen; he had hoped for a river view and I was happy because he deserved everything he wanted.

We busied ourselves putting his things out and then everything swung into action. Swabs were taken for the supervirus, Paul was wired up for ECGs, he pulled on unsexy white stockings to prevent thrombosis, he was given blood tests and then he had to fill in more forms about his general state of health. It was still only four o'clock in the afternoon and the operation wasn't going to be until early evening. There was more activity when the anaesthetist arrived, checked him out, shared a joke and then disappeared. As quickly as everyone had piled in, now they were gone, and there was silence.

Paul reached for the TV remote control and daytime quiz shows filled the void. We were alone, accompanied by boats plying up and down the river. He lay on his bed in his operation gown playing with his iPad. Probably on Facebook where he had been absolutely upfront about the cancer in all his postings, or playing Candy Crush. 'What do you win?' I asked of Candy Crush. When he told me that you just went up levels and you won nothing I was amazed and ribbed him about it for months afterwards. Especially as you paid for the privilege!

I probed but he ignored me. He was connected to his friends from around the world who were all there with him: watching him, waiting with him, loving him, supporting him and even some praying for him. Not for the first time I saw what a lovely community he had kept alive, and nurtured to continue growing.

I looked over at him and I dearly wanted to swap places; I knew Paul had so many fears that he had never spoken about. He saw me looking and winked: 'All right Sweet?'

'Yes, thank you, Sweet,' I replied.

Neither of us remembered why we habitually repeated these inane endearments – I think it started because we were taking the piss out of each other, sending ourselves up, playing at sincerity. But it had now become our way, our private signature tune. In a strange way it had found its own hyper-sincerity because no one understood why we did it.

He looked at me. I looked at him. And he went back to his iPad.

I glanced away, out of the window. Knowing that this amazing man was about to have his face cut open and stitched back together again was almost too much to contain. That this fucking cancer had ripped our lives up. Everything had changed. But I knew too it had made me realise that I could lose him and that our time together was finite. It had made us be positive, and it had brought out a side of him that I never knew existed.

I thought he would fold, that he would give in. But he had become my hero. He had shown a strength that had always been there but I had somehow never noticed. The same strength that he showed years before when I had tried to sabotage our relationship. The same strength he drew on to deal with the disappearance of his father. And the same strength he needed to cope with being gay, being different.

He told himself that he was going to live through this cancer, not with it. And that is why, at every twist and turn and piece of shit news, we went out and tried to have a good time, to turn the negative into a positive.

Finally, in her blue theatre garb, Jenny arrived. Paul signed the consent form. She confirmed where she was going to cut: in the middle of his forehead, then down, around the left side of his nose and up to the lower eyelid.

'Tighten it up a bit while you're there,' he added cheekily.

'Course I will,' she laughed.

They had a lovely relationship.

She looked over to me. 'You okay?'

'I'm fine,' I nodded.

Jenny put a couple of ink marks on Paul's face and thigh and said that quite a few people were in the operating theatre waiting to see him. She added that he should be back in his room within two hours.

Paul looked at me and said: 'Make sure you go out and have something to eat. I don't want you getting ill on me.'

I took a deep breath and nodded.

'Okay,' said Jenny. 'We've done enough talking. Shall we get it done?'

'Yes,' he replied. 'Yes.'

Alone, before he was taken to theatre, I hugged him and we told each other how much we loved one another. 'I love you, Sweet.'

'I love you too, Sweet.'

I said that I would be waiting in the room when they brought him back.

Without sedative or pre-med, Paul walked with the porter to the operating theatre, and I followed. We all got into the lift together, they got out at the second floor and in his dark blue dressing gown, slippers and long white stockings I watched the love of my life walk away. His utter, utter bravery shocked me and I leant back against the lift wall, struggling to breathe.

I followed his instructions and found somewhere to eat, and though I physically filled those two hours my head was filled with him. Silently I questioned if he would be okay after the op, if it was proceeding as planned and how much of his beautiful face they would cut.

Inside his hospital room I waited, my senses heightened for any signs that he was coming back. Then the doors quietly opened and he was brought in on a bed with tubes and wires coming from all directions. I called out gently to him but he looked at me without any recognition. The left side of his face was covered with bloodied dressings. Unable to move, I stood in the corner and watched in wonderment and overwhelming relief; he was back. He responded to the nurse's questions and they continued to check on him every half hour. As the medical team left, silence enfolded the room. Outside it was getting dark. Then he looked over at me in the corner and smiled; and I wanted nothing more.

A few hours later, at about one in the morning, he was tucking into a plate of hot food and, against all rules, I produced a bottle of red wine from the bedside cabinet. He screamed with joy, then his face dropped: 'You silly sod. We haven't got a corkscrew!' I searched in the bag and produced another bottle. To my relief, and his, it had a screw cap.

For the next ten days he coped with the pain, the discomfort, the hole in his face and the stares from people in the street, with huge dignity. This would be another part of the journey that he had to travel on his own, the psychological support for dealing with people's reactions to disfigurement. It is shocking how insensitive people can be.

The pathology report on the removed tissue confirmed angiosarcoma, and we were lucky that it was within the five-centimetre operable boundary. Jenny explained that she would take out a bit more from the sides, but that there was no need to go any deeper, before doing the reconstruction. Everyone was positive. When Jenny did her plastic surgery, she was happy with her work. Paul was delighted because she did tighten him up a bit and all things considered, his face looked amazing. I joked that after twenty-seven years I suddenly had a new model. He said he wished he could say the same. The process continued with a trip to a make-up artist, Lady Mimi, at Chelsea Hospital, who showed him how to blend the different skin tones with stage make-up. Finally he was sent to the psychologist who, after just two sessions, told Paul that he already knew how to deal with his 'new, challenging world'.

I found a cruise, and put the details in front of him. 'Three weeks, to the Antarctic. The Cruise of a Lifetime.' I squashed the sadness that I still felt deep, deep inside, and said: 'We deserve it, babs.'

'We do,' he smiled.

I started to notice that my own health was erratic. I often broke out into sweats but would feel cold and I was getting increasingly breathless, but I dismissed it as stress. Paul noticed it too and insisted I see the GP. My blood pressure was through the roof, understandably so, but a blood test came back with an unsatisfactory report and I was duly sent for a scan of the kidneys.

I felt like I was sailing through it all, that it was not happening to me. My only concern was Paul and I compared everything to what he was going through. So, it was with this mentality that I suddenly found myself sitting opposite a surgeon who was explaining to me the best way to remove the cancer from my left kidney.

'Cancer' – would it ever leave us alone, I wondered?

Paul joked that it was typical of me to be diagnosed so soon after him, that I hated being left out of the 'limelight' and that whatever he had, I had to have. We both laughed, and we did the best thing to do, poured another drink.

Alone, I sat in St Thomas's Hospital with the brilliant professor of interventional radiology, Andreas Adam. He asked if the surgeons had explained the complications of renal surgery. I told him that they hadn't, so gently and patiently he talked me through it. My cancer was small and there were a range of options for treatment: watch, wait and see if it grows, or get it out now. I decided on the latter; I wanted to move forward with my life as soon as possible, so I chose the interventional radiology.

The tables were turned, as so often in our relationship, and Paul remained in the hospital room as they took me to the operating theatre. Unlike his experience, I was in a wheelchair and barely able to keep my head up because of the pre-med. There were complications with the operation and what should have taken an hour lasted three. Upstairs, waiting in my room overlooking the House of Commons, Paul asked the sister if everything was all right. She replied dismissively that I must be alive, or they would have called.

Drowsy, but happy, the first thing I saw was Paul waiting in my room.

'I've been worried about you.'

I just replied that the drugs were brilliant and then dipped in and out of a wonderful sleep.

The next day Professor Adam discharged me and, pain free, Paul and I walked out of St Thomas's and made our way home. Now we were both on the watch list. We would need a check-up every three months, six months, then hopefully only every year. He worried about me. I worried about him. Sharing our cancers and celebrating our lives.

55

We had dealt with two cancers, taken the time and trouble to dispatch them both, and now we decided it was the time to live like there was no tomorrow. We started looking forward to our first big treat, the cruise to the Antarctic, which was in December, just before Parliament went into recess.

Then, out of the blue, I received a letter from the Cabinet Office; I read it and then I slumped into a chair in stunned silence. Paul was concerned, grabbed the letter and then looked up and shouted 'Yes! A CBE. You've got a CBE!'

The letter, very carefully worded, informed me that the prime minister, David Cameron (on Ed Miliband's nomination), proposed to submit my name to the Queen that 'she may be graciously pleased to approve that you be appointed a Commander of the British Empire...' It stipulated that the letter was in strict confidence and that I had to inform them if I wanted to accept. I shot a letter straight back that I was chuffed to be awarded the CBE for my political service, and thereby, for equality. I had no hesitation in accepting.

Paul and I were flushed with pride and he immediately started organising who would come with us to the palace and, of course, the resulting party! Before then, though, it was the holiday.

We had two days in Rio de Janeiro, where the cruise started, and from there the ship sailed along the breathtaking South American coast, stopping off at Buenos Aires, Montevideo, the Falkland Islands and then on to the Antarctic Sound. We had booked a cabin with a large bed and a balcony that looked out to sea. Once unpacked we rushed around the ship like a couple of kids in a playground and then, after a few days, we found the other gay men and a small group that we socialised with, especially in the evenings.

Paul and I would begin in the cocktail lounge and, Martini in hand, watch the dancing couples glide around the floor displaying their well-practised routines, or others who barked out orders as they stamped through their choreography. After dinner we headed for the variety show and the dancers, divas and drag queens. Then we rounded off the night supping and singing in the piano bar before heading off to our bunk. We loved every single minute of it, particularly taking our exercise on deck, walking lap after lap as the sea shouted, screamed and threw rainbows into the air. And those other days when the storms were unbearably cruel and the only safe place to be was tucked up in bed, drugged.

In the midst of all of this, on 28 December 2012, the New Year Honours list was announced and there among the names was Commander Cashman! So we partied some more, shared our news, and phoned our families.

As we approached the Antarctic the ship's engines slowed and we glided through the death-cold seas, past penguins flying out of the water, gigantic icebergs carrying lazy seals, the killer whales basking patiently, and always accompanied by the silence that was both indescribably calm and unsettling. It was there that we celebrated New Year's Eve, the sun never quite setting and the ship just turning in a circle as if to defy time, as nationality after nationality clocked the arrival of New Year in their far-off countries. Some Russian passengers, previously cold and distant, draped themselves across Paul and me – and we didn't object – as the Aussies, who never held back, raised yet another glass, and the wondrously open Americans were staggered by this sudden eruption of bonhomie.

We disembarked after sailing along the Chilean fjords and made our way to the airport; it really had been the experience of a lifetime. It had been like travelling in your own hotel, dipping for a day or two into countries that once experienced we vowed we'd visit again; how we laughed as we stood outside the Casa

Rosada in Buenos Aires singing 'Don't Cry for Me Argentina'. More holidays were lined up. Nothing was going to stop us.

There were other exciting times ahead, including my investiture at Buckingham Palace. Paul completed all the organising for the day. We splashed out and bought new outfits, and Paul looked incredible. I didn't realise it at the time but I was rediscovering him all over again; he looked smart, chic and handsome, the make-up skilfully applied, those blue eyes glittering, and that slight break in his nose making him look like a sexy young boxer.

Inside the palace it was once again spectacle and pomp, and it worked – they did theatre well. My brother Johnny and friend Michelle Collins sat with Paul in the ballroom while I was separated off with others to be told what would be expected of us; how we were to address Prince Charles – his mother had other things to do – the handshake that would signal our audience was at an end, the steps backwards and then exit stage left.

I waited to be called forward, an orchestra played in the gallery, and with my heart beating another rhythm I walked towards Charles, who charmed the socks off me.

'LGBT equality?' he said.

'That's right,' I replied.

'We deal with quite a bit of that here too,' he quipped. It was a lovely, relatively long exchange and I saw a side of the man that is rarely captured by the media – a genuine warmth.

The excitement afterwards was palpable as everyone gathered in the inner quadrangle with friends and relatives, while television cameras and interviewers bobbed in the background and everyone queued for their souvenir photos. We celebrated at the Ivy restaurant with Paul O'Grady, Barbara Windsor and her husband Scott Mitchell, Michelle and her partner Mike Davison, Anna Yearley (Ed Miliband's political secretary), Olivette Cole-Wilson (Stonewall founder), Ian McKellen and my brother Johnny. The restaurant lavished us with free champagne and we finally finished upstairs in the club, staggering home at about 11.30.

Through all of this intervened the reality from which we escaped: the hospital visits and the search for secondaries; blood tests, X-rays, scans, then waiting for the results. The reassuring smiles of Stephen and Jenny (and for me Professor Adam) as they gave us the all-clear. At times, as Paul and I struggled to cope with the sharp reminders of the uncertainty that we were living with, our minor disagreements would erupt; we would avoid contact when we went to bed and all too often I would have that last glass of wine and sink into a darkness. Then quickly it would all be forgotten.

The end of the year approached. I had managed work well and I still enjoyed it: Brussels, Strasbourg, the West Midlands – and South Africa. Following that first successful trip, Paul always came with me and we found a way of getting a few days in the African bush where we were endlessly seduced by its astonishing beauty. In late December we went to Beijing for a few days and Paul and I celebrated my birthday, with hardly another soul present, on the Great Wall of China. In Hong Kong we boarded a ship and set off for Vietnam, Cambodia and Thailand. We celebrated New Year 2014 on board, the celebrations going on late into the night, and we cuddled up in bed knowing that this was the year of my retirement. It was also the end of another year of living differently, not worrying about money or the future, a year of living in the present and of living together. Instead of dreaming of places we had decided to visit them; instead of thinking about friends and families, we spent time with them. And the added bonus was the European elections loomed large on the horizon and I would not be taking part in them. Despite our occasional petty rows we had changed our lives together for the better.

It was a golden period and Paul was determined it would continue. When we finished the last floating hotel cruise Paul decided to celebrate my retirement by booking a fifty-six-day cruise, starting in Alaska, sailing across the Pacific then around Australia and New Zealand. We both wanted to do it. Back at home he was straight onto the iPad booking the flights and hotels. He believed procrastination was the thief of a good time. I was the careful one, always thinking about the future and worrying about finances. He worried about not living life to the full, and in response to my gentle nagging about cost he would rub his hands together and shout: 'Spend it.' I would scream in mock horror and cover my ears and he would shout it again: 'Spend it!' It was great.

56

We invested in two shows in New York, and as far as we were concerned this made us 'Broadway producers'. *Waiting for Godot* had been a big hit in London and now it was opening on Broadway with a rarely seen Harold Pinter play, *No Man's Land*. Both shows, starring Ian McKellen and Patrick Stewart, were directed by Sean Mathias, our good friend who'd been instrumental in setting up Stonewall through the gala production of *Bent*.

We decided to see 'our' shows, so after a few days in the Hamptons we arrived at our favourite hotel, the Sofitel, famous for sexual misdemeanours – though thankfully not ours; rather those allegedly engaged in by the French politician Dominique Strauss-Kahn. A couple of days into the trip my mobile rang: it was Tim Livesey, Ed Miliband's chief of staff. They knew I was away, so I took the call in case it was urgent. Paul watched as I sat down and listened to Tim.

I don't remember what I said, but when I had finished Paul said: 'What's wrong?'

I didn't know how to say it.

'What?'

'Ed wants me to go into the Lords. Labour have been given three places to put people in the House of Lords and he wants me to be one of them.'

He hugged me and kissed me and we jumped around: 'I am proud of you babs. You deserve it.'

I was staggered. I sat for ages just smiling and shaking my head. Although I had dreamed of becoming a member of the House of Lords, and the incredible honour that came with it, I never believed it could happen to me, especially as so few places in the

Lords came up for Labour now that we were in opposition. Tim had been clear that Ed supported me wholeheartedly and stressed that it was in recognition of the changes that I had worked for on equality issues and much more. It was true Ed and I had a good relationship and I had served him well in difficult times when I was chair of the NEC.

Tim told me that they would prepare the citation for the Lords and pass it on to me before sending it with their recommendation to the House of Lords Appointments Commission, and he was adamant that it would also refer to my work before entering politics. And so it was, that for the first time in a Lord's citation, a gay kiss on TV was mentioned. I had never expected recognition; we had all achieved equality together. Of course it had been difficult in the early years, but Paul, his family and mine had probably paid a greater price. I just got on with it.

I was on cloud nine and I felt deeply humbled, but it was also sad that my mum and dad were not around to see it.

I recounted to Paul the conversation with Tim again and again. Tim had advised keeping it a secret, 'just in case'. Besides, we needed to respect protocol. 'We won't tell anyone,' said Paul, but we both knew that we would.

Never did we tire of New York. Walking the streets at any time, night or day, in the heat or the blistering winds, we found it a magical city. Harsh, brash, difficult, funny, but alive, New York defies you to accept its challenge to live, to belong where no one really belongs. We would queue for tickets for Broadway shows, nuzzle round the half-price ticket booth for bargains in Times Square and stroll along Broadway, Greenwich Village, up to Central Park and beyond. We walked for miles and never got bored. And Paul's 'new look' was very attractive to New Yorkers. Gorgeous men threw themselves at him, especially when they heard his accent!

It was nice being in the city again with Ian, and also Patrick Stewart, as it felt like a home away from home. Then came the day when we went to see both 'our' shows, one at the matinee and the other in the evening! The productions were finely tuned, beautifully acted and the New York audiences loved them. There was not a weak link and the reviews were really good as a result. It was also certain that we would get back our investment.

Afterwards we went out with Ian to Bar Central, where artists often went after their shows. That's when we told Ian about the peerage. His reaction was incredibly warm and generous and funny. On the street he kissed us goodnight and promised not to tell a soul. Then off he swept in a taxi to the formidable apartment that the film director Peter Jackson had lent him for the duration of his time in New York. Unusually for us, Paul and I walked arm in arm across the avenues until we reached the hotel. The February snow had started to fall.

The next day would be our last full day, when Michelle Collins and Mike were flying in, along with Rod McNeill, friend and dentist to the rich, famous and infamous, and his partner Luke. There was lots of shopping to be done. I was looking for bargains while Paul hunted for designer wear.

We had lunch in Greenwich Village and Paul complained that his asthma was playing up. Early on in the trip he had to see a doctor at a pharmacy because of his breathlessness. It was a chest infection and we walked away with the usual antibiotics.

That night we had a lovely dinner with Michelle, Mike, Rod and Luke, throughout which we kept changing places because we wanted to share and shape gossip. I was at the other end of the table when I heard Michelle scream with excitement: 'No? No?'

Tables around us went quiet and people looked over. I looked at Paul. And I knew he had told her. Everyone on our table looked over to her.

'What?' said Rod.

'Nothing. Nothing,' as she waved her hand and turned back to Paul.

The wine continued to flow as fast as we all could drink it and eventually we teetered out into the freezing February night.

'What's going on?' asked Rod.

I looked at Paul, who looked back at me eagerly. We both knew there was no point in having a secret if we couldn't disclose it to our mates, so we told him.

'You deserve it,' he said, then added, 'in fact I was a bit worried when they gave you the CBE. I thought that might be it!'

The next morning Paul wasn't well, and it wasn't a hangover. He had a temperature, his lungs ached and he was having trouble breathing. I went to the pharmacy and got some advice and medication. Then I told the hotel that we wanted the room for the rest of the day – our flight was around ten that night – and I checked availability in case we needed to stay on a few extra days.

I forced Paul to stay in bed. He needed sleep, medication and lots of hot drinks. If he wasn't well enough then we would rearrange the flights home. Uncharacteristically, he just agreed. I put the TV on in the background, which he always loved, and sat in the corner keeping a close eye on my 'patient'.

One by one our friends responded and wanted to come over, or to help out. Ian offered his apartment and the services of his New York doctor. Thankfully it wasn't necessary. By about five in the afternoon Paul was back to normal. We put it down to exhaustion: doing too much in New York, the late nights and the booze. We landed at London City Airport the next morning, got home, unpacked and settled back into the routine.

57

It was nearly three years since Paul was diagnosed, or rather misdiagnosed, by that ward orderly of a consultant dermatologist. Nearly three years since he found the wonderful team at St Thomas's. In that time it surprised us how we had modified our lives and got used to it. We had developed coping mechanisms, like promising to live life differently, which we were doing, but accepting that daily life lulled us back into old routines.

On the Antarctic cruise they had a 'walk for life' for cancer research. You paid $10 for the T-shirt and then walked many laps of the ship. They asked if there were any 'cancer survivors' among the participants. Our hands went up, along with others, and we were asked to step forward. Paul looked at me quizzically and said: 'What cancer have you had?'

He had forgotten.

We were asked to say what cancer we had and how long ago we had been given the all-clear. 'Two years and nine months,' said Paul.

'Two years and six months,' said I.

Later a woman said to us how lovely it was that father and son had come on the cruise together, and both survivors! 'Husbands. We are a couple,' corrected Paul.

The woman beamed, 'Even better.'

But I had survived nothing compared to what Paul had gone through: the knife physically cutting into his face and the constant threat of secondaries. My kidney was tucked away, I could ignore it or forget about it, and if the worst happened I could live without a kidney. But each time he looked in the mirror the scars looked back at him. Each time someone took an additional second look at him, or he saw them wince, it was a reminder. The constant processes of thoughts taking hold of your mind and having to deal with the different futures they presented. But deal with them he did. His strength and his tenacity made me love him beyond all imagining.

Back in Brussels we were approaching the election period so I started packing up the office and throwing away fifteen years' worth of papers and records. At times like these Paul normally helped me, but he was busy in Turkey and preparing for Eurovision, so I just got on with it. I sensed he wanted me to, to see if I could do it on my own.

I had decided that it would be better if I stayed away from most of the European elections, particularly in the West Midlands. It was important that I left the space for others to occupy, and I hated it when people wouldn't let go. So, when I went up for my 'farewell', I gave my heartfelt thanks. The people there, the party members, had shown Paul and me real support, understanding and love. We were accepted as a couple without hesitation, and when Paul had been diagnosed the compassion was deeply moving. They knew too that I had to make the break for our life together. With all the goodbyes done, I walked out of my office to West Bromwich and took the tram into Snow Hill, where I had appeared fifty years before as a thirteen-year-old actor at Birmingham Rep. I quietly said goodbye to the city of Birmingham, and I took the train home, to Paul.

During the election the hostility on the streets had been ferocious and the dehumanisation of politicians was mean. We were all accused of being the same as one another, of feathering our nests. I was so pleased that I was standing down. Nationally Labour had suffered badly and UKIP did well, but we gained a seat in the West Midlands and crucially London bucked the trend. There we doubled our number of MEPs.

I had stayed in London and had occasionally gone out campaigning. Paul disappeared to Denmark for Eurovision and was thrilled to see Conchita Wurst, resplendent in full drag and with a beautifully trimmed beard, win the contest. It was a classic Eurovision win, full of irony, drama, musical key changes and lots of camp.

Texting me from the hall in Copenhagen he was already planning his trip to the host country, Austria, for the following year. He partied like an animal and the next day, with a monstrous hangover, he said farewell to the gang he knew so well, including Graham Norton, and joined me in Malta for three days.

I was there as a keynote speaker in the LGBT+ conference organised by the Maltese government, which was shaking off the Catholic Church's hold on the political establishment and forging ahead on equality. Paul arrived tired but happy and I convinced him to rest and get ready for his fiftieth birthday celebrations at home in London.

The eighteenth of May arrived and the birthday party started at three in the afternoon, the final guests not leaving until about two in the morning. Paul produced a bound book of photos to celebrate his fifty years and no one was left out of it. He was meticulous. Both Michelle and Savage had to leave part-way through to do a TV awards ceremony, but returned immediately afterwards. Everyone who said they would come, did.

The Bangladeshi guys from the local restaurant ran the drinks service, while Mahmut Dal and Rebecca Wheatley served home-made Turkish food. Everything worked and everyone got on. Family and friends mingled as one.

At one point I looked across the room and I was momentarily astounded: I watched him at the centre of our life, comfortable, in his element, and I thought back to the nineteen-year-old boy that I had met all those years before.

A little later I grabbed him and said: 'Mr Cottingham, do you know we have been together nearly thirty-one years?'

He looked at me in mock horror: 'Thirty-one years! That's longer than my inside leg,' and off he went back to the centre of it all.

June Brown and Neil and Glenys Kinnock sat putting the political world to rights, and wrongs. Miss (Francis) Lynch dished gossip about me to anyone who would listen. Paul's *Rocky Horror* cast mates stirred up the past, then in the midst of all this John Reid, and husband James, arrived with a great big painting.

Paul loved presents and started tearing at the wrapping. 'No!' shouted John. 'You'll have to unveil it in private.'

'Ooh, let's have a look,' said June, sensing mischief.

In the bedroom we stood with the present – a very expensive and pornographic painting of two men with their dicks hanging out. Savage's eyes were out on stalks. 'You don't get many of them to the pound,' he said knowingly.

'Be nice to weigh them, though,' said June, dryly, as she puffed on her fag.

By the time everyone left, the place was a wreck, the empties were piled up precariously in a corner, Paul was still up to party and I was put to bed by two gorgeous men.

A few days later we attended the Queen's garden party and the week was topped off by the most brilliant, but more sedate, party in celebration of Ian's seventy-fifth birthday, where Paul got dressed up in Gandalf's hat and staff.

Summer was beginning, there was so much to look forward to and so much to look back on. Paul and I were as one in our amazing life and friends, in a way that beforehand had been unimaginable. We had got here through hard work, love and commitment, and above all by his patience. Our backgrounds hadn't held us back; they'd inspired us so that we could become true to ourselves. In our lifetime the world had spun forwards and what made us feel safe now was remembering how it had been, and how it could become again. We took nothing for granted, certainly not each other.

On 17 June in Brussels I held a farewell party in my bare office and friends from fifteen years in the European Parliament came to say goodbye. Newly elected MEPs, colleagues from across various EU countries, the commissioner Kristalina Georgieva, who had been a wonderful colleague and ally, our Socialist Group staff, the president of the Socialists, Hannes Swoboda, and president of the Parliament, Martin Schulz, all attended to party and to wave me off. Comrade Schulz made a warm and funny speech about our years working together, and I reciprocated in what was an emotional evening, the end of my time in the parliament.

The Brussels office was empty and my stuff was in boxes awaiting shipment to the UK, but Renaud and Bruno were still trying to hang onto things. 'Throw it all away,' I kept saying. 'The work will speak for itself, or it won't. Throw it away.'

The wall outside our office was lined with posters of campaigns, hearings and inquests from our years in the parliament. I physically took the boys into the corridor and made them help me take the posters down. Before we began we took a photo, a memory of fifteen years' worth of activism. Then I took down the first poster, 'Pro-choice', which over the years had been ripped and torn by our opponents as they passed. Down came the trans posters, LGBT+, the environment, public health, and one by one they all went into the bin. I knew our legacy would not be remembered by the posters but hopefully by the lasting change we had helped to effect.

Then the day arrived, my last as a Member of the European Parliament. That morning I left the hotel and walked into the building that I had loved working in for the last decade and a half. It was quiet, almost deserted. I had already said my farewells to the wonderful staff who worked in the bars and the restaurants, the attendants who brought us coffee in committee and the admin staff. Now, I was saying goodbye to the building and the silent memories. I collected my few things from the office on the thirteenth floor, took one last look and left, without looking back. A departure had never been more decisive. Renaud came with me to the ground floor. We hugged, and masking my sadness at not working with him any more, I muttered that I would speak with him on the phone before climbing into a car, and leaving.

I found my mobile and called Paul: 'That's it, babs. I've left.'

Now it was going to be just him and me. Me and him.

58

Both of us were now back in London, but I was taking a while to adjust. I no longer had the routine of Brussels or indeed even Strasbourg. The novelty of the lie-in, the nothing-on-the-agenda attitude, was starting to wear off. I was beginning to get bored, edgy, fidgety. And Paul hated fidgets.

The phone didn't ring, the emails didn't come through. We were still waiting for the list of new Lords to be agreed by the Appointments Committee, but there were problems with a couple who were Tory donors. Everything seemed to be on hold, it was frustrating.

I knew I needed to find something to focus on and I could tell that Paul had to get used to having me around in 'his space'. I took myself out for little walks to the post office or the super-market, and stopped off to have coffee to fill the time. I started counting down the days to the summer holiday in Turkey because I was used to that, almost conditioned to it. There I had a different routine, and I belonged with him.

During one of Paul's routine hospital visits, Jenny told him she needed to have another go at his face, for cosmetic purposes. He went in to the hospital overnight, and when he was discharged they were both happy. His recent bloods and scans had come back okay – so it felt like perfection when he received the 'all clear' from pathology.

The day before we went to Turkey, Paul had an event to organise and he insisted I went with him. It was a Labour Party fundraiser reception and from there he wanted us to pop into an LGBT+ Labour event. The Tavistock Rooms in Holborn were packed, and I headed straight to the bar. Suddenly I realised by the mischievous smile on his face that all was not as it seemed.

'What?' I asked.

'Nothing,' he said. 'Nothing.'

Then I heard my name and I was called to the stage. There followed an unbelievable tribute to me, and to Paul, for the LGBT+ work we had done over the long years, recognising my decade and a half in the European Parliament and as co-president of the LGBT+ intergroup. It was very moving and, unable to control my feelings, I grabbed Paul and hugged him. He held onto my hand like we rarely did in public, and it felt marvellous. Then to top off the tribute there was a video presentation from Tony Blair, Gordon Brown, Neil and Glenys Kinnock, Paul O'Grady, Ian McKellen, and Michelle Collins. I was overwhelmed.

I mixed and thanked people individually; so many party staff and Members of Parliament had turned up. Just when I thought it was time for us to go I heard spontaneous applause, Tony and Cherie entered the room, and we joined them in conversation.

The night ended as we jumped into a taxi like two elated Cheshire cats. He was breathless. I was overwrought. I held his hand in the darkness of the taxi and I thanked him again. I loved the brilliant understated way that he had coaxed me to the event, and that he still had the capacity to amaze me. He knew about it all, helped organise it, yet I had been completely unaware.

'Did you know Cherie and Tony were going to be there too?' I asked.

In the darkness he nodded and I squeezed his hand tighter.

'Fish and chips?' he asked.

And we stopped off at the Turkish fish and chip shop in Limehouse. A week later we flew out to have fish and chips in Turkey!

59

'I can't breathe,' he said. We had been there three days and his health had deteriorated. I knew it wasn't his asthma because he complained of being bloated too. I told him if it didn't get any better by tomorrow we would go to the local hospital in the Turkish town.

The next day his stomach was clearly distended. We phoned our friend, Sylvie, who came over and cast her nursing eye over him. It was obvious we needed to go to the hospital. There, among the confusion of languages, we paid our fee to see the doctor and took our place in the long corridor, alongside the mothers and children and old people. With Sylvie offering some translation and Paul doing the rest, he was given an ultrasound. The doctor muttered to Sylvie that he hoped it was not the liver.

Finally, he announced his diagnosis: Paul had an inflamed and bloated gall bladder. He prescribed a strict diet, no alcohol, medication, and lots of rest. The latter was not going to be a problem, he just wanted to sleep. Two days later things had not improved. Paul was now extremely bloated, his stomach protruding and painful. We decided to take the sixty-kilometre journey to the hospital at Marmaris. He was obviously not well because he was okay with me doing the driving.

We placed a couple of calls to medical friends in London. We needed reassurance. At the Ahu Hetman hospital we satisfied them that we could pay, which we did in advance, and he was given another ultrasound and blood test. It was a smart, clean, modern building and well organised, very different from our local Turkish hospital. The doctor spoke perfect English and told us that Paul had chronic liver disease. It sounded serious, but I said nothing. Paul and I exchanged a worried glance.

'Should we fly home?' Paul asked.

Almost disinterestedly the doctor said we could finish our five weeks' stay, then go home. Another prescription, the ultrasound results in our hands, and we began the sixty kilometres back. The fact that it was obviously not so serious that we could finish our holiday lifted Paul's spirits. We even stopped off for a cup of coffee and a browse in a Turkish Tesco.

I scanned the internet for liver disease; it was serious. Despite the passing of another couple of days and the new medication there was no progress. On the contrary, his legs were swollen to an incredible size, so too his testicles. Inside I panicked but calmly told him that we needed to get him back to the hospital.

'Can't it wait?' he pleaded.

'Babs, this is serious. You are not pissing, and with your balls and dick like this you are not going to be able to, which means your organs will drown.'

I packed an overnight bag. It was already getting dark as we drove the precarious night journey over the mountains.

As soon as the on-call doctor saw his physical condition she admitted him. In the morning he was seen by two doctors, one of whom was the chief medical officer. Their English was good, and they complimented Paul on his Turkish. They found it hard to believe that he was sent home three days before. I produced the evidence of their doctor's report and the ultrasound. They took them for their records and we never saw the papers again. After more tests, bloods and X-rays they confirmed chronic liver disease and promised to do their best.

There was a fold-down bed in the corner, and after a brief trip back to Datça to collect some things, I moved into the room with him. It was calming to be there together. I called Paul O'Grady, who was in Turkey and on his way to stay with us. He offered to undertake 'an errand of mercy', but we convinced him and Andre, his partner, to stay in their hotel in Bodrum.

Paul started on a series of medications, including diuretics to get rid of the volume of water. Doctors explained that his kidneys and liver were malfunctioning, and his body wasn't excreting. His breathing began to deteriorate and his blood pressure had dropped. On one occasion the fall in blood pressure was so dramatic that they had to perform resuscitation in front of me. Paralysed with fear I stood there and watched. I observed him, almost in slow motion, fade away and drift off, but they got him back.

Paul got used to them not being able to find a vein for the syringes, and he hardly winced as they dug around incessantly. Familiar, too, was the door crashing open in the middle of the night and the lights being blasted on so that one thoughtless nurse could do her observations. I took a break each morning in the shopping centre, drinking coffee after coffee. In the evening I invariably went to the same small restaurant. 'How is your friend?' the owner always asked. I would tell him.

As Paul had to give up alcohol so did I, even when I was eating alone. I started to look forward to Cola-light, and rice cakes. I agreed to speak to his family for the most part, and when he was up to it he chatted to his mum.

After about ten days there was a breakthrough. He started to excrete more than he was taking in; he was looking less bloated and his weight was coming down. We never thought we would get so excited about how much he could piss! Now we looked forward to it with eager anticipation. He was looking and feeling better. Though he was still on oxygen most of the time his breathing had improved and we started going for walks along the corridor, even boldly venturing downstairs to the hospital café.

By the middle of the second week the doctor said that if he kept up the improvement then they would allow us to fly home at the weekend. It was brilliant news, but Paul was exhausted and he asked if we could have a few days in Datça before returning to London. He wanted to rest away from hospitals and illness. The doctor hesitated and said that he would prefer us to go home while Paul was improving, but would decide on Friday. When we were alone I hugged and kissed him, and we whispered wistfully that were going 'home'.

Home.

On Friday lunchtime the doctor prepared to do a couple of final tests. Providing the results were okay we could go to Datça for a few days, but bound by the promise to fly back to the UK soon.

We promised.

Paul, full of smiles, was taken away in a wheelchair for the tests. I started packing the things that we had accumulated over the last two weeks. I could not wait to get out, to get back to some degree of normality.

Soon he was back in the room. 'They're not going to discharge me,' he said, devoid of any emotion whatsoever.

The ultrasound on his chest revealed fluid around his heart. An hour later we were speeding to the nearest big city, Bodrum, in an ambulance, the blue light flashing, and the driver talking on his mobile phone.

It was a state-of-the art hospital and the cardiologist, Dr Aksu, had the air of a UK professor. He explained the situation: in the pericardium, the sac surrounding the heart, there was a large amount of fluid. In his opinion Paul was not suffering with chronic liver disease, but with pericarditis, which is not common. The volume of fluid was so large that it was preventing the heart from pumping effectively, hence the organs had slowed down, and he was unable to pass urine or anything else.

It seemed to make sense.

Later the liver specialist arrived, certain in his diagnosis that it was chronic liver disease and that as soon as the fluid was drained he would need to perform a biopsy. In this hospital, which functioned and felt more like a four-star hotel, we settled down for the night, with me on a more upmarket fold-down bed. Paul was reassured when Dr Aksu told him that the procedure would be done the next day under a local anaesthetic.

I waited in his room for his return. The door clunked open and they brought him in on his bed. Dr Aksu revealed that he had drained two-thirds of a litre of fluid from the sac which should normally contain approximately thirty-three millilitres. He was certain that it was not the liver, but acute pericarditis, and he was hopeful that if the fluid didn't recur we should see a return to normal organ function. It was the best news. We could hardly contain our sense of joy. The liver specialist made one more attempt to claim his patient but then gave up and we saw no more of him. The battle had been won.

Each day there was improvement; Paul's weight was stable and so too were the observations. His breathing was back to normal and once again we started to hope. We talked with the doctor about having a few days in Datça before flying home to have the pericarditis checked and, if necessary, a surgical procedure so that any recurring fluid would drain into the thoracic cavity and be absorbed by the body.

Meanwhile, I received a couple of calls from the Labour Party press office in London about the list for the Lords. Rumours had started in the UK press and my name had been mentioned. It had been almost six months since we had first got that call in New York, and the brilliant thing was that all the people we trusted with the secret had kept it. Six months – but it felt like a lifetime, and I had rarely thought about it during the time in those hospitals. Paul was thrilled about the news and we agreed to celebrate in Datça. As it was not liver disease, we could do so with copious amounts of red wine. The confusing, chilling journey finally seemed to be coming to an end. Paul looked thinner, but better, and three weeks of hospital life were coming to a close.

The following morning at eight, UK time, I got a call from London. The list for the Lords had finally been released. We agreed a statement, which also mentioned Paul, and I agreed to do limited interviews. Our mobile phones vibrated across the room as our friends and families sent their love and messages about the peerage; Lord and Laddie Cashman!

On the dot, as promised, Dr Aksu appeared with his junior. The pathology report on the fluid he removed from the pericardium had come back. They had detected cancerous cells.

60

Paul was discharged on the proviso that we would return on Monday when Dr Aksu would make a final decision on whether Paul was fit enough to face the stress of flying home. The Lords suddenly paled into complete insignificance. Nothing mattered. That word, cancer, had followed us to Turkey. But we hung onto the doctor's words of hope; he wasn't positive that they were cancer cells, as often old blood cells showed up as such. He would get another pathology opinion for Monday.

On the other side of Bodrum we booked into a beautiful hotel, nestled into a small bay. We would try and have a good weekend; early morning or early evening swims, keeping out of the sun, rest and good food. And wine. Now we both needed a drink.

We decided to make contact with Paul's oncologist, Stephen Morris, and through him we made an appointment with a cardiologist in London. It was a beautiful weekend. Paul looked stunning, if a little fragile, and we continued to reassure ourselves that things would be fine. We had been through shit before and we would get through it again, so long as we had one another. It was such an utter joy when we both went into the sea together, repeating over and over again how wonderful it was to begin to feel normal again.

On Monday morning I took a gamble and checked us out of the hotel. I was hopeful that Dr Aksu was going to be positive and my hunch was confirmed. At the hospital Paul was declared fit for discharge and permitted to fly. But the angiosarcoma cells were also confirmed in the fluid. We promised that we would see the specialists in London immediately when we got back, and fell into a waiting taxi. During the journey we said very little and discreetly my hand touched his. It had been an unbearable three weeks but at least we would have a few days free from medics, we were liberated.

Throughout the silent, tense, two-hour ferry ride, I sensed Paul wanted to be back in the hospital where he felt safe. Our dear friend, Metin Tunç, was there to meet us at the ferry and after the short car journey we were back home in our beautiful old house and garden in Datça. But inside we were both stunned.

We slept well, did a little gentle exercise and Paul kept to his medication. After four perfect days with our friends, we rose early, locked the house, climbed into the taxi and as the sun rose, we crept over the mountain towards the airport. On the way we separately took photographs of the soft August sunrise, and said very little. I committed every minute to memory, and I watched Paul sitting in front of me, his head turning in every direction, capturing it all too. We were going home to London and yet more uncertainty, but with new determination to get it sorted once and for all. The four days in Datça had done us good. We were ready.

Stephen Morris's referral letter to the cardiologist had been encouraging, saying he had 'never known secondaries for angiosarcoma to appear in the pericardium'. We physically punched the air when we read that. But now it was back to the hospital for further tests and scans. They told us that fluid had again accumulated in the pericardium. A cardiothoracic surgeon would perform a procedure so that the fluid could just seep away. The operation was a success and two days later we went home to await yet more pathology reports. But Paul was in a lot of pain. His neck and chest areas started to swell.

We tried to get back to normal, to cling onto a routine that would keep us sane. I went to do the shopping and returned home to find him in agony. He'd sneezed and there was a small rupture in the lung, a pneumothorax, protruding through his back. He was readmitted to hospital, and a drain was fitted to extract the excess fluid or air.

I couldn't stay overnight like we did in Turkey, so I stayed in the hospital as late as I could and returned early. I was starting to get exhausted. Paul told me to have an early night and then a lie-in but I told him I didn't need it. Our friends were wonderful; they would pop in to the hospital on the off-chance, which lightened our days and nights. The eagerly anticipated fifty-six-day cruise was a few weeks away and we took the difficult-yet-easy decision to cancel it. I suggested we look for another as a consolation and the clouds lifted. Paul smiled from ear to ear. I knew that we must have something to look forward to.

Our mood improved again when they moved us to a room overlooking the Thames, and when Michelle visited the three of us, trawling through the internet, found a cruise to Alaska and booked it.

After three nights Paul was discharged and it was brilliant cuddling up on the sofa and sleeping together again, my foot curling around his every night. We got out of the flat and even managed to get to the West End for dinner with Helen Worth, from *Coronation Street*, and her new husband Trevor. Despite some breathing difficulties, it really felt like Paul was on the mend.

At home in the middle of the afternoon the phone rang. I was in our bedroom but I could hear Paul talking. Everything sounded normal so I carried on doing whatever I was doing. Then I noticed the silence. It was longer than it should have been. I moved quickly to the sitting room and Paul was standing in the hallway, the phone still in his hand.

'Babs?'

His face started to crumble and I took him in my arms. The cancer was back. The cardio surgeon told him on the phone. On the fucking phone. We stood there silently hugging one another, then held each other at arm's length, repeating that we had fought this before and we would fight it again. We wouldn't get depressed. We would see what Dr Morris had to say.

That evening Stephen quietly repeated the news in his office. Unusually the secondaries had formed on the pericardium and remained unseen. He said: 'Paul, it is the worst news.' Stephen then looked to me and I nodded.

I felt tears welling up as our life started to fall apart. I heard 'palliative care' and I ran cold. Stephen was trying to tell us to prepare. My mind rushed back over the weeks. All of those imagined moments when I sat alone in the Turkish cafe, all those terrifying moments that came unbidden into my mind were suddenly real. I had pushed them so far away into an eternity that I never wanted to reach. Now we were facing the truth. In this small office I was numb, I was lost and I didn't think Paul had truly taken in the news. He gently pleaded that we go on the short cruise to Alaska, flying out the next day, and I didn't try to dissuade him. Stephen reasoned the escape out of Paul's mind. He wanted us to meet his colleague at the Royal Marsden, the sooner the better.

We said very little as we walked out of the hospital and into the outside world. But it felt our world no longer. There was a wine bar nearby that I had been to before and we went there. Sitting outside as people hurried past, we drank a glass of red and quietly, unemotionally picked over Stephen's words. We were in search of positives, and there had been some in the conversation. After a meal at the crazy Italian restaurant with the singing Elvis, which provided some much-needed absurdity, we arrived home.

Outside the Thames was lapping and crashing on the stony beach. The sound was hypnotic, and we decided to lie on the floor so that we could be lulled to sleep by its rhythms. Our mood was good and we had each other.

In the early morning light though it felt different; colder and more real. Our families had to be told, but we concentrated on being constructive. The Royal Marsden was one of the best hospitals in the world, and its sarcoma unit was famous.

At the Marsden we met Dr Ayşe Miah. She was small, energetic and full of optimism. We liked her enormously. She talked about improving the quality of Paul's life, about the palliative chemo that he would undergo for the next few months, plus the support from the heart specialist. She emphasised that any new treatments would be offered if they came on-line and we met the team of palliative nurses who worked alongside her. As we walked off to see the heart specialist at the nearby Royal Brompton, we were strangely hopeful.

'She isn't talking in terms of weeks, she is talking months,' said Paul, adding: 'I just thought I had days.'

I agreed how good it felt, so much better, and that we had found the right place. A place to feel safe, where we could think about and plan for a future. Paul would start the first six-weekly cycle of chemo, which they hoped would arrest the growth of the cancer, on 1 October, just a few days away. Riding on a wave of assurances, and with a wedge of material to read about chemotherapy and its side effects, we spent a lovely weekend with Neil and Glenys, who insisted on travelling over to see us, and then another party at Ian's.

On Monday we took the train to Manchester to the Labour Party conference. Paul was insistent that we went. He wanted to see his friends. Every year he had done conference, taking the senior politicians around the exhibitions, arranging the celebrities for the gala dinner and being a lynchpin in so many ways. He wanted to be there. And I understood. This year it had to be different, however, because he was an observer.

We booked into the conference hotel, the luxurious Midland, and then it was off to see friends, who gave him an ecstatic welcome. It wasn't easy though. Those who hadn't seen him for a year were visibly shocked because the weight he'd lost in Turkey had aged him; he looked gaunt. Yet he didn't let it affect his humour or his enthusiasm. He charged through it all. Sticking to his conference routine, that night we had dinner with our mates at the San Carlo restaurant, then early to bed.

The Tuesday of the conference was the leader's speech followed by a reception for high-value donors, then finally the gala dinner. A leader's speech was always the highlight of the week and never more so than when an election was close. Paul and I had decided to have a rest beforehand but it was interrupted by a call from Tim Livesey, who wanted to come to our room. Tim needed to talk urgently and confidentially so we adjourned to the tiny sitting room.

When he left Paul asked: 'What was all that about?'

'It's a secret,' I joked, then I spilled the beans. Miliband's office had done it again; I was gobsmacked. Ed wanted me to be his LGBT+ global envoy. It was groundbreaking – a huge promotion for the equal rights movement, and if we won the next election I would effectively be the prime minister's global envoy! So we did what any decent, sane couple would do, we skipped and whooped around the room like two-year-olds. Later that afternoon Ed Miliband announced in his speech that he would appoint 'Lord Cashman' as his envoy. It was the first time I had heard my title being used and Paul and I were chuffed. As conference applauded, Paul discreetly squeezed my arm as the cameras closed in.

At the gala dinner we sat down with Anna Yearley, Sadiq Khan and Stella Creasy MP, as Paul's mates in the photographic team captured a simple photograph of us. When I looked at it later I saw that it was profound, deeply profound in what Paul was radiating: it was as if he was carefree and saying: 'It's okay, I know. It's okay.' Unlike the other years we only stayed for one drink in the hotel bar, but he was crowded around by so much warmth and love. There were hugs and tears, and we slipped away to the great big bed. After breakfast we went to say goodbye to his friends in the conference unit. When Ann Kennedy waved him off she said to me: 'You take care of him. See you soon Paul.'

We walked out of the office and there was a moment of tremendous sadness. Ed Balls was doing his tour of the exhibition stands, something Paul always did with him. As ever, Ed was popular and engaging and funny. We stood watching on the outside of the small crowd. Paul said something to Ed as he passed, but he didn't hear. The small group with Ed at its centre started to move on and we turned to walk away. 'Paul! Paul!' we heard from behind, as Ed rushed up to him.

They chatted and laughed, and Paul grew, visibly. 'Missed you mate. See you soon. Okay?' said Ed. Then off we went, back to London. Paul felt enormous satisfaction that he had come to conference and I was proud of him. The reception he got had been really moving and encouraging.

Over the next few days we saw Paul's heart specialist, who was now working in conjunction with the Royal Marsden. He had a port implanted so that the chemo and other drugs could be pumped into him directly, as opposed to always searching for another vein. The procedure was painful but he took it with his usual stoicism. I could only wait outside and imagine. When the session was finished the consultant thanked us for all that we had done for gay rights and told us that she and her partner had recently had their civil partnership. She was about Paul's age, and we shared our thoughts that what we had now – our equality and our rights – was unimaginable before.

The day of the first chemo arrived. We sat in the unit at the Royal Marsden for three hours. Paul was attached to the machine and slowly all our hope for the future dripped into his veins. A lovely staff nurse in her mid-fifties told him she wanted him to keep away from this place. He is too healthy, she said. Other couples were there too. Some patients had lost their hair, some looked absolutely fine, while others looked as though they had given up. All of us shared at least two things in common: cancer and a desire to live.

During the first week we looked for a pattern. Paul felt good for the first day after the chemo, followed by two awful days and nights, then a kind of resurgence. So, on the days he felt up to it, we managed to do what he loved doing: going out and living, not just sitting waiting.

One such event was the European Diversity Awards dinner at the Natural History Museum. It was a magnificent evening during which April Ashley was given a lifetime achievement award for her courage and leadership as a trans woman. I watched him in these surroundings and he was in his element: glass in hand, usually red wine, laughter all around and always on the lookout for a celebrity he could capture to do something for a charity, or for the Labour Party. It was heart-warming to see, and I knew that despite the deep foreboding that I had these weeks, if anyone could beat this disease it was him. I watched him and I smiled, and smiled and smiled.

For me, though, the real joy was getting home – our home overlooking the Thames that was just 500 yards away from where I was born and brought up and that he had brought me back to. Home, and having him all to myself, curling up on the sofa, where we could doze and chat, or the bliss of holding one another in our bed, then drifting off to sleep; but I knew Paul needed more. He needed to feel life, the buzz, he needed to live. And I knew he needed to prove to himself that he was not just living to be medicated. At the weekend he started to feel exhausted again, and I told him he had to rest. He ignored me, then fell asleep on the sofa for most of the day. He complained about it but I told him how brilliant and important it was to rest and let the body repair itself, to cope with the poison that had been pumped into him. The next morning he could hardly get off the sofa because his head was 'like a dead weight', but by the afternoon he had recovered and was looking forward to the celebration dinner that Ian was giving for us, in honour of the peerage, at the Dickensian riverside pub, the Grapes, close to where I grew up.

I watched Paul putting on his camouflage, his make-up, and marvelled at how much more revived he looked. The dinner was perfect. The room upstairs looked exquisite; it was packed full of candles, flowers and our friends from the neighbourhood. Ian made a warm, generous speech, then I said a few words and recounted many shared memories, my childhood on these streets and my amusing theatrical meeting with the Garter King of Arms, to agree my title prior to entering the Lords. My eyes fixed on Paul looking at me from the corner. I saw his love and I knew beyond any doubt that he adored me. I started to melt. Deep in my heart I knew I was where I was because of him. That we had achieved this together. And I found the strength to say it to everyone there.

After the speeches he sidled up and kissed me. Everyone was chatting, it was so lively, and happy, but I saw that he was fading. He told me he would walk the few doors along to our apartment but that I was to stay. I started to protest but he silenced me with a look. A short while later I left too.

At his next chemo session Paul was having trouble breathing and the oxygen levels in the blood were not good. There was talk about a blood transfusion but luckily it was put on hold. Once the session concluded we were asked to return at lunchtime to see his consultant, Ayşe Miah. She was accompanied by a thoracic surgeon from the Royal Brompton. After scans and X-rays, we headed home but en route we got a call to turn back immediately. They had found a bed at the Brompton and they wanted to operate that night to put a drain into the cavity between his lungs and chest wall.

It was late, approaching nine o'clock, as we waited for the surgeon. At night hospitals take on a totally different atmosphere; there is a lull, as if a tsunami has been, and everyone was now patiently waiting for another to begin. Patients demanding medication, support machines pumping and exhaling in the background, and the call button for the nurse or doctor going off relentlessly. We had been waiting two hours. Paul was ready for the operation and he was relieved that he wouldn't be put under a general anaesthetic. The surgeon and his registrar arrived and joked that they were his porters for the evening, and once again I watched him disappearing into the distance on a hospital bed.

I walked outside into Chelsea, aimlessly wandering along the King's Road. I decided to have something to eat and chose the Pheasantry at Pizza Express, where Paul and I had seen so many cabaret performances. In the corner of the restaurant was an old acquaintance from Equity and acting, Harry Landis, from *EastEnders*, who sent his love to Paul. Always love, never regards.

Later I was back at the hospital, looking at the empty space for Paul's bed, waiting for his return.

61

'You should feel a lot better,' the surgeon said to Paul, explaining that they had drained the fluid from the pleural cavity. The next day we would be shown how to operate the drain in Paul's side. Before the surgeon left, Paul insisted that he needed to be discharged by tomorrow afternoon at the latest. I now thought that he had totally lost it.

'What?' I asked.

The surgeon was amused and reasonable, especially when Paul told him the need for the early discharge: 'I am taking some friends to see *The Book of Mormon*.'

I did my best to reason with Paul, but he told me it was late and I should go home and get some rest. I took a taxi home but we got into gridlock along Stepney Highway, my advice to avoid the route being totally ignored, so I got out and walked. I was angry with the taxi driver, but really I was angry that Paul was putting his health at risk and would rather go to see a show we had already seen than stay in hospital where he could get better.

At home I opened a bottle of wine, determined to finish it. I knew I could drink some of the pain away, and the anger welled up inside me. But I managed to quash the destructive impulse no matter how much I wanted to sink into it. Before I went to bed, Paul and I exchanged text messages. He was having a rough time trying to sleep, despite the red wine I had smuggled in, and another patient was calling out in pain. The night was going to be a long one. I went to our bed in need of sleep; it was the first time I had slept without him in weeks. It seemed so huge and empty.

I awoke to a couple of text messages. Paul seemed on good form and I was feeling better after my low, lonely moment the night before. He had finally got some sleep and had been moved to another ward. I arrived at the hospital just before twelve. Paul told me he would be discharged at about three and I marvelled at how he managed to curl people, even surgeons, around his little finger, but said nothing.

Back at home we looked at the paraphernalia laid out on the table: the drainage packs and sterile equipment we needed for the next few days. We'd been put through our paces at the hospital on how to use it, but it seemed so complicated. They must have seen the look on our faces because they assured us that it was easy and we would get used to it.

Paul needed to rest after the hospital, but he couldn't, no he wouldn't – because he was determined to go to the theatre. I called a minicab and we got stuck in the evening traffic. Incredibly he decided that we should get out at Holborn and walk. Walk! This from a man who could hardly breathe, and with a drain coming out of his side. I felt my anger rising in me, again. Why, I kept asking myself, why was he doing this? It was utter madness. I kept telling him to slow down, that it was okay if we were late. Anna Yearley and her husband Jonathan Pearse would understand.

The streets were as packed as the roads, and there were no shortcuts, no easy spaces, there was just the obstacle, this journey to the theatre. We arrived and Anna waited with the tickets. Paul, deeply out of breath, finally sat down and I got us all a glass of wine. In truth I just wanted to lift Paul up in my arms and carry him away. He was exhausted but he put on a good show. He wanted everyone to enjoy the evening.

And, of course, they did, even I finally let go and laughed out loud. I looked at him and I saw a man who was satisfied, who had accomplished what he had set out to do, who was getting so much pleasure from others enjoying themselves. So now we could go home and he would rest easy.

Although the swelling around his neck and chest had diminished, Paul's breathing had not improved. At times when he was sleeping, now at an upright angle, he sounded like a bowl of Rice Krispies. We gingerly approached the draining process, trying to keep it sterile at all times as the last thing he needed during chemo was an infection. The first drain produced about half a litre of bloody fluid.

We exchanged looks. I told him it wasn't blood and that he was absolutely not to worry. I think he believed me. Then there were a myriad of different pills, including his morphine and other painkillers to administer. He slept for most of the day, again at the crazy angle to help his breathing, and we awaited the pattern to the reaction of the chemo. It was horrible but we knew the worst was yet to come.

Sunday was not a good day. Paul again had a heavy head that he was hardly able to lift and no appetite, not even for a glass of wine. I tried to coax him into drinking some other alcohol and he said he fancied a Baileys, so I rushed to the off-licence like a thing possessed.

He woke me in the night, which was not uncommon. Although I was on sedatives to get me off to sleep they didn't appear to affect my reactions. In seconds I was alert, or was I on autopilot? His breathing was getting worse. I helped him to the toilet then back to bed, gave him his shot of morphine and found more pillows to get him in a position so he could sleep again. I clung onto him as we tried to drift off to sleep, him towering above me at the top end of our bed on the pillows, me slumped below.

I was called awake again, and this time I found him sitting on the edge of the bed. 'It's getting worse, babs,' he said, trying to snatch a good breath.

I checked his temperature and his blood pressure. The temperature was high. Blood pressure was low. I told him we would give it fifteen minutes then check it again. I spent the entirety of that intervening period wishing and hoping that his temperature would drop, that his blood pressure would return to near normal. But it didn't. We agreed that I had to phone the emergency nurse. There were no emergency services at the Marsden so we were told to get Paul to the nearest A & E.

I started to get him dressed, we joked that this was all part of the process, that we had better get used to it, and I asked him if he wanted an ambulance or a taxi. It was just gone five in the morning. Outside the October morning was dark and wet. We sat in silence and waited. The phone rang and we jumped. The taxi was outside.

I picked up the overnight bag that we had kept on standby; I gathered up our keys, held the apartment door open for him and we left together for the last time. He would never come back again.

62

Three nights in the Royal London at Whitechapel felt like a bloody lifetime. There was a sense that nobody really cared whether you were there or not. From the window of Paul's room on the eleventh floor we could just about see our apartment. Everything was so near, and yet so far.

In the entire hospital there wasn't a single drain to attach to his implanted port. I made various calls to his surgeon, to the Royal Brompton and to the district nurse services, but no one knew where we could get these vacuum packs. The priority was to get him over to the team at the Marsden, but there wasn't a bed. Nothing was straightforward, everything was going wrong.

Frustrated, and not wanting to show Paul my anger, I went home to sleep, exhausted, but then he rang. A junior doctor had taken the initiative and sent a taxi to the Royal Brompton to collect a couple of vacuum packs. We both shouted 'Yippee!'

In the morning there was a slight improvement, but he was so miserable: 'Get me out of here, babs, get me out. It's awful. I never see anyone. It's like I don't exist.' I looked around the grey, colourless room, devoid of TV or radio, and I understood completely. Friends and family came to visit, but he was so unhappy.

Ayşe was out of the UK at a conference; late at night she phoned me and promised that they would get him over to the Marsden as soon as possible.

After three days of persistent pestering, of mind-numbing indifference to him, Ayşe saved us – there was a bed. I rushed over, packed Paul's things, washed and dressed him. And we waited. After an interminable four hours the ward sister said we could go. I asked for his medication but they didn't give us his morphine.

When I specifically asked for it she told me it mustn't have been transferred with him from the other ward. Paul insisted that he had had the morphine while he was on that ward, so it must have come with him. She shrugged her shoulders. They knew we wanted to get out of there.

Stalemate.

Silence.

The nursing sister shrugged her shoulders again.

The doors barged open, the transfer ambulance had finally arrived. In came the paraphernalia and two hot, cheeky young Asian guys. Paul smiled and winked. Sod the morphine. It was going to be a nice ride to the Royal Marsden after all.

63

The transfer ambulance turned into the King's Road in Chelsea and we knew we were minutes away. Suddenly it appeared, the Royal Marsden, and we looked at one another and sighed with relief. 'We are here!' I said, and I felt everything was going to be okay.

'We've been waiting for you,' said the ward sister with a big smile as she ushered us into his room. The lovely ambulance guys wished us well, the nurse said she would return in a minute, and then the door closed behind them and we were alone.

I stood and hugged him. 'We're safe, babs, we are safe!'

We kissed, and all our fears fell away. Paul was smiling, no longer carrying that deep frown, and I even thought he was breathing better.

It was a small room with a TV, which he was thrilled about – he could gorge on daytime reality shows and house makeovers – a bathroom, and a couple of windows that looked out to the inner courtyard. I started to unpack our things, which made the room look like ours. He rested on the bed while I found an armchair and we switched on the TV to ease the waiting. As expected everything fell into place.

The oncology team didn't have the finesse of Ayşe, but they were good, really good. They told us what we already knew: that the antibiotics weren't working. The collapsed left lung needed to be inflated again, and Paul went to theatre for another drain to be inserted.

The thoracic consultant visited and we heard him say that the next three days would be 'critical'. Paul asked Ayşe's young registrar to explain but she failed to find the right words to reassure him. Ayşe returned from overseas and quietly took command. Again we felt confident. Paul told her that he didn't want any 'doom and gloom' but just wanted to know what was going on. She agreed and told us that they needed to beat the infection before they could restart the chemo. The good news was that one area of the tumour had shrunk, so we all agreed the chemo must be doing its job. As she was about to leave she asked if he would like anything else, and I was staggered by his response.

'Is it okay if Michael stays with me?'

'Yes,' she replied.

'I mean that he sleeps overnight.'

'Of course, Paul. Anything.'

After that, sometimes on a chair, then on a fold-down bed, I spent my days and my nights with him. I watched as he battled and struggled, hardly able to lift a leg, or get to the side of his bed without gasping for breath. I watched as they prepared us to go home, and I laughed with him when we sat eating dinner together – my food bought at Waitrose – and drinking our red wine. When he woke in the night, needing more morphine, or for his observations to be done, I watched. I observed, and I could do so little. Eventually he started coughing up blood. Ayşe was concerned.

No doom and gloom, said Paul.

No doom and gloom, she repeated.

He and I made a pact that once he had coughed up he would hand me the tissue and I would examine it and tell him. I lied. I saw him starting to cough up bits of his lung, and I discreetly passed the tissue or pathology tube to the beautiful staff nurse.

Ayşe popped in one night, it was late and she saw us sipping wine.

'Is it okay?' he smiled.

'Perfectly okay,' she replied, then added, 'but won't it taste nicer out of glasses?'

So I ran round to Waitrose and bought us four wine glasses. On the way back I choked back thoughts of losing him, of my life beginning its end. For a moment on those journeys it would always bubble up, but I pushed it away. I rejected it.

The palliative team told us they were going to move him to a bigger room to prepare for our return home, but first they would assess our needs for turning our apartment into a version of his room here. His mum and sisters, his nieces – and his newly tracked-down dad – made the journey from Newark to be with him. The ward became a bit excited when Paul O'Grady turned up and spent a couple of hours with us, followed by Michelle Collins, Helen Worth and Cherie Blair. But none of the magic worked on him any more.

His morphine was gradually increased and another small machine was fitted to pump it regularly into his veins. Again and again Paul asked me to massage the back of his lungs, which I did. He said it helped his breathing. But I was not sure. I knew it was the feel of my hands on him. Telling him he was alive. Telling him we belonged.

His blood oxygen levels were dropping. No matter how much oxygen they increased he was still unable to breathe properly. Then the lies fell away and I saw the end begin to start. He couldn't lie back, he couldn't breathe, he couldn't rest. I sat beside him on the bed trying to help him find an angle that might just allow him to drift into sleep. At his insistence we piled the table full of pillows and sitting on the edge of the bed he leant forward onto them and his breathing eased. I took a hospital blanket and sat beside him on the bed, the two of us leaning forwards, and I wrapped us in it. I held him throughout the next few hours and, as gently as I could, I hugged him.

The ward was busy in the early morning. The day staff were trying to see what they could do; Paul just wanted to sleep, but he couldn't. Suddenly he asserted himself and told everyone to leave.

Around eleven o'clock Ayşe appeared in our quiet room. He looked up slowly from his morphine-induced state and smiled. The conversation began.

'Now Paul, you have not had a good night, and I always told you I wouldn't give you doom and gloom.'

'Yes,' he said, still smiling.

'But I have to tell you I can do no more for you. I will be with you every step of the way, as will all the palliative team, but there is nothing else I can do.'

My heart choked. And choked.

'Okay,' he said, 'okay.'

She took his hand and then she looked and I knew instinctively that she wanted to speak with me. Paul asked her if we could be alone. The door closed silently behind her as she went.

I sat opposite him on the bed. 'Well babs, now we know. Now we know,' he said quietly.

'I know babs, I know.'

I had no more words. None. We gazed at each other in the silence.

'And I am ready,' he said.

He held his words.

'I am ready.'

We hugged each another and I knew I was not ready, that I could never be ready. Over and over again we told one another how much we loved each other. How we would always love each other. We talked about what a wonderful life we had shared together and we brushed away tears laughing at how silly we were.

Then I gently held his face and asked, 'You do know I love you, don't you?'

He held my face and said, 'I do now. I do now.'

He said how upset he was that he would never see his lovely Datça again, and I told him that he could see it in his mind. And suddenly how I wished I had lied to him and said, 'You will, babs, you will.'

Even now a routine started to take over: I was in another room with Ayşe having the conversation that she wanted, talking about the next few hours, telling her that above all else I did not want him to suffer. When I returned to his room his palliative nurse was with him and they were talking about how they could get him to the House of Lords in five days' time to see me formally take my seat there.

Then quietly they slipped away and left us alone.

I held onto his hand, my eyes never leaving him. He closed his eyes and started to sleep. His breathing was still difficult.

No words were said but his morphine was increased. His family arrived, and his mother Mary and his dad stood at their son's bedside. His eyes opened and when he saw them he smiled. He fell into a deeper sleep but his body caught a sharp breath for every one that left him.

At one point he wrestled with me, trying to get out of the bed to pee and I physically restrained him. He smiled and shook a weary fist. And then he slept.

A young doctor arrived to fit a catheter, to touch him where only I should touch him. And I wondered to myself, was this the last invasive act or was it their final gesture of love? After that the observations stopped and there were no more intrusions as we were left in transition.

My brothers, Johnny and Danny, arrived.

All was quiet.

Inexplicably I started to pack our things: the toilet bag, the clothes, the pyjamas, the iPad, books, the computer, and the neatly packed bag placed in the corner with his jacket and mine. I didn't even know why I was doing it, and I wasn't even sure I was.

I walked outside and down the stairs and found a bench in the courtyard. I looked up at the cloudy sky and a voice inside my head told me to get back to him, to stay with him.

The night shifted into the early morning but I never left the room. I sat holding him and stroking the hairs on his legs, or holding his arm. His mum and dad and sisters similarly came to sit with him. I had been with him like this for over twelve hours, watching his chest rise and fall, wiping the collection of saliva from his oxygen mask, watching as the nurses tried to get him into a more comfortable position. Now I was sitting in the corner in the armchair. Watching. Waiting. Suddenly I flinched, and I knew. I said to someone to get the others because he was going.

I watched him take a deep breath. He breathed out. And breathed in no more.

I rushed towards him. 'Go my darling. Go!' I shouted.

His sisters crammed into the room, my brothers too, they were all there.

I took him in my arms and embraced him.

His sister Karen tried to close his eyes. I held him, I looked at him, and he opened his eyes and looked into mine. Then it was over.

Over.

He was gone.

I looked at him in the bed, slumped slightly to his right, and once we were alone again I talked to him. It was a final conversation only heard by us. I said goodbye, and as I left the room I turned back to take my last look at my beloved partner and best friend, at the man who had saved me so many times.

At home exhaustion overtook me and I went to our bed. This was the first time in over a week that I had been here, that I had slept here.

The dawn was beginning to break. I knew I must go to the hospital to collect his death certificate and the remainder of our things. I needed to register his death. These things didn't crowd into my head, they just placed themselves there. I lay in our bed and I had no sense of life, or living. All I could see was Paul, the colour draining away from him, and slumped slightly to the right in that hospital bed.

Back at the hospital ward they gave me the remainder of our belongings. They caressed me with kindness and I knew it was the living that they must take care of now. The living who really occupied their minds. I took the letter in which the junior doctor certified that Paul died from words and words related to angiosarcoma. I smiled and thanked them. Then I walked down the narrow staircase from his ward for the last time, heading towards the Chelsea streets.

I passed by mornings and nights of memories. Of snatched minutes at the coffee bar that I wished I had never stolen. Of outpatient visits and preparations for chemotherapy. And empty chairs in the pharmacy where we waited in hope. I walked along the streets of white stuccoed self-important houses. Onwards, glancing at churches that could never deliver and garden centres that did. Onto the King's Road, Chelsea. There I saw a teenaged Michael in search of love in gay bars long painted over and gone. Or driven in flash cars, by flash men, because youth was what he had. And what they wanted.

At Chelsea Town Hall my brother and I registered Paul's death. Johnny and I waited a short time, and when the registrar arrived he was gentle and kind. He even tried to open the envelope without making too much noise. I told him what a lovely day it was outside, and he said he hoped that would it last for the weekend. I had forgotten there would be a weekend.

Paul's death was certified, my place in his life officially recorded for the last time, and I was back on the street. Going home.

Four days later I entered the House of Lords. We rehearsed the ceremony, and people were nobility itself in their kindness and understanding. I stood there in my fake ermine and listened to the summons being read, with our friends and my family looking down from the gallery, the Labour benches packed in support. My heart started thumping in my chest like it was going to explode, and I looked up and I thought of Paul. And I smiled.

We gathered for his cremation, the celebration of his life. The Labour Party family took over for me. His wonderful friends organised everything. I stumbled through the mist of it all. Routine again dictated my actions and reactions and emotions. His body was laid in a beautiful wicker casket and thirty-one white roses were placed on top, one for each year we were together. The City of London Crematorium spilled over with friends and love and loss. People stood outside too, individuals in a crowd. I saw our friends from Turkey and Holland – I was so moved that they came.

Michelle did a reading for him, I read his eulogy – making no apology for its length – and Ian gave him Shakespeare. Of course, only Paul Cottingham could get Ed Miliband, Neil and Glenys Kinnock, Tony and Cherie Blair, Margaret Beckett, Sadiq Khan and everyone else to sing Barry Manilow's 'Mandy' in public.

A wish he suggested to me once was realised when he entered the crematorium to the Prelude to Charpentier's *Te Deum*. Some thought it posh, others knew it was the Eurovision anthem, and smiled.

His wake was an incredible affair and his spirit took it over. It was in the White Swan, at Stepney, where we had spent countless years at the gay disco, seeing Savage in the early days, and Michael Barrymore jumping out of the closet and then rushing back in. The place came alive. It was not long before people were dancing to Abba and Eurovision, networking and liaising for the future, and I saw his magic at work.

After a few hours I could stay no more. I needed to get away and be on my own. I walked the streets of the East End, the streets that we walked. There I talked to him. This wasn't the way it was supposed to be, I said. This was not what I had planned in my head. I was older. I would go first, he would be taken care of and could rebuild his life. Paul loved life and I just lived it.

In the hospital I had talked with him of us both dying together but he wouldn't accept that. I had to promise him I would take care of myself. But I no longer wanted to. And he even foresaw that.

When I collected his ashes from the City of London Crematorium, a place where we had visited my mum, dad and relatives so often, I lifted up the box containing his ashes and hugged it close. I took him home, his remains. His spirit was in the ether, his energy all around. I kept saying to him that this was not how it was meant to be.

But, ever the organiser, Paul didn't leave me unprepared. In a drawer I found a piece of paper with all his passwords and pin numbers. On a chair was a notebook. When I opened the notebook, I read his thoughts and feelings from the past: how lonely and depressed he had been in London, how he ached for love and how hurt he was by his father walking out on him all those years ago. He kept asking: why. Why?

My eyes stopped on the words: 'Michael my friend and soul mate I adore and love' and I could read no more.

I went to the desk that we shared, opened the middle drawer and took out the envelope marked 'Open in the event of my Death'. My similar envelope was beside it. Inside was his will, which we knew had been invalidated by our civil partnership. There was nothing else. My hands delved into pockets of suits and trousers and jackets. I checked the same pockets again, and again. I was surprised by how little paperwork he had left; even though he took over most of the drawers of the desk, there was hardly anything. It crossed my mind that perhaps he had thrown a lot of stuff away, that he had prepared for this and that I never knew. I pored over thousands of photographs, looking for something, yet I didn't know what.

Weeks later I opened the drawers under the bed. Underneath were hundreds of theatre programmes and Notts Forest football programmes. Among them I spotted an old, ripped, grey folder, covered in dust. Inside was a diary from 1984 accompanied by all the letters and the cards we had sent one another when we first met, and the original invitation to Barbara Windsor's 'Grand Soirée' on 9 September 1983. A pile of letters, of love, hurt, confusion and elation. And I knew. These were his last letters to me. What we started and what we became was all there. Like a prediction from a fortune teller's booth in Scarborough. Finally I read the words written thirty-one years before, from me to him:

It was smashing talking to you over the weekend, and I was so pleased about the honest chat we had late on Friday.

It does worry me that you are having some difficulties. I want to help you all I can, and so the best I can do is to love you. I will love you, give you the knowledge that whatever happens to you, whatever you do I will love you and give you the security of a relationship as long as you (and I) need it. I hope that it is forever, but only time will tell, and we must not live for tomorrow, but for now, for today.

All I am trying to say in my confusing style is that whatever anyone thinks, feels, or says about you, remember

that you love someone, they love you. That is enviable. Not
everyone experiences that. End of lecture.

I placed the letter back in its envelope, addressed to him at the Butlin's Grand Hotel, Scarborough, and closed the folder.

The House of Lords became my saviour. It gave me something to do. It got me up in the mornings and gave me somewhere to go. It helped me make it through the days to the nights when I could get quietly drunk, fall asleep and try to forget that he was gone. And get to the next day, to do the same.

Ian showed me kindness beyond words or understanding and chose his moment to tell me that Paul had gently taken him aside a few weeks before, to ask 'you will look after Michael, won't you?' I grew aware that he had said this to others too.

Their friendship was sublime. It lifted and supported me, but I was lonely for him. His name was my last word at night, and my first when I awoke. When the weekends came I was lost. Literally. I took trains to places only to take another train elsewhere. Along the seafront at Southend I walked for miles in the rain and, aloud with the wind, I talked with him. On the underground I heard the trains approaching and I knew I could throw myself on the line, yet I never did. I had made Paul a promise. I started returning to self-harm, and the addiction of self-abuse. Finally, sharing an office at the Lords with Glenys Kinnock and Gordon Brown's ex-political secretary, Baroness (Sue) Nye, I asked Sue for help. She found me someone at the Priory.

Addiction was big in the City of London; the Priory had opened a clinic there. I met with Dana. I was not there for bereavement counselling, I told her. She nodded and said of course not. But eventually, when I acknowledged that I was, I opened up and let go. I started to recognise my addictions. How I tried to hurt people I loved and who loved me. I began to see that I found it easier to be hurt. I could cope with that, it felt natural, it felt normal. If someone loved me they would have to hurt me in order to prove it.

Finally I was on the journey. The one he had asked me to take so often. It had taken me thirty-one years to start down this path that would lead I knew not where. Only now, I started it alone. But because of Paul I would never be alone. To be alone is never to have been loved.

EPILOGUE

I must make my maiden speech, my formal contribution in the House of Lords. Until I do so I cannot take part in debates or questions and I cannot carry out my job as Labour's global LGBT+ envoy. I choose the Modern Slavery Bill on which to make the speech, a deep reminder of the endless fights we must always undertake.

In it I speak of my experiences before entering the House, of Paul's death just four days prior to my introduction and of the extraordinary kindness I have been shown. I speak of my hopes for the future, and I speak of the privilege I have been given. Finally, I print the speech, tuck it into my suit pocket and get ready to leave home.

Looking out across London from our flat I watch the dark, sluggish Thames slowly winding its way upstream, and decide to take the boat to work. The pavement is wet and I remember to button up my coat. My mind is racing ahead to standing up in the chamber but I remind myself to be present.

I look across to the park and the Japanese maples clinging to leaves of embarrassed red, to a street where I ran and played as a kid, and where my mum trudged daily in snow, or hail, in the hours before dawn, to go to work. Where my dad searched for jobs as a young docker, and often staggered home on borrowed beer. I think of our lives lived out along this street, no more than 500 yards away from where I was born and where we grew up. And I recognise that it was Paul who brought me home to the East End. Brought us home.

I turn towards the river and Canary Wharf looms ahead, built upon the foundations of Lou Clench's corner shop and the never-present Ned. I find a seat near the front of the boat so I can see London's riverscape ahead of me, enveloping me. In my head I go over the speech and again my heart races. I look out at places where Paul and I lived together along the river, on the south bank and the north bank. I sail under bridges we have walked over and I sigh as I pass the hospital that knew us so well.

The stark, silver Shard thrusts into the sky, clouds gently airbrushing the landmark. Tower Bridge rises majestically into sight; passing the Tower of London a defiant St Paul's Cathedral stands proud against the tower blocks, as London's iconic red buses nudge their way across Southwark Bridge. Life is all around me, begging to be lived. I smile as I recall the nights that Paul and I sat at the back of these boats, fresh from the theatre or a late-night meal, a glass of red wine pressed to our lips and laughter cascading everywhere. Next we reach Waterloo Bridge, and I remember Paul's love of the view from here as I pass beneath it. London woven into us, and us, as one, woven into it.

I disembark, walk west along the Embankment, Big Ben in the distance. The London Eye spins slowly and effortlessly, the traffic moves fitfully. I hear nothing. Not a single sound. I am doing this. And no matter how much I wish otherwise, I know it will never be. Paul would have loved this new chapter so much and enjoyed every single second. That would have made it complete for me. Now I can only imagine.

The Lords is in sight; I see the Union Jack flying from the Victoria Tower. Grey clouds give way to a brightening sky, but the cold wind picks up to remind me that winter is going nowhere.

So this is it. I navigate the excited crowds of tourists and turn onto the vast forecourt of the House of Lords. I lift up my head as I approach the peers' entrance. A doorkeeper dressed in a gold-braided top hat and three-quarter-length royal red overcoat stands waiting. I smile softly and nod.

He smiles back, 'Good morning, my Lord.'

ACKNOWLEDGEMENTS

To paraphrase Shakespeare: how do I thank thee? Let me name the names: the amazing orchestra of Bloomsbury led by the superlative editor-in-chief Alexandra Pringle; the incredible Elise Burns, David Mann, Emma Bal, Lauren Whybrow, Allegra Le Fanu; and the man who shifted my story into reality with his editorial skills, Callum Kenny. If that wasn't lucky enough I had the most amazing copy-editor Kate Johnson and the encouragement from Paul Stevens, Debbie Owen and Martin Sherman (who always has his best ideas over an Italian – meal).

Alexandra Pringle is an author's dream: she never let the book leave her from first reading and throughout has nudged me gently along my virgin (book-writing) path.

And there, behind the bins sometimes puffing on a cigarette, the reader, Antonia Till, avidly looking for something to recommend, a story to reveal.

There are so many people not named in the book without whom I probably would not have got here: Sonya and David Newell-Smith, Mark Greenburg, Vanessa Bowcock, Jane Hogarth, Rebecca Wheatley, Rachel Kinnock, Colette Meurey, John Roberts and Tom Thorpe, Nigel and Julia Sheinwald, Paul and Caroline Stanley, Jonathan Pearse and Anna Yearley, Simon Milson, and Beechy Colclough who reached out and grabbed my hand when it seemed the darkest.

Knowing my brothers were always there, quietly in the background, has been my rock, so too Paul's sisters Janet, Karen, Sharon and their late mum, Mary.

Special thanks to Aunt Mary McDermott (from Canada), my dad's sole surviving sibling, who gave me so many insights into his early life – aged 91, she is as sharp as a knife!

My journey to the final page of this book has been an experience I will never forget and one that I could never imagine to be better. Thank you to the countless people without whom this book would never have reached you.

And finally, an all-embracing thank you to Robert Caskie, my agent and mentor, who always knew exactly the why and the how.

A NOTE ON THE TYPE

The text of this book is set in Linotype Sabon, a typeface named after the type founder, Jacques Sabon. It was designed by Jan Tschichold and jointly developed by Linotype, Monotype and Stempel in response to a need for a typeface to be available in identical form for mechanical hot metal composition and hand composition using foundry type.

Tschichold based his design for Sabon roman on a font engraved by Garamond, and Sabon italic on a font by Granjon. It was first used in 1966 and has proved an enduring modern classic.